Historical Sketch and Roster Of The Tennessee 24th Infantry Regiment

By John C. Rigdon

Historical Sketch and Roster of
The Tennessee 24th Infantry Regiment

9th Printing – DEC 2016 4/1/2/3

© Copyright 2003. All Rights Reserved. No part of this book may be reproduced by any means without the express written consent of the copyright holder.

Published by:
Eastern Digital Resources
31 Bramblewood Dr. SW
Cartersville, GA 30120
http://www.researchonline.net
EMAIL: Sales@Researchonline.net
Tel. (678) 739-9177

Contents

Aye, But Its Hopes Are Dead 6

A Turtle On A Fence Post 7

The Flag of the Tennessee 24th Infantry Regiment 8

Officers 10

Brigade/Division/Corps Commanders 11

Assignments 21

Battles 22

Companies Of The TN 24th Infantry Regiment 23

TimeLine of the Atlanta Campaign 24

TimeLine of the Atlanta Campaign 24

The Franklin – Nashville Campaign 43

TimeLine of the Carolina's Campaign 51

A Confederate View 59

The Death Of An Unsung Confederate Hero 64

Historical Sketch 69

A Civil War Filler: 138

The Twenty~Fourth Tennessee Regiment 139

Last Surviving Officer. 142

One Man Company & Regimental Flag 144

Chaplaincy Of The 24th Tennessee Regiment. 147

Comrades True 151

Field Staff and Band 165

Company A 168

Company B 180

Company C 196

Company D 207

Company E 217

Company F 225

Company G 240

Original roster of "The Duck River Riflemen" 255

Company H 262

Company I 277

Company K 293

Company L 302

Company Unknown 306

Bibliography 315

Index 317

For Further Research 344

The Historical Sketch & Roster Series 359

Aye, But Its Hopes Are Dead

Sir Henry Houghton - England

Sir Henry Houghton, of England, in 1865, wrote these beautiful lines as a reply to "The Conquered Banner." The Southern people never expect to see that sacred banner unfurled except to typify the noblest deeds of the human race.

> Gallant nation, foiled by numbers,
> Say not that your hopes are fled;
> Keep that glorious flag which slumbers,
> One day to avenge your dead.
> Keep it, widowed, sonless mothers,
> Keep it, sisters, mourning brothers,
> Furl it with an iron will;
> Furl it now, but keep it still,
> Think not that its work is done.
> Keep it till your children take it,
> Once again to hail and make it
> All their sires have bled and fought for,
> Bled and fought for all alone.
> All done! aye, shame the story,
> Millions here deplore the stain;
> Shame, alas! for England's glory,
> Freedom called, and called in vain.
> Furl that banner, sadly, slowly,
> Treat it gently, for 'tis holy,
> Till that day---yes, furl it sadly,
> Then once more unfurl it gladly,
> Conquered banner, keep it still.

A Turtle On A Fence Post

If You ever see one, you'll know he didn't get there by himself.

This work has been compiled from a number of different sources. I have concentrated on first hand accounts and primary sources when available. It is my hope that this sketch will help in your research and become the basis of future in depth research into this regiment and the men who served.

If you have additional information on the men who served in this unit, or the regiment's actions, drop me a note at JRigdon@researchonline.net. I will incorporate them into future editions.

The Flag of the Tennessee 24th Infantry Regiment [1]

Courtesy Sheila Green TN State Museum

****

William Hearn - Nashville, Hearns art gallery was on Market Street. Sometimes, in conjunction with Mrs. J.T. Lord, wife of a local sewing machine shop proprietor, he made flags for Tennessee units. Among those colors that he executed are the flags of the 3rd Tennessee Infantry (adorned with a knight in armor), and the regimental colors of the 23rd and 24th Tennessee Infantry (the latter two

---

[1] Source: Flag Makers Of The Confederacy
http://www.confederateflags.org/FOTCflagmakers1.htm

definitely with Mrs. Lords help). No other flags have been connected to Hearn as yet.

Mrs. J.T. Lord/Singer Sewing Machines Agent - Nashville, TN: Mrs. Lords husband, J.T. Lord, ran the Singer sewing machine franchise in Nashville. After the secession of the state, she used the stores ability to work with cloth to begin making flags. According to one source, Nashville papers ran advertisements of the store offering , 'Southern flags made to order.' Mrs. Lord worked with local painter William Hearn to produce a pair of flags for the 23rd and 24th Tennessee Infantry in 1861.

Officers

Colonels:

- Robert D. Allison
- Hugh L.W. Bratton
- John A. Wilson

Lieutenant Colonels:

- Thomas H. Peebles
- Samuel E. Shannon
- John J. Williams

Major:

- William C. Fielding

Brigade/Division/Corps Commanders

Maj. Gen. Patrick R. Cleburne

Born March 17, 1828 Bridgepark Cottage on River Bride,
County Cork, Ireland
Killed November 30, 1864 Franklin
Buried Helena AR

Maj. Gen. William Joseph Hardee

Born October 12, 1815 Camden County GA
USMA 26th in 1838
Died November 6, 1873 Wytheville VA while on trip
Buried Selma AL

Maj. Gen. Benjamin F. Cheatham

Born October 20, 1820 Nashville TN
Died September 4, 1886 Nashville TN
Buried Mount Olivet Cemetery

Lt. Gen. Alexander Peter Stewart

Born October 2, 1821 Rogersville TN
USMA 12th in 1842
Wounded at Ezra Church
Died August 30, 1908 Biloxi MS
Buried St. Louis MO

Brig. Gen. Joseph Eggleston Johnston

Born February 3, 1807 'Cherry Grove', Farmville VA
USMA 13th in 1829
Wounded at Seven Pines/Fair Oaks
Died March 21, 1891 Washington DC as result of cold contracted while walking bareheaded in US General William Tecumsah Sherman's funeral procession
Buried Green Mount Cemetery Baltimore MD

Maj. Gen. Leonidas Polk

Born April 10, 1806 Raleigh NC
Uncle of CS General Lucius Eugene Polk
USMA 8th in 1827
Killed June 14, 1864 Pine Mountain near Marietta GA
Buried Christ Church Cathedral New Orleans LA

Maj. Gen. Braxton Bragg

Born March 22, 1817 Warrenton NC
USMA 5th in 1837
Died September 27, 1876 Galveston TX
Buried Mobile AL

Maj. Gen. John B. Hood

Born June 1, 1831 Owingsville KY
USMA 44th in 1853
Wounded at Gettysburg and Chickamauga
Relieved of duty January 1865
Died August 30, 1879 New Orleans LA of yellow fever
Buried Metairie Cemetery

Maj. Gen. Earl Van Dorn

Born September 17, 1820 near Port Gibson MS
USMA 52nd in 1842
Murdered May 7, 1863 Spring Hill TN by Dr. George Brodie Peters
Considered 'lady's man', Peters claimed Van Dorn 'violated the sanctity of his home'
Buried Wintergreen Cemetery Port Gibson MS

Maj. Gen. Edward Cary Walthall

Born April 4, 1831 Richmond VA
Wounded at Missionary Ridge
Died April 21, 1898 Washington DC
Buried Hill Crest Cemetery Holly Springs MS

Assignments

After taking part in the conflicts in Shiloh and Perryville, the Tennessee 24th was attached to General Stewart's, Strahl's, and Palmer's Brigade, Army of Tennessee.

Battles

Cave City - KY Oct. 25, 1861

Shiloh - April 6th & 7th 1862

Farmington Mississippi (May 28, 1862)

Perryville (Oct. 8, 1862)

Murfreesboro

Tullahoma

Missionary Ridge

Chickamauga

The Atlanta Campaign

Nashville

Franklin

The Carolina's Campaign

Companies Of The TN 24th Infantry Regiment

The men were from the counties of Hamilton, Monroe, Knox, Union, Claiborne, Hawkins, Jefferson, Bledsoe, Bradley, Polk, Hancock, Blount, and Sullivan.

Co. A, Rutherford Co., Capt. John C. Jackson
Co. B, Williamson Co., Capt. W.E. Shannon
Co. C, Macon Co., Capt. J.M. Uhles
Co. D, Williamson Co., Capt. John A. Wilson
Co. E, Sumner Co., Capt. J. A. Baskerville
Co. F, Smith Co., Capt. James Dowell
Co. G, Maury Co., Capt. James A. Billington
Co. H, Hickman Co., Capt. C. W. Beale
Co. I, Hickman Co., Capt. E. W. Beasley
Co. K, Franklin & Wilson Co. Capt. T.C. Goodner

Capt. Buck Hart's Company from Sumner, Trousdale & Smith Counties & a Company commanded by Capt. Mays were afterwards added to the 24th.

TimeLine of the Atlanta Campaign

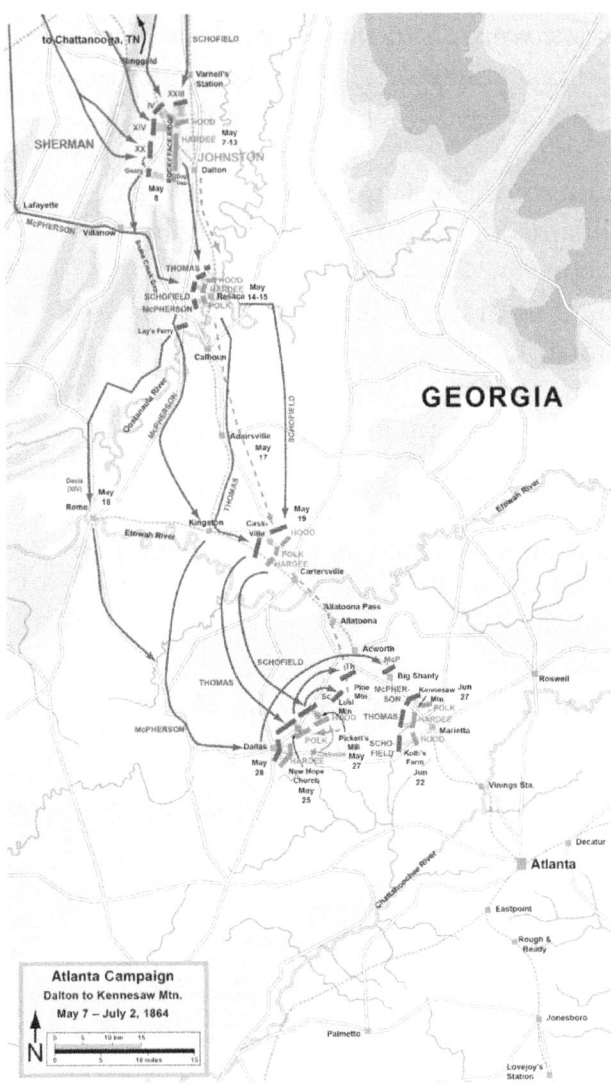

WEEK 142

December 16, 1863

General Joseph E. Johnston was ordered to Dalton, Georgia to replace Braxton Bragg as commander of the Army of Tennessee.

WEEK 144

December 27, 1863

Gen. Joseph Johnston arrived to take over command of the western army.

WEEK 150

February 12, 1864

Grant directed Maj. General George H. Thomas commanding the Union Army of the Cumberland, to conduct a "reconnaissance in force" against Johnston's Confederate Army of Tennessee, in their winter quarters at Dalton, Georgia. Heavy rains delayed the departure of 25,000 Union troops from Chattanooga until February 22nd. In addition to the rain, Thomas was suffering from an attack of neuralgia and was unable to take personal charge of mission. He placed his senior corps commander, Major Gen. John M. Palmer, in command.

WEEK 152

February 23, 1864

The GA 1st Sharpshooters moved from their winter camp to the Confederate lines a mile north of Dalton. They held this position during the Federal demonstration at Dalton until February 28th.

February 24 1864

The 3 Union divisions of the XIV Corps under Palmer skirmished with Confederates on the north end of Rocky Face Ridge and down into Crow's Valley for 3 days.

February 25, 1864

Brigadier General Alfred Cumming received orders to move his brigade up Crow's Valley about 3 1/2 miles northwest of Dalton to relieve Brigadier General Clayton's command. After establishing a battle line and while engaged in relieving Clayton's skirmishers, which were posted about 2/3 of a mile in front of the line, the enemy advanced a strong line of skirmishers, supported apparently by two brigades. Cumming's skirmishers by his orders fell back to a ridge several hundred yards nearer to his lines where they briskly engaged the enemy and held them in check during the whole day. From this position, Cumming's skirmishers made several partial advances, which always occasioned a corresponding withdrawal on the part of the enemy. This continued until dusk. During the greater part of the day the 34th. Ga., being the left of Cumming's lines, was exposed to brisk and almost continuous fire. During the night the Federals withdrew. Early on the morning of the 26th, skirmishers were again thrown forward. A fight developed and 6 prisoners were taken.

WEEK 153

February 28, 1864

By command of General Joseph E. Johnston, issued at Headquarters of the Army of Tennessee at Dalton Georgia, Stevenson's Division was transferred to Hood's Corps. Hood's Corps now consisted of Hindman's Division, Stewart's Division and now Stevenson's.

WEEK 160

In the latter part of April, 1864, Major General Stevenson received orders to break up his winter camp on Sugar Valley Road and move his division to the position assigned it in front of Dalton. He was charged with the defense of a portion of the line that extended from the signal station on Rocky Face Mountain to Alt's Creek. General Pettus' Brigade was placed on the left, General Reynold's Brigade on the left center, General Cumming's Brigade, on the right center, and Brown's Brigade on the right.

WEEK 161

April 24, 1864

Scouts begin to probe Confederate strength south of Ringgold, Georgia. This is the first activity that can be directly associated with the Atlanta Campaign

April 27, 1864

This is the earliest generally accepted date for the start of the Atlanta Campaign. Rear echelon troop movement began for the Army of the Tennessee (General John B.

McPherson). Union scouts probed troop strength at Tunnel Hill.

WEEK 162

May 1, 1864

Skirmish at the old Stone Church, east of Ringgold, Georgia. This date is the "official" date of the start of the Atlanta Campaign, listed as such in the Official Records.

May 2, 1864

Skirmish at Lee's Crossroads, near Tunnel Hill and near Ringgold Gap.

May 3, 1864

Skirmishes at Catoosa Springs and Red Clay.

May 4, 1864

This is one of the generally accepted dates for the start of the Atlanta Campaign. General George Thomas (Army of the Cumberland) [US] began to move slowly east along the Western and Atlantic Railroad from Ringgold. Union troops in all departments began to move into position for what will be the final summer of war. Skirmish at Varnell (Prater's Mill)

May 6, 1864

Skirmish at Tunnel Hill.

May 7, 1864

This is the latest date for the start of the Atlanta Campaign. The Army of the Tennessee [US] moved south from Lee and Gordon's Mill along Taylor Ridge, using it to cover McPherson's flanking movement. A division of the Army of the Cumberland [US] attacked Confederate skirmishers at Tunnel Hill.

Gen. Joseph E. Johnston had entrenched his army on the long, high mountain of Rocky Face Ridge and eastward across Crow Valley. As Maj. Gen. William T. Sherman approached, he decided to demonstrate against the position with two columns while he sent a third one through Snake Creek Gap, to the right, to hit the Western & Atlantic Railroad at Resaca. The two columns engaged the enemy at Buzzard Roost (Mill Creek Gap) and at Dug Gap. In the meantime, the third column, under Maj. Gen. James Birdseye McPherson, passed through Snake Creek Gap and on the 9th advanced to the outskirts of Resaca where it found Confederates entrenched. Fearing defeat, McPherson pulled his column back to Snake Creek Gap. On the 10th, Sherman decided to take most of his men and join McPherson to take Resaca. The next morning, Sherman's army withdrew from in front of Rocky Face Ridge. Discovering Sherman's movement, Johnston retired south towards Resaca on the 12th.

WEEK 163

May 8, 1864

Fighting commenced along Rocky Face Ridge west of Dalton, specifically at Mill Creek and Dug Gap. The enemy pushed forward vigorously. Skirmishers were supported by a line of battle against Pettus' portion of the line, but were repulsed. Fighting along this spine of high mountains continued until May 11th. In compliance with instructions from Lt. Gen. Hood, Brown's Brigade was moved from the right of Stevenson's line to the left of Pettus' Brigade. This made Cumming's Brigade now the extreme right.

May 9, 1864

McPherson's Army of the Tennessee ran into stiffer than expected Confederate resistance as he moved towards the Western and Atlantic railroad bridge near Resaca. In hostile territory, the general decided to dig in and await reinforcements. Sherman spent the night at the Clisby-Austin house in Tunnel Hill. Moving south after disembarking at the Red Clay depot, Schofield's Army of the Ohio encountered Joseph Wheeler's Confederate Cavalry near Varnell.

Casualties of Stevenson's Division during the demonstration on Dalton was 138 killed and wounded.

May 11, 1864

Carter Stevenson awoke to silence. He communicated to Johnston that his men could find no soldiers immediately west of Rocky Face. Johnston ordered a cavalry sweep of the area. Wheeler's cavalry found almost no Union soldiers.

May 12, 1864

Outflanked, with superior numbers to his rear, Johnston withdrew to Resaca

May 14, 1864

Battle of Resaca, Day 1 - Almost 100,000 men poured out of Snake Creek Gap west of the town of Resaca. Major General Stevenson established his battle line at a position just north of Resaca in two lines, immediately on the right of the Resaca and Dalton road. Cumming's and Brown's brigades were in the first line, Reynold's and Pettus' brigades in the second. Fighting occurred along the entire line although the heaviest fighting occurred to the north of the city. Among the wounded was the Battalion Commander Major J.W. Johnson. At 5:00 p.m. Stevenson ordered Cumming's and Brown's brigades forward to dislodge the enemy.

Cumming's and Brown's brigades were facing the following Union elements of Major General George H. Thomas' Army of the Cumberland.: Cruft's, Whitaker's and Grose's brigades of Stanley's First Division of Brigadier General Oliver O. Howard's IV Corps supported by elements of Ward's Brigade of Brigadier General Daniel Butterfield's Third Division of Major General Joseph Hooker's XX Corps, and Ireland's Brigade of Geary's Second Division also part of Hooker's Corps.

Brown's Brigade supported by Reynold's Brigade, was directed to move out in front of their trenches and then swing around to the left. After the movement commenced, Brigadier Gen. Cumming was also directed to wheel his brigade which was to the right of the ridge, to the left in front of the Union's breast-works. The regiment on the crest of the ridge was the pivot and the movement was successful.

WEEK 164

May 15, 1864

Battle of Resaca, Day 2 - Engagements continued along lines around Resaca. Hood's Corps [CS] (Brown's, Reynold's, and Cumming's brigades) and "Fighting Joe" Hooker's XX Corps [US] bore the brunt of the day's fighting north of the city. The battle continued with no advantage to either side until Sherman sent a force across the Oostanaula River, at Lay's Ferry, towards Johnston's railroad supply line. Reports of Union troops at Lay's Ferry (Oostanaula River) forced Johnston to withdraw. On the evening of the 15th, Stevenson received orders to withdraw his troops in the direction of New Hope Church.

The losses of Stevenson's Division in killed and wounded during the two days of fighting at Resaca was 575. Total casualties to the C.S.A. was 300 killed 1,500 wounded and 1,000 missing or captured. The Federal troops suffered 600 killed and 2,147 wounded.

May 17, 1864

Rome falls. After a small skirmish at Adairsville Johnston set up at Cassville. Sherman mistakenly ended up at Kingston.

May 18, 1864

General John B. McPherson spent the night at a present-day Georgia landmark, Barnsley Gardens.

May 19, 1864

Johnston withdrew to the Allatoona Mountains south of the Etowah River after an attack at Cassville, Georgia was cancelled. Sherman decided to regroup in Kingston.

WEEK 165

May 23, 1864

In 1844 the General had visited the Etowah Indian Mounds near Cartersville, Georgia. The W&A cuts through Allatoona Pass east of Cartersville, which Sherman remembered and avoided. He decided to leave the Western and Atlantic and head south across country from Kingston.

May 24, 1864

Polk and Hardee's Corps reached the road a few miles south of Dallas, Georgia; and Hood's Corps was four miles from New Hope Church on the road from Allatoona. It was discovered that the enemy was entrenched near and east of Dallas.

May 25, 1864

Battle of New Hope Church-- Johnston, forced by Sherman to abandon his stronghold in the Allatoona Mountains, moved to block the Union advance on Atlanta meeting Sherman's Army at a small church some 25 miles northwest of Atlanta.

Lieutenant General Hood's Corps was placed with its center at New Hope Church. Stevenson's Division was placed to the right of Stewart's Division. The brigades from left to right were in the following order; Brown's Brigade commanded by Brigadier General John C. Brown, Pettus' Brigade commanded by Brigadier General Edmund W. Pettus, Cumming's Brigade commanded by Brigadier General Alfred Cumming, and Reynold's Brigade commanded by Brigadier General Alexander W. Reynold.

Cumming's Brigade formed in this order from left to right, The 34th Ga., The 36th Ga., The 39th Ga. and the 56th Ga..

An hour before sunset, Stewart's Division, Maj. General Alexander P. Stewart commanding, was fiercely attacked by three divisions of General Joseph Hooker's XX Corps. Robinson's. Ruger's, and Knipe's Federal Brigades of William's Division ran directly into Stewart's left and encountered Stovall's and Clayton's brigades. The Federal brigades of Bushbeck and Candy, of Geary's Division hit Stewart's center and came face to face with elements of Clayton's and Baker's Brigades. Butterfield's Federal division, consisting of Ward's, Coburn's, and Wood's Brigades attacked Stewart's right and Stevenson's left, encountering Baker's Brigade of Stewart's Division and Brown's, Pettus', and Cumming's Brigades of Stevenson's Division. The attack was repulsed after a hot engagement of 2 hours. Skirmishing was kept up on the 26th and the 27th.

May 27, 1864

Spreading their respective lines east from New Hope Church, Sherman and Johnston battled at Pickett's Mill.

At 5:30 P.M. Howard's Corps assailed Cleburne's Division, part of Hardee's Corps, located just south of Dallas and was driven back with "great slaughter". Confederate losses in each of the last two actions were approximately 450 killed and wounded. The enemy dead, except those borne off, were counted at 600. General Joe Johnston therefore estimated the total Union loss to be at least 3,000.

May 28, 1864

After 2 defeats in three days Sherman realized that fighting here was a mistake and moved east towards the railroad. Johnston tried to take advantage of this move by testing Sherman's right flank. Confederate General William Bates ran headlong into McPherson's regulars at Dallas after misunder-standing a signal from his cavalry.

One regiment from Cumming's Brigade, equipped with long range rifles was sent to Brigadier General Alpheus Baker commanding a brigade in Stewart's Division. This Brigade was formerly Moore's Brigade. Baker had transferred from Cheatham's Division. Their purpose was to dislodge an enemy artillery battery in front of Baker's defensive works.

WEEK 166

June 1, 1864

General George Stoneman's cavalry captured Allatoona Pass. Realizing the mistake he made, Sherman ordered his men to return to the railroad in Acworth.

June 4, 1864

Johnston took a position on Lost Mountain and Pine Top and moved to Brush Mountain to protect the railroad.

WEEK 168

June 14, 1864

Leonidas Polk died during fighting at Pine Mountain.

June 18, 1864

The advances made by Sherman forced Johnston to withdraw and reform a line at Kennesaw Mountain.

WEEK 160

June 19, 1864

Fighting began at Kennesaw Mountain.

June 22, 1864

Hood attacked at Kolb Farm, halting Sherman's attempt to bypass Kennesaw.

WEEK 170

June 27, 1864

Battle of Kennesaw Mountain. General George Thomas was repulsed in a bloody attack on the center of the Confederate line.

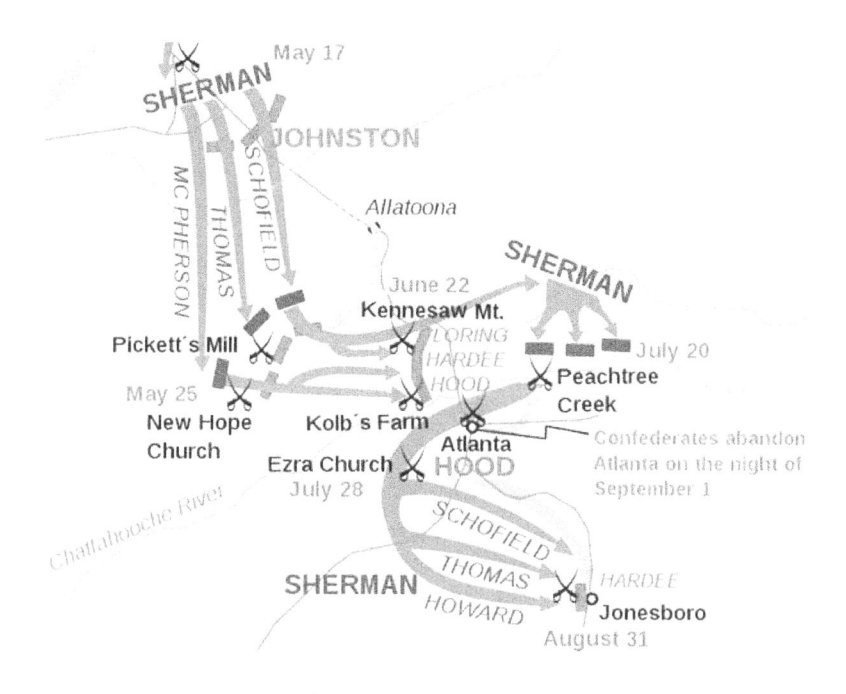

WEEK 170

July 2, 1864

After McPherson moved to outflank Johnston, the Confederate General withdrew to Smyrna.

WEEK 171

July 4, 1864

Intense fighting at Ruff's Mill turned Johnston's left flank. Johnston pulled back to the Chattahoochee Line.

WEEK 172

July 10, 1864

Johnston withdrew to the outskirts of Atlanta, carefully destroying all bridges over the Chatta-hoochee River. There was skirmishing in Alpharetta. Braxton Bragg traveled to Atlanta to meet with Johnston as a representative of President Davis.

July 11, 1864

Davis informed Robert E. Lee of his decision to remove Johnston, asking Lee about his feelings on Hood as a replacement.

July 16, 1864

Sherman's forces moved east from Marietta and spread across the open land north of Atlanta. Replying to an inquiry about his plans made by Davis, Johnston says, "As the enemy has double our number, we must be on the defensive. My plan of operations, therefore, must depend upon that of the enemy."

WEEK 173

July 17, 1864

President Davis relieved Johnston of command and placed John Bell Hood in charge. In a meeting with his men two days later, Sherman instructed them to expect an attack at any moment, given Hood's aggressive nature. Sherman had found out about the change in command thanks to the Atlanta newspapers.

July 20, 1864

Hood attacked and lost at Peachtree Creek. From a point northeast of Atlanta along the Decatur Road (at the corner of present-day Dekalb Avenue and Degress St.) the first artillery shells fall on the city.

July 21, 1864

A "bald hill" east of the city fell to men under the command of Mortimer Leggitt. Renamed Leggett's Hill, this rise offered Sherman an elevated place to fire artillery into the heart of downtown Atlanta. Sherman believed the city would be quickly abandoned. Forward troops reported large-scale movement of Confederate forces.

July 22, 1864

The large-scale troop movement was not the retreat of the Army of Tennessee, but the movement of Hardee's Corps on a 15-mile circuitous route to attack the Federal left flank in East Atlanta. Confederate losses may have exceed 10,000 in this battle.

Following the Battle of Peachtree Creek, Hood determined to attack Maj. Gen. James B. McPherson's Army of the Tennessee. He withdrew his main army at night from Atlanta's outer line to the inner line, enticing Sherman to follow. In the meantime, he sent William J. Hardee with his corps on a fifteen-mile march to hit the unprotected Union left and rear, east of the city. Wheeler's cavalry was to operate farther out on Sherman's supply line, and Gen. Frank Cheatham's corps were to attack the Union front. Hood, however, miscalculated the time necessary to make the march, and Hardee was unable to attack until afternoon. Although Hood had outmaneuvered Sherman for the time being, McPherson was concerned about his left flank and sent his reserves—Grenville Dodge's XVI Army Corps—to that location. Two of Hood's divisions ran into this reserve force and were repulsed. The Rebel attack stalled on the Union rear but began to roll up the left flank. Around the same time, a Confederate soldier shot and killed McPherson when he rode out to observe the fighting. Determined attacks continued, but the Union forces held. About 4:00 pm, Cheatham's corps broke through the Union front at the Hurt House, but Sherman massed twenty artillery pieces on a knoll near his headquarters to shell these Confederates and halt their drive. Maj. Gen. John A. Logan's XV Army Corps then led a counterattack that restored the Union line. The Union troops held, and Hood suffered high casualties.

WEEK 174

July 26, 1864

General George Stoneman left for the raid on Macon, Georgia, in an attempt to cut Hood's supply line.

July 28, 1864

Concerned with Federal troop movement west of the city, Hood attacked and lost at Ezra Church.

WEEK 175

August 4, 1864

Slow encirclement of the city of Atlanta continued with Federals crossing Utoy Creek. Over the next several days heavy skirmishing occurred in this area.

WEEK 178

August 25, 1864

Sherman tired of waiting for Hood to leave Atlanta. Orders went out to six of seven divisions telling them to begin moving towards the Macon and Western Railroad, the last of the supply lines for Atlanta.

WEEK 179

August 30, 1864

Forward units of Howard's Army of the Tennessee crossed the Flint River and took high ground west of Jonesborough, Georgia.

August 31, 1864

Battle of Jonesborough--Day 1. Georgia native, General William "Old Reliable" Hardee moved to Jonesborough to protect the Macon and Western Railroad and launched an attack against Howard. Hood withdrew S. D. Lee from the "diversion."

September 1, 1864

Battle of Jonesborough--Day 2. Defending the small city of Jonesborough, Hardee bore the brunt of a massive assault, but Atlanta was about to be abandoned. With his communication and rail line cut, Hood realized he could no longer hold the city of Atlanta and retreated to Lovejoy Station (now Lovejoy in Clayton County).

September 2, 1864

Henry Slocum's XX Corps moved into Atlanta, accepting the surrender of the city from Mayor James Calhoun.

September 3, 1864

Sherman wires Washington "*Atlanta is ours, and fairly won...*"

The Franklin – Nashville Campaign [2]

Allatoona (October 5)

Resaca, Dalton, and the movement into Alabama

Forrest's West Tennessee raid (October 16 – November 16)

Decatur (October 26–29)

Columbia (November 24–29)

Spring Hill (November 29)

Battle of Franklin (November 30)

Pursuit to Nashville

Forrest at Murfreesboro (December 5–6)

Battle of Nashville (December 15–16)

At the conclusion of his Atlanta Campaign, Sherman occupied the city of Atlanta on September 2, 1864, and Hood, who was forced to evacuate the city, regrouped at Lovejoy's Station. For almost a month, the normally aggressive Sherman took little action while his men sat about idly, and many left the army at the end of their enlistments. On September 21, Hood moved his forces to

---

[2] Adapted from
https://en.wikipedia.org/wiki/Franklin%E2%80%93Nashville_Campaign

Palmetto, Georgia, where on September 25, he was visited by Confederate President Jefferson Davis. The two men planned their strategy, which called for Hood to move toward Chattanooga, Tennessee, and operate against Sherman's lines of communications. They hoped that Sherman would follow and that Hood would be able to maneuver Sherman into a decisive battle on terrain favorable to the Confederates.[3]

During the conference, Davis expressed his disappointment in Hood's performance during the Atlanta Campaign, losing tens of thousands of men in ill-advised frontal assaults for no significant gains, and implied that he was considering replacing Hood in command of the army. After the president's departure for Montgomery, Alabama, he telegraphed Hood that he had decided to retain him in command and, acceding to Hood's request, transferred Lt. Gen. William J. Hardee, one of Hood's corps commanders, out of the Army of Tennessee. He also established a new theater commander to supervise Hood and the department of Lt. Gen. Richard Taylor, although the officer selected for the assignment, Gen. P.G.T. Beauregard, was not expected to exert any real operational control of the armies in the field.[4]

Although Sherman was planning to march east to seize the city of Savannah, Georgia, he was concerned about his lines of communications back to Chattanooga. One

---

[3] Connelly, pp. 477-78; Eicher, pp. 736-37; Jacobson, pp. 29-30; Sword, pp. 45-46.

[4] Connelly, pp. 472-77; Sword, pp. 46-49; Jacobson, pp. 30-32.

particular threat was the cavalry commander Nathan Bedford Forrest, who had long bedeviled Union expeditions with lightning raids into their rear areas. On September 29, Lt. Gen. Ulysses S. Grant urged Sherman to dispose of Forrest and Sherman sent Thomas to Nashville, Tennessee, to organize all of the troops in the state. Sherman sent another division, under Brig. Gen. James D. Morgan, to Chattanooga. [5]

Sherman had some advance notice of the nature of Hood's proposed campaign. In a series of speeches given at stops along his way back to Richmond, President Davis rallied his listeners by predicting success for Hood, speeches that were reported in the press and read avidly by Sherman. In Columbia, South Carolina, his speech included:

General Hood's strategy has been good and his conduct has been gallant. His eye is now fixed upon a point far beyond that where he was assailed by the enemy. He hopes soon to have his hand upon Sherman's line of communications, and to fix it where he can hold it. ... I believe it is in the power of the men of the Confederacy to plant our banners on the banks of the Ohio, where we shall say to the Yankee, "be quiet or we shall teach you another lesson." [6]

---

[5] Welcher, p. 583; Esposito, map 148.

[6] Sword, pp. 51-52; Kennedy, p. 389. Connelly, p. 479, discounts the specific nature of Davis's rhetoric and states that there is "little in Davis's several messages to indicate that any plan was in the making for leaving Sherman behind and invading Tennessee and the Ohio Valley. ... such

Confederate attacks on Sherman's supply line

So far, the Confederate strategy was working, because Sherman was being forced to disperse his strength to maintain his lines of communications. However, Sherman was not about to fall into Hood's trap completely. He intended to provide Thomas with sufficient strength to cope with Forrest and Hood, while he completed plans to strike out for Savannah. On September 29, Hood began his advance across the Chattahoochee River, heading to the northwest with 40,000 men to threaten the Western & Atlantic Railroad, Sherman's supply line. On October 1, Hood's cavalry was intercepted by Union cavalry under Brig. Gens. Judson Kilpatrick and Kenner Garrard in a raid on the railroad near Marietta, but Sherman was still uncertain of Hood's location. For the next three weeks, Sherman had difficulty keeping abreast of Hood's movements. Hood moved rapidly, screened his march, and maintained the initiative. The Union cavalry, which Sherman had neglected to train adequately, had a difficult time following Hood and reporting his movements. [7]

On October 3, the day that Thomas arrived in Nashville, Stewart's corps captured Big Shanty (present-day Kennesaw) with its garrison of 175 men, and the following day Acworth, with an additional 250. Sherman left Maj. Gen.

---

comments had been made often by Confederate leaders attempting to whip up the western morale.

[7] Welcher, p. 583; Esposito, maps 148, 149. Sword, p. 84, states that the best horses were reserved by Sherman for his March to the Sea.

Henry W. Slocum in Atlanta and moved toward Marietta with a force of about 55,000 men. Hood split his force, sending the majority of his command to Dallas, Georgia. The remainder, a division under Maj. Gen. Samuel G. French, moved along the railroad toward Allatoona. [8]

The weeks that followed saw the virtual destruction of Hood's Army of Tennessee. The Battle of Nashville was one of the most stunning victories achieved by the Union Army in the war. The formidable Army of Tennessee, the second largest Confederate force, was effectively destroyed as a fighting force. Hood's army entered Tennessee with over 30,000 men but left with 15-20,000. [9]

Casualties from the two-day battle were 3,061 Union (387 killed, 2,558 wounded, and 112 missing or captured) and approximately 6,000 Confederate (1,500 killed or wounded, 4,500 missing or captured). [10]

Retreat and pursuit of Hood

The Union army set off in pursuit of Hood from Nashville. The rainy weather became an ally to the

---

[8] Sword, p. 54; Esposito, map 149; Welcher, p. 583.

[9] Jacobson, p. 428: the field returns for Hood's army on January 20, 1865, listed 20,700 effectives. Jacobson surmises that missing men from Franklin and Nashville gradually rejoined the army during and after its retreat.

[10] Eicher, p. 780.

Confederates, delaying the Union cavalry pursuit, and Forrest was able to rejoin Hood on December 18, screening the retreating force. The pursuit continued until the beaten and battered Army of Tennessee recrossed the Tennessee River on December 25. On Christmas Eve, Forrest turned back Wilson's pursuing cavalry at the Battle of Anthony's Hill. [11]

Although Hood blamed the entire debacle of his campaign on his subordinates and the soldiers themselves, his career was over. He retreated with his army to Tupelo, Mississippi, resigned his command on January 13, 1865, and was not given another field command. Forrest returned to Mississippi, but in 1865 he was driven into Alabama by James H. Wilson, and his command became dissipated and ineffective. [12]

By the time of Hood's defeat in Nashville, Sherman's army had advanced to the outskirts of Savannah, which they captured just before Christmas. Five thousand men from the Army of Tennessee were later employed under Joseph E. Johnston against Sherman in South Carolina, but to no avail.

---

[11] Welcher, p. 610; McPherson, pp. 207-08.

[12] Esposito, map 153; Niven, p. 144; Kennedy, p. 397.

The TN 24th Infantry Regiment 49

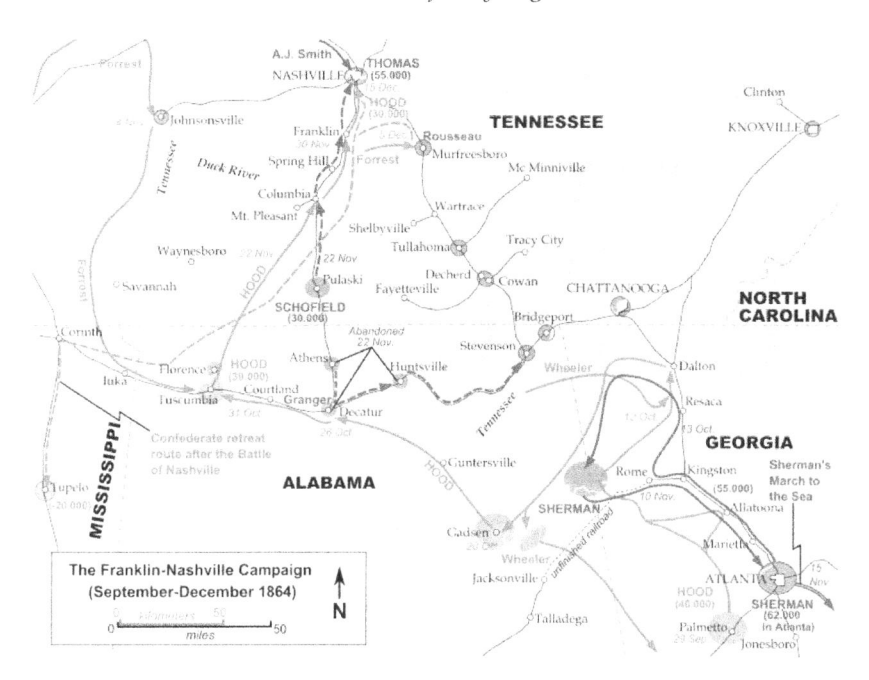

"Franklin-Nashville campaign" by User:Andrei nacu at en.wikipedia - Own work. Licensed under Public Domain via Commons - https://commons.wikimedia.org/wiki/File:Franklin-Nashville_campaign.svg#/media/File:Franklin-Nashville_campaign.svg

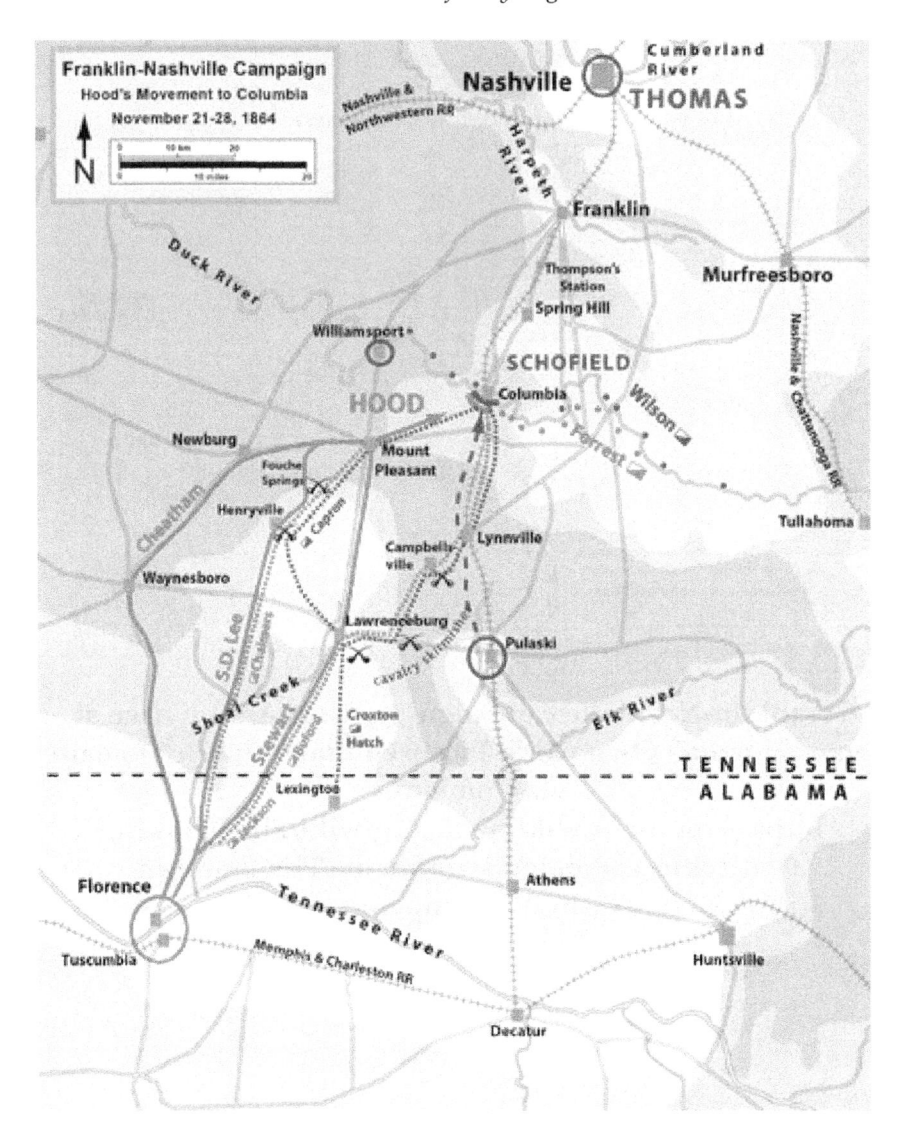

Map by Hal Jespersen, www.posix.com/CW
Hood's advance from Florence to Columbia

TimeLine of the Carolina's Campaign

"Carolinas Campaign" by Map by Hal Jespersen, www.posix.com/CW. Licensed under CC BY 3.0 via Wikimedia Commons - https://commons.wikimedia.org/wiki/File:Carolinas_Campaign.png#/media/File:Carolinas_Campaign.png

JANUARY

3, 1865. -Skirmish near Hardeeville, S. C.

3-17, 1865. -Transfer of the larger portion of the Army of the Tennessee, under Major-General Howard, from Savannah, Ga., to Beaufort, S. C.

8, 1865. -Major General John A. Logan, U. S. Army, resumes command of the Fifteenth Army Corps, relieving Major General Peter J. Osterhaus.

14, 1865. -Advance of Union forces from Beaufort to Pocotaligo, S. C., and skirmishes.

15, 1865. -Destruction of the U. S. monitor Patapsco, in Charleston Harbor, S. C.

20, 1865. -Reconnaissance from Pocotaligo to the Salkehatchie River, S. C., and skirmish.

25, 1865. -Reconnaissance from Pocotaligo to the Salkehatchie River, S. C.

26, 1865. -Skirmish near Pocotaligo, S. C.

27, 1865. -Skirmish at Ennis' Cross-Roads, S. C.

28, 1865. -Skirmish at Combahee River, S. C.

*29, 1865. -Skirmish at Robertsville, S. C.

30, 1865. -Skirmish near Lawtonville, S. C.

31, 1865. -The Department of North Carolina constituted, to consist of the State of North Carolina, and Major General John M. Schofield, U. S. Army, assigned to its command.

FEBRUARY

1, 1865. -Skirmish at Hickory Hill, S. C.

Skirmish at Whippy Swamp Creek, S. C.

2, 1865. -Skirmish at Lawtonville, S. C.

Skirmish at Barker's Mill, Whippy Swamp, S. C.

Skirmish at Duck Branch, near Loper's Cross-Roads, S. C.

Skirmishes at Rivers' and Broxton's Bridges, Salkehatchie River, S. C.

3, 1865. -Action at Rivers' Bridge, Salkehatchie River, S. C.

Skirmish at Dillingham's Cross-Roads or Duck Branch, S. C.

4, 1865. -Skirmish at Angley's Post-Office, S. C.

Skirmish at Buford's Bridge, S. C.

5, 1865. -Skirmish at Duncanville, S. C.

Skirmish at Combahee Ferry, S. C.

6, 1865. -Action at Fishburn's Plantation, near Lane's Bridge, Little Salkehatchie River, S. C.

Skirmish at Cowpen Ford, Little Salkehatchie River, S. C.

Skirmish near Barnwell, S. C.

February 7, 1865. -Skirmish at Blackville, S. C.

Skirmish at the Edisto Railroad Bridge, S. C.

Reconnaissance to Cannon's Bridge, South Edisto River, S. C.

8, 1865. -Skirmish at Williston, S. C.

Skirmish near White Pond, S. C.

Skirmish at Walker's or Valley Bridge, Edisto River, S. C.

Skirmish at Cannon's Bridge, South Edisto River, S. C.

9, 1865. -Major General Quincy A. Gillmore, U. S. Army, assumes command of the Department of the South, vice Major General John G. Foster.

Major General John M. Schofield, U. S. Army, assumes command of the Department of North Carolina.

The advance of the Twenty-third Army Corps arrives at Fort Fisher, N. C.

Skirmish at Binnaker's Bridge, South Edisto River, S. C.

Skirmish at Holman's Bridge, South Edisto River, S. C.

10, 1865. -Skirmish at James Island, S. C.

Skirmish at Johnson's Station, S. C.

11, 1865. -Action at Aiken, S. C.

Action at Johnson's Station, S. C.

Attack on Battery Simkins, S. C.

Action near Sugar Loaf, N. C.

11-12, 1865. -Skirmishes about Orangeburg, S. C.

12-13, 1865. -Skirmishes at the North Edisto River, S. C.

14, 1865. -Skirmish at Wolf's Plantation, S. C.

Skirmish at Gunter's Bridge, North Edisto River, S. C.

15, 1865. -Skirmish at Congaree Creek, S. C.

Skirmish at Savannah Creek, S. C.

Skirmish at Bates' Ferry, Congaree River, S. C.

Skirmish at Red Bank Creek, S. C.

Skirmish at Two League Cross-Roads, near Lexington, S. C.

16-17, 1865. -Skirmishes about Columbia, S. C.

17, 1865. -Union forces occupy Columbia, S. C.

MARCH

7–10 - Wyse Fork

10 - Monroe's Cross Roads

16 - Averasborough

19 – 21 Bentonville

While Slocum's advance was stalled at Averasborough by Hardee's troops, the right wing of Sherman's army under Howard marched toward Goldsboro. On March 19, Slocum encountered the entrenched Confederates of Gen. Joseph E. Johnston who had concentrated to meet his advance at Bentonville. Johnston had increased his forces to about 21,000 men by absorbing the troops under Bragg, who had abandoned Wilmington. Late afternoon, Johnston attacked, crushing the line of the XIV Corps. Only strong counterattacks and desperate fighting south of the Goldsborough Road blunted the Confederate offensive. Elements of the XX Corps were thrown into the action as they arrived on the field. Five Confederate attacks failed to dislodge the Federal defenders, and darkness ended the first day's fighting. During the night, Johnston contracted his line into a "V" to protect his flanks, with Mill Creek to his rear. On March 20, Slocum was heavily reinforced, but fighting was sporadic. Sherman was inclined to let Johnston retreat. On March 21, however, Johnston remained in position while he removed his wounded. Skirmishing heated up along the entire front. In the afternoon, Maj. Gen. Joseph Mower led his Union division along a narrow trace that carried it across Mill Creek into Johnston's rear. Confederate counterattacks stopped Mower's advance, saving the army's only line of communication and retreat. Mower withdrew, ending fighting for the day. During the night, Johnston retreated across the bridge at Bentonville. Union forces pursued at first light, driving back Wheeler's rearguard and saving the bridge. Federal pursuit was halted at Hannah's Creek after a severe skirmish. Sherman, after regrouping at Goldsboro, pursued Johnston toward Raleigh.

Aftermath

When Joseph E. Johnston met with Jefferson Davis in Greensboro in mid-April, he told the Confederate president:

"Our people are tired of the war, feel themselves whipped, and will not fight. Our country is overrun, its military resources greatly diminished, while the enemy's military power and resources were never greater and may be increased to any extent desired. ... My small force is melting away like snow before the sun."

On April 18, three days after the death of President Abraham Lincoln, Johnston signed an armistice with Sherman at Bennett Place, a farmhouse near Durham Station. Sherman at first offered terms of surrender to Johnston that encompassed political issues as well as military, without authorization from General Grant or the United States government. The confusion on this issue lasted until April 26, when Johnston agreed to purely military terms and formally surrendered his army and all Confederate forces in the Carolinas, Georgia, and Florida.

A Confederate View

[The following narrative is excerpted from Confederate Military History – Georgia Volume and presents the events in and around Waynesborough from a Southern perspective.]

Gen. G. W. Smith, in command of the First division, Georgia reserves, had at Lovejoy's Station a force numbering about 2,800 effective infantry, 200 or 300 cavalry, and three batteries. Brigadier-General Iverson with two brigades of cavalry covered his front. On the 12th, Major-General Wheeler arrived in person and his cavalry division soon followed from Alabama. After the cavalry had skirmished with Howard's advance, Smith fell back to Griffin, and there learning of the Federal movements eastward, moved rapidly to Macon. Wheeler notified Generals Bragg and Hardee, General Beauregard at Tuscumbia, Gen. Howell Cobb, General Taylor at Selma, General Hood and others, of the enemy's movements and evident intentions, and General Cobb also advised those high in command of the danger that was threatening. General Cobb, at Macon, had but a small force, and reinforcements were urgently called for. But there were few that could be spared. Beauregard could only send Gen. Richard Taylor to take command, and himself follow, but he had no forces to take with him.

The war department extended Hardee's command to the Chattahoochee, but he could only spare the Fifth Georgia without stripping the coast. President Davis instructed General Cobb to get out every man who could render service, and promised that Colonel Rains, at Augusta, would furnish torpedoes to plant in the roads. Stirring appeals were made to the people of Georgia by Senator Hill and the

Georgia congressmen to fly to arms, remove all subsistence from the course of Sherman's army, and destroy what could not be carried away; burn all bridges, block up roads, and assail the invader night and day.

Meanwhile Sherman marched on, creating a charred avenue over 40 miles wide through the unprotected State, destroying the railroads, seizing all provisions, pillaging, plundering and burning. There was no force available to obstruct his onward course. He had simply to accomplish the military feat of "marching through Georgia."

The forces of Generals Wheeler, Smith and Cobb being concentrated at Macon on the 19th, General Hardee took command, and sent Wheeler up to Clinton to reconnoiter. Six of his men dashed into Clinton and captured the servant of General Osterhaus, corps commander, within twenty feet of headquarters. Charging and counter-charging followed, ending in the repulse of a Federal cavalry command by Wheeler's escort. On the 20th there was active skirmishing by Wheeler.

Kilpatrick advanced as far as the redoubts about Macon, held by the infantry and dismounted cavalry, and the head of his 'column entered the works but were repulsed.

On the 22d, Howard having approached Gordon, sent Wood;s division and Kilpatrick's cavalry toward Macon for another demonstration. This force was met by Wheeler's men, who charged early in the morning and captured one of the Federal picket posts, causing the loss of about 60 to the enemy. A considerable cavalry fight followed, and in the afternoon Walcutt's Federal brigade behind barricades was attacked by the Confederate infantry and a battery. with great vigor. Walcutt was wounded, but managed to hold his ground with the assistance of cavalry.

On another part of the line of invasion the Federal Twentieth corps, opposed only by desultory skirmishing of small Confederate bands, had made a path of destruction through Madison and Eatonton. Geary's division destroyed the fine railroad bridge over the Oconee, and the mill and ferryboats near Buckhead. On the 19th he also destroyed about 500 bales of cotton and 50,000 bushels of corn, mostly on the plantation of Col. Lee Jordan. This corps entered Milledgeville on the 20th, and Davis' corps, accompanied by Sherman, arrived next day.

The State legislature hastily adjourned, and under the direction of Gen. Ira R. Foster, quartermaster-general of the State, great efforts were made to remove the State property and archives, but on account of the scarcity of wagons and the demoralized condition of the people, adequate help could not be obtained. As the penitentiary had been used for the manufacture of arms, and was expected to be destroyed, Governor Brown released all the convicts and organized them into a regularly mustered-in and uniformed battalion under Captain Roberts, which subsequently did good service in removing property and in battle.

Upon the arrival of the Federals, two regiments under Colonel Hawley, of Wisconsin, occupied the capital city, and according to his own report, burned the railroad depot, two arsenals, a powder magazine and other public buildings and shops, and destroyed large quantities of arms, ammunition and salt. A general pillage followed these acts of war. Then the two Federal corps pushed on by way of Hebron, Sandersville, Tennille and Louisville, and Howard's wing crossed the Oconee at Bali's ferry and advanced in two columns by the 1st of December to the neighborhood of Sebastopol.

Howard at this date reported that he had destroyed the Ocmulgee cotton mills, and had supplied his army from the country, which he found full of provisions and forage. "I regret to say that quite a number of private dwellings which the inhabitants have left have been destroyed by fire, but without official sanction; also many instances of the most inexcusable and wanton acts, such as the breaking open of trunks, taking of silver plate, etc. I have taken measures to prevent it, and I believe they will be effectual. The inhabitants are generally terrified and believe us a thousand times worse than we are." The wanton destruction went on, however, with rarely such efforts to restrain the soldiery from depredations.

As Howard advanced, Gen. H. C. Wayne, with the cadets of the Georgia military institute and part of the reserves, fell back across the Oconee. Maj. A. L. Hartridge in a gallant fight defended the Oconee railroad bridge. The Federals by the feint at Macon had managed to hold General Hardee there with some forces in their rear, and the similar feint toward Augusta detained Gen. B. D. Fry, with about 4,000 troops. On the 23d, Austin, with the cadets, successfully held the railroad bridge against the enemy, and Hartridge, at the ferry, drove back across the river a Federal detachment which had forced its way over. This permitted the removal of the stores from Tennille. Gen. A. R. Wright took command in this quarter under authority of a telegram from President Davis, all communication between the east and the west sides of the State being broken. Augusta was reinforced by troops under Generals Chestnut and Gartrell from South Carolina. Beauregard, arriving at Macon, where Lieutenant-General Taylor also was, reported that Sherman was doubtless en route to the sea, thence to reinforce Grant, and he instructed Hood that he should promptly crush Thomas in middle Tennessee, to relieve Lee.

On the 24th, Wayne reported to General McLaws that the Federals were shelling him at Oconee bridge, but he kept up a gallant fight till night, holding one end of the bridge while the enemy set fire to the other. Finally parties crossed the river to his right and left, and he was compelled to withdraw his few hundred men. Wheeler crossed the river to the south on the same day and moved to the support of the Confederates.

On the 25th General Bragg reached Augusta and took command. Wheeler, pushing on to Sandersville, reinforced the local troops which were skirmishing with the Federal cavalry advance, and drove the latter back with some loss. On the same evening, learning that Kilpatrick had started out toward Augusta, he left Iverson before the Federal infantry, and overtaking Kilpatrick at midnight, drove him from the main Augusta road. Pushing on rapidly he struck the enemy several times during the early morning, capturing prisoners. The way was lighted with the barns and houses, cotton gins, and corn-cribs fired by the Federals. Kilpatrick was forced to turn off by way of Waynesboro, where he destroyed the bridge and set fire to the town, but Wheeler arrived in time to extinguish the flames. Beyond Waynesboro, Kilpatrick hastily barricaded a line which

Wheeler assailed with great spirit, Humes and Anderson attacking on the flank. The enemy was routed, losing a large number in killed, wounded and prisoners, General Kilpatrick himself escaping with the loss of his hat. In a swamp the fight was renewed, and the enemy again stampeded with the loss of about 200. Retreating over Buckhead creek, Kilpatrick fired the bridge but could not hold his ground long enough to see it burned, and Wheeler repaired the structure and crossed in pursuit. His worn-out troopers had now been riding and fighting a night and a day, but before night again arrived he attacked the Federal line behind their barricades and again sent them flying. "During the night," Wheeler reported, "Kilpatrick sought the protection of his infantry, which he did not venture to forsake again during the campaign."

First Hand Account

The Death Of An Unsung Confederate Hero

[The following is the relatively unknown account of a Confederate soldier's wife regarding the death of Robert Newton Hull at Binnaker's Bridge, South Carolina. It details the attempt of the woman and a chivalrous Federal officer to save the life of the young Major.]

As I passed through the parlor on my return from the dining-room I chanced to overhear several words of a conversation going on between two officers. They were discussing the events of the day, and among other things spoke in terms of the highest admiration of the dauntless bravery of a young Confederate officer who, throwing himself in the rear of his men, had tried to rally them even after they had commenced to retreat, and was shot down in the act. My sympathy was at once aroused. He was a "boy in gray," he had fallen fighting for the cause we both loved in common. I must know all that I could about him. If still alive he must be found and taken care of; if dead then his body must have such burial as became a soldier and a hero.

Stepping to the side of the officers I asked then to tell me the name of the brave young commander. They answered,

"Major Hulsey."

My feelings of sympathy were now changed to keen pain and intense solicitude, for Major Hulsey was a relative of my husband's and sister-in-law's families.

"Is he dead?" I asked.

"I suppose not, madam," he replied, "or at least he was not when we found him."

"Where is he now?"

"In the branch at the head of the lane," they answered, as coolly as if they had said, "In the next room on a feather bed."

"Gentlemen," I entreated, "will you not have him brought to the house? If really Major Hulsey, he is related to us; and if he is not Major Hulsey, it is all the same; he is one of our soldiers, a brave defender of our rights, and as such I crave - nay, beg the privilege of ministering unto him."

I think I touched the right chord when I addressed them as "gentlemen," for that they were gentlemen, as well as officers, their after conduct showed plainly. My earnest, entreating words seemed to have the desired effect upon them. They arose at once and went out, and a half hour later the wounded young officer was brought in on a stretcher. I had him at once carried into the dining-room, where a large fire was now blazing, and laid upon a mattress placed upon the floor.

Soon a crowd had gathered within, whether from pure curiosity, or a desire to warm themselves before the roaring fire, I could not decide. Doubtless it was from both. One glance into the face of our brave young soldier, ashy gray in its pallor where it was not covered with clots of congealed blood, convinced me that he had not long to live. The bullet had done its fatal work, passing in through the left temple and lodging in the brain. I saw, also, that it was not Major Hulsey, but a stranger. However, I made up my mind that I would, for certain reasons, keep this knowledge to myself.

As I stooped above him to render what assistance I could, it was all that I could do to keep from crying out in nervous horror as I caught sight of the ugly ghastly wound, which looked ten times ghastlier now as the warmth from the fire caused the congealed blood to flow afresh. I knew this would never do, and, making a brave effort at control, I strove zealously, but, alas! vainly to staunch the flow of blood. Just as I had almost given up in despair a kind-faced young officer made his way to my side, and bending above me said gently: "Madame, I have a flask of brandy here. Get a spoon and we will see if we cannot force him to swallow some." I did as bidden; but, alas! it proved fruitless. With all our efforts we could not force it past the tightly clenched teeth, and in a little while his struggles ceased, he lay passive for a few moments, and then with a few hoarsely muttered, disconnected sentences and a nervous twitching of the muscles of the lips, the brave young soldier had Fought His Last Battle.

As the last breath escaped him I burst into tears, folded the hands, still stained with their own lifeblood, across the pulseless heart that would never stir again at the sound of the martial reveille. Tenderly bathing the face and hands of the dead young soldier, and smoothly brushing the soft dark hair, I prepared to leave him in the charge of two of the soldiers, who, through the sympathetic interest of the young officer who had proffered me the flask of brandy, were detailed to watch over him until morning, when I had determined to see the commanding officer and arrange for a proper burial.

I can never forget the kindness of this young officer, whom I afterwards learned was Capt. L. M. Dayton, aide-de-camp to Gen. Sherman. He was considerate, courteous and gentlemanly in every intercourse with us, and but for him our trials and sufferings would have been increased tenfold. Wherever he may be now, if living, should these lines chance to meet his eye, I beg he will accept this grateful tribute from a Southern woman, who admired him for the generous, chivalrous man he was as well as the brave and noble officer - though he wore the blue.

While arranging the clothing of the dead young soldier I had noticed that all his pockets were turned wrong side out as though they were hastily rifled of their contents; while a portion of his watchguard, which had evidently been cut, still hung from a buttonhole in his vest. I at once made known these discoveries to Capt. Dayton, who upon instituting a series of inquiries, soon found out that the burly officer, who had attempted to give me the rebuke, was the one who had shot him down; that he, also, was the one who had rifled his pockets of their contents and that he still had in his possession his horse, watch, pocketbook, some letters and papers and one or two photographs.

Then and there I made up my mind that I would never rest until I had each one of those articles, with the exception of the horse, of course, in my possession. They would be sacred treasures to his relatives and friends, whoever and wherever they were. I believed that I could trace them up by means of the letters. I then enlisted Capt. Dayton in the work, and he promised he would return them to me if it lay within his power.

Historical Sketch

The Tennessee 24th Infantry regiment was organized in July 1861 and completed at Camp Trousdale, Sumner County, Tennessee August 23, 1861. The 24th Tennessee was originally composed of 12 companies, each containing over a hundred men. Its companies were recruited in the following counties: Rutherford, Williamson, Macon, Sumner, DeKalb, Maury, Coffee, Hickman, and Wilson.

The first battle for the 24th was an expedition from Cave City, KY Oct. 25, 1861 against Camp Joe Underwood about 5 miles away which succeeded in breaking up the Federal Camp of instruction. The Regiment was at this time in the 3rd Brigade, Col. R. G. Shaver commanding in Hardee's Division but was transferred to the 2nd Brigade under Col. Patrick R. Cleburne on Jan. 1st 1862 where it remained until the reorganization at Tupelo. While this unit did not participate at Ft. Donelson, they did join the retreating forces under Albert Sidney Johnson from Bowling Green and became part of the Central Army reorganization at Murfreesboro on Feb. 23rd 1862.

At the Battle of Shiloh on April 6th & 7th 1862, the 24th fought bravely losing 12 killed and 24 wounded of the 406 men they took into the two days of fighting. Cleburne's Brigade went into the battle 2,750 strong and lost an even thousand men with 32 missing. Field returns for April 26, 1862 show that the 24th was reduced to a total of 106 effectives.

Next in line of duty was the Battle of Farmington, Mississippi on May 28, 1862. Here Colonel Allison was criticized severely and Major Bratton commended very highly.

At the reorganization at Tupelo on July 8, 1862 Company G was consolidated with B of Williamson County becoming part of the 2nd Brigade commanded by Brig. Gen. Alex P. Stewart, Maj. Gen. Frank B. Cheatham the Division, and Maj. Gen. Leonidas Polk the Left Wing. Under this organization the Regiment took part in the Battle of Perryville on Oct. 8th, 1862 suffering 68 casualties. Company G lost another 2 men with 1 wounded. Afterwards, the Confederate Army traveled through East Tennessee with a supply wagon train forty miles long headed toward Nashville and took position around Murfreesboro in the Autumn of 1862. In the last of December of that year the regiment went into battle there suffering 43% of the 344 engaged. It entered the fight with 31 commissioned officers and 313 men, taking a total of 344 effectives it lost 3 officers with 6 men killed, & 5 officers and 39 men wounded. Here Colonel Bratton was mortally wounded, Lieutenant Colonel Wilson was wounded and Major S. E. Shannon took over the command.

The 24th remained in line until Jan. 4th and were one of the last commands to be withdrawn on the retreat to Tullahoma.

On April 1st 1863, the army was reorganized and Col. O. F. Strahl commanded Stewart's Brigade, Cheatham the Division, and Polk the Corps Commander. Then they were sent to Sweetwater, Tennessee for a short time, fought at Tullahoma and returned in time for Missionary Ridge where they had 45 casualties. At Chickamauga they suffering 43 casualties. Company G had 4 wounded, 6 captured, 1 missing, & 1 discharged for disability.

By December 14th, 1863 the field returns showed that the 24th then had an effective force of 211, total present 257, number of arms, 148 with 40 rounds of ammunition per man.

The 24th participated in the Atlanta Campaign from early 1864 through the fall of Atlanta and Jonesboro.

Soon afterwards, Hood began his march into Tennessee heading towards Nashville. He established headquarters two and a half miles from Spring Hill, TN on November 29, 1864. The next day the 24th fought at the bloody Battle of Franklin. The 24th was in the Granny White Pike area and formed part of the force under General Walthall covering the retreat to Corinth, Mississippi.

In the aftermath the 24th Tennessee Regiment as a whole had the Colonel, Lieut. Colonel, Major, Adjutant, and every Captain and First Lieutenant killed or wounded, the ranking officer being a Second Lieutenant. Field Returns November 6th shows Stewart's Army Corps to have 8,708 total effectives present, and Cheatham's Corps 10,519. The next field return is December 10th after Franklin and before Nashville and read 5,321 and 7,272 showing a loss of one third. Nashville proved to be Hood's final downfall where he was absolutely routed. By this time the Tennessee 24th had become so absorbed in reorganizations and consolidations that it had lost all semblance of existence as a separate organization. The original twelve companies were made into: Company F of the 3rd Consolidated Tennessee

Infantry and as such was paroled at Greensboro, North Carolina on May 1, 1865.

On December 20th 1864 Forrest was placed in command of the rear guard of the army, and Walthall was ordered to support him with eight brigades of "picked infantry". These eight brigades gave him an effective force of 1900 men, of whom about 400 were without shoes, and many more were practically bare-footed and made up the famous "Rear Guard". Maney & Strahl's brigades were commanded by Col. Hume R. Field and field returns next day show 113 effectives total. In the last consolidation in North Carolina March 21st 1865, the 3rd Tennessee Consolidated Regiment was organized and was composed of the 4th, 5th, 19th, 24th, 31st, 33rd, 35th, 38th, and 41st making up newly formed Company K.

On the way home from the surrender the few retiring members of this unit had to stop at the home of a widow's house about ten miles east of Greenville, Tennessee to care for John H. Derryberry who had suffered with chronic dysentery. In a few days he died leaving no means to bury him. That night four of the Riflemen (Co. K) led by Anderson Daniel made a charge on the combined Commissary, Quartermaster, Paymaster, and Ordnance Train and captured four bales of spun cotton yarn. With three of these a coffin was procured from town and the other bale was given to the widow for her attention to the deceased and a grave for him in her apple orchard. This was the last official act of the Duck River Riflemen.

First Hand Account [13]

The Duck River Rifles

by Judge Frank H. Smith

(The Herald published below the first installment of a series of articles from the pen of Judge Frank H. Smith, on the Duck River Riflemen being an historical sketch of the deeds of one of the most remarkable companies of Confederate soldiers in the Civil War. The company was made up largely of Maury Countians, and most of the companys history, as written by Judge Smith, is totally unknown to the vast majority of Maury Countians, yet at the same time it is intensely interesting, and each installment will be not only worth reading, but well worth preservation)

My friend, Capt. R. W. Tindall, of Leftwich Bridge, has a roster of Captain J. M. Billingtons company, The Duck River Riflemen, which was made up in the eastern part of Maury County and western part of Marshall County, and which served with distinction in the Civil War, in the 24th Tennessee Volunteer Infantry. This original report is on pieces of Confederate paper, written with Confederate ink, which like other Confederate things has faded. As this

---

[13] Historical Sketch by Judge Frank H. Smith published in the Columbia Herald April 7, 15, 23, May 6, and May 13, 1904)

roster was made at the end of the war, without access to the Muster Rolls of the previous four years, it does not contain all the names of the Company as there were many recruits and additions, and some served for only a short time.

In this series of articles I wish to give a Historical Sketch of this Company and incidentally of the other and larger commands with which it was connected. While many persons are acquainted with most of the facts there are some incidents that are not so generally known, and which nave never been published. I trust that this Sketch will prove of interest, not only to the families of the Duck River Riflemen, but also to the general reader.

Where the Company Was Organized.

The Duck River Riflemen were organized at the old Napier Hole, a noted place on Flat Creek just north of the Bear Creek Pike; here they met regularly for drill under Capt. Billington, and here they were sworn in by Dr. J. M. Parks.

The Company originally numbered 112 men, but no record is now available giving all the names.

Thomas Hosford was so small and so young that he was afraid he would not be accepted; the left of the line being very close to the creek, he jumped in the water, where it was about waist deep so Dr. Parks made no objection to his height, and Hosford took the oath while in the creek. He was the last man sworn in, and one of the first killed in battle on that fateful Sunday morning at Shiloh.

Captain Jas. M. Billington.

James M. Billington, a member of a prominent Maury County family, was elected Captain. He was the 29 years old, in the prime of manhood, with a face and form that would attract attention in any assemblage. Capt. Billington commanded the Company in the engagement at Camp Joe Underwood, and in the battle of Shiloh, with great credit to himself and the men. His health failing, he resigned at Tupelo and returned home. He had planned to have a family reunion at his home near Rally Hill on his birthday Sep. 5, 1885; the reunion was held, but it proved to be for his funeral.

Leaving Maury County__

This Company marched to Columbia, taking cars here for Nashville and Murfreesboro, and at the latter place went into quarters at Camp Anderson, three miles from town. The regiment organization was made in July 1861, and completed at Camp Trousdale August 24, 1861, the Duck River Riflemen becoming Company G, in the 24th Tennessee Volunteer Infantry.

The Twenty-Fourth Tennessee,--This Regiment was originally composed of 15 companies, each containing over a hundred men.

Col Samuel E. Shannon, who is now living near

Nashville, writes me that the organization of the regiment was as follows:

Co. A, Rutherford Co; Captain John C. Jackson

Co. B, Williamson Co; Captain S. E. Shannon

Co. D, Macon Co;. Capt. J. M. Uhles

Co. E, Sumner Co. Capt. J. A. Baskerville

Co. F, Smith Co; Capt, James Dowell

Co. G, Maury Co.; Capt. J. M. Billington

Co. H, Hickman Co.; Capt, C. W. Beale

Co. I, Hickman Co. Capt. E. W. Beasley

Co. K, Franklin and Wilson Co.; Capt. T. C. Goodner

Capt. Buck Harts Co. from Sumner, Trousdale and Smith Counties, and a company commanded by Capt. Mays were, afterwards added to the twenty-fourth.

How Pat Cleburne Got His First Brigade and Made an Enemy.

The Colonel, Richard D, Allison, was from Smith County, and was energetic in the enlistment of a company there. He was elected Captain, and on the organization of the regiment was made its Colonel. He had served with credit in the Mexican War, and naturally supposed that his previous military experience would procure him the command of the Brigade. Great was his disgust when he found that an Arkansas lawyer, and an Irishman at that, had received the appointment, and he never forgave Pat Cleburne for winning the Commission that he had himself expected. And there seems to have been no love lost on Cleburnes part, for I find that at Shiloh, Cleburne or some higher power, had placed Allison temporarily in arrest, and thus deprived him of the command of the Twenty-Fourth in that battle. But Allison did not sulk in his tent, like Achilles of old at Troy, but taking a musket, he fought in the ranks as a common soldier.

The friction between Cleburne and Allison became so great especially after Cleburnes report on an expedition near Corinth in the later part of May, in which he accused Allison of unsoldier-like conduct that Allison resigned and formed a command known as Allisons Cavalry Squadron, which remained under Gen. Joe Wheeler throughout the war.

Gallant Colonel Peebles.

Thomas H. Peebles, the Lieutenant Colonel of the 24th, was from near Spring Hill, at which place and Franklin he had achieved great success as a teacher. He made up Company B in the southern part of Williamson County, and was elected its Captain. After Allison was chosen Colonel of the 24th, Peebles was given the next highest office, and Sam C. Shannon became Captain of Company B.

Col. Peebles commanded the regiment at Shiloh,

and was highly complimented by Cleburne in his official report for the excellent manner in which he handled the men. Almost at the first fire his horse was killed under him. And he fought on foot throughout the rest of the battle, escaping unhurt, although his coat was pierced by three minie balls. Just after the battle he resigned ad accepted a position with Cleburne and was not actively connected with the regiment afterwards.

Daring Work as a Spy.

A year or two later he was detailed on a hazardous secret mission into Middle Tennessee, then occupied by the Federals. He had accomplished the object of his trip, but just before reaching the Confederate lines was captured by a roaming squad of Federal cavalry. As they were proceeding to search him, he recognized one of these soldiers as having been a former member of his old Company, who, having deserted, had joined the enemy. The renegade prevailed on his comrades to desist, and treat the Colonel with more consideration. At the first convenient moment, Col. Peebles took the information he had been at so much pains to collect, and which, if discovered, would have hung him, and slipping the paper in his mouth, chewed it up. He was sent as a prisoner to Camp Chase, but was soon exchanged and returned to service. Col. Peebles was killed near Spring Hill in an unfortunate personal encounter in November 1870 on the very day on which he had been elected State Senator.

Major Jack Williams--

Jack J. Williams, who was commissioned to First Major of the 24th, enlisted in Hickman County, and was first elected Captain of Co. I. When the regiment was organized he was the general choice for Major, and Lieut. Edward W. Beasley was elected to succeed him in the command of the Company. We went through the battle of Shiloh with great gallantry, but in the reorganization at Tupelo three months later he resigned.

Hardships Caused Much Sickness During the Early Days.--

The regiment was in Kentucky in the autumn of 1861, forming a part of the Central Army, under the command of Albert Sidney Johnston. These troops were so largely recruited from the rural districts, that they were soon suffering from diseases which, in a more urban population are usually incident to childhood, and comparatively harmless. Mumps, whooping cough and measles were the chief of these, and were almost epidemic. While many of the Duck River Riflemen were in the hospital only three cases terminated fatally: James Hardison, Samuel Jones and Sam Secrest. Dying in October 1861, from measles contracted at Camp Trousdale. These were the first losses this Company sustained. Judge Spences History of Hickman County gives the names of ten members of Company H, and eleven of Company I of this regiment, who died of sickness in the eight months preceding the battle of Shiloh.

The Riflemens First Battle.--

The first engagement of the Duck River Riflemen was in an expedition from Cave City, October 25. 1861, against Camp Joe Underwood, about 5 miles away. Biffles and John B. Hamiltons troops, largely from Maury County, joined a detachment of the 240 men from the 24th, the whole under the command of Col. Allison. The expedition was successful, breaking up the Federal Camp of instruction, and returned without any loss to the command. The Regiment was at this time in the Third Brigade, Col. R. G. Shaver, commanding, in Hardees Division; but on January 1st, 1862, it had been transferred to the Second Brigade under Col. Patrick R. Cleburne, where it remained until the reorganization at Tupelo on July 1862.

The Retreat from Kentucky.--

The 24th did not take part in the battles of Fort Donelson in Feb. 1862, where so many of the Maury County soldiers distinguished themselves. Retreating directly to Nashville with the main forces from Bowling Green, under the command of Albert Sidney Johnston, Central Army was reorganized at Murfreesboro Feb. 23rd, 1862, and in the further withdrawal of the Confederate forces, the 24th reached Decatur on March 17th. On this retreat from Bowling Green, Joseph Dean, the kettle drummer of the Duck River Riflemen, was lost. He as about 70 years old, and it seems strange that the enlistment of a man his age would be accepted; and yet Gen. Winfield Scott, Commander-in-Chief of the United States Army, was almost an octogenarian.

The Riflemen at Shiloh--

In the battle of Shiloh, April 6th and 7th, 1862, Capt. Billington commanded the company, and Lieutenant Colonel Peebles commanded the Regiment, First Lieutenant J. Lou Secrest and many of the privates were in hospital with measles. In the first days fight on Sunday, the regiment was on the extreme left of Cleburnes Command. In the first fire from the Federals the Duck River Riflemen lost nine men killed outright, sixteen wounded, before there was an opportunity of retuning the fire in spite of this frightful sudden loss the troops moved gallantly forward under the command of such officers as Cleburne, Peebles and Billington; making four successive advances, taking the Federal encampment.

The ammunition being exhausted in this brilliant movement, and the nature of the ground rendering it impossible for the ordnance trains to be moved up to supply it, a detail was made which (as Forrest often said) toted the ammunition forward for over a mile. The Command then advanced again nearly to the Tennessee River, where it was finally checked by the Federal gunboats, and by orders from Beauregard, who had succeeded to the command on the death of Albert Sidney Johnston. Gunboats were a great terror to the Southern soldiers then, and like so many other terrors, distance and unfamiliarity increased the danger, Beauregard was at his post in the rear, and the shells from the gunboats were much more destructive there than nearer the river.

A Roll of Honor an Bravery. --

The Duck River Riflemen sustained the following losses in the two days fight at Shiloh:

Andrew Jackson Derryberry, shot through the heart

M. E. Dowell, Jr., shot through the breast.

James Evans, shot in the temple.

James Fuller, shot through the brain.

E. Fitzgerald, shot in the head.

Thomas Hosford

Jeff Weatherly. Shot in the breast

Tom A. Orr, shot through the breast

Newton Reid, shot in the head.

The above nine were killed dead at the first fire.

Merrill Hinson was shot through and through below the collar bone, and died a day or two later in the field hospital. Sid Evans was wounded, and fell into the hands of the enemy, dying in prison about two months later. Hiram Williams was detailed with the infirmary corps, and was lost in the second days fight, and never heard of afterwards. Wm. L. Dougherty was shot through the body; and John Johnson was shot through both hips; these two men finally recovered and were discharged. David A. Jackson, Jr., was terribly wounded in the right leg, losing the free use of the limb; after a partial recovery, he joined the cavalry and was killed at Pulaski in Hoods retreat in December 1864. George G. Daimwood was wounded in the thigh. Sert. David M. Hardison received a flesh wound in the right arm.

Wm. J. Lovett was wounded in the arm. Jacob Bennett was wounded in the leg. James Clark was wounded in the hip. Tom Harmon was wounded in the knee. Martin V. Hardison was wounded in the arm. Simon L. Mc Fadden was wounded in the shoulder. Franklin J. Wright was wounded in the leg. John L. Biggers was wounded in the right arm, losing the use of the limb. He remained with the army doing light duty and was captured at Nashville in Dec. 1864. Though he lived twenty-one years after being wounded, he suffered constantly from its effects. Sergt. Sam W. Daimwood, Corporal James A. Dougherty,

Corp. Wm. A. Collins, T. Anderson Daniel, Geo. W. Pinkleton, Thomas A. Sharp, Pole King, Porter Mayfield and Sergt. Geo. W. Rummage were wounded, but not seriously. Sergt. Ira Shires was cocking his gun, when a Minie ball knocked the hammer off, wounding him slightly in the hand, taking the gun of a dead comrade he continued through the fight.

Edom Edward was shot through the chest and lay on the battlefield from early Sunday morning until Monday night; the litter corps though his sound so certainly mortal that they would not bring him in. Monday night he was put in a wagon and carried to the field hospital, where Dr. Hutton said it would be a waste of time to even dress his wound when there were so many others needing care that had a chance of life. He laid out in the rain all that night, and Wednesday morning Dr. Sam Hardison (now a banker at Lewisburg) began attending him by drawing a silk handkerchief entirely through the wound from front to back. Edwards never fully recovered, but was discharged and died many years after the war at Joe Allens on Bear Creek.

Hickman County Losses.--

Referring to Judge Spences History of Hickman County, I find the following losses in the two companies from our sister county in this regiment at Shiloh.

Company H lost and killed:

Corp. W. D. Baker, E. R. Beasley, W. A. Parker, G. H. Pritchard, W. D. Parker, B. S. Cornwell, Wm. R. Beasley, Dixon Dyer, Thomas M. Haynie, Jesse Powell, John D. Taylor and Henderson M. Winkler.

These were wounded: Captain H. C. Campbell, R. M. Anderson, D. C. Anderson, Thomas Cunningham, W. C. J. Giles, J. B. Hooten and S. J. Reeves.

Company I had killed:

J. M. Duke, A. S. Garrett, W. C. Griffin, Perry Gunter, Wilson Pace, J. M. Reece, and Thomas Curl.

These were wounded: Major Jack J. Williams, formerly captain of Company I, Captain Edward R. Beasley, Lieut, T. S. Easley, Sergt. R. F. Green, arm amputated, W. J. Campbell, W. C. Garner. Died in prison, Wm. Jenkins, W. N. Milam, mortally, Wm. Pinkerton, Jr., W. M.Sanders, Wiley Stuart, W. P. Wofford, T. J. Walker and Babe Sisco.

The effective force of the Duck River Rifleman was greatly reduced before the battle by discharges. Absences and sickness in hospital. Yet this dimished Company lost 12 killed or mortally wounded, and 24 wounded in this bloody fight. Lieut. Joel Hardison was complimented for bravery in this battle.

Pat Cleburnes Brigade. –

Cleburnes Brigade went into the battle 2,750 strong, and lost an even thousand men killed and wounded , and 32 missing. There is no report in the official records of the separate regimental losses, but the field return and April 26, 1862. show that the 24th was reduced to a total of 106 effectiveness. In his report of the battle of Shiloh, Cleburne charged of the men with cowardice and failure to stand fire; he also speaks of the reprehensible conduct of a few stopping to plunder the Federal Encampment that had just been captured.

Captured a Trunk full of Money and Lighted Cigars with it.--

And speaking of despoiling the camp of the enemy, a queer incident occurred on the same Sunday of the first days fight a Shiloh. A well-known citizen of Columbia, whose modesty forbids the use of his name, in print, was then a private in Company H, In Colonel Schallers 22 Miss. Infantry, in the Brigade commanded by Col. Statham. About one oclock that afternoon Lieut. John C. Evans, commanding Co. H, was killed the charge through the Federal encampment and fell close to the sutlers tent of the Douglass Brigade. Just after dark, the Quartermaster of the 22nd Mississippi detailed this present predominent Columbian to take a wagon, and with two other privates of the same Company (Ben S. Jumper and Sam Graham, of near Oxford.) to bring off the remains of Lieut. Evans.

After placing the body in the wagon, these three soldiers put in a lot of crackers, oysters, sardines, and other things from the sutlers tent; they then noticed another large tent close by; and going into it, found a table and camp chairs that indicated its use for office purposes. There were also some large chests or cases, that , seemed very securely made, and without more ado, they broke one of these open with an axe, and found to their disgust, that it was a paymasters chest, containing nothing but greenbacks money, in the original big sheets just as it had been issued by the Treasury Department at Washington. Not wishing to be outdone, however, they took a few armfuls of the money, and dumped it loose into the wagon with the corpse, cigars, oysters, etc., and drove back to the field hospital, where they remained that night.

The money was considered a curiosity merely, and none of the soldiers thought of preserving it, or supposed it would be of any value. This present, prominent Columbian, gave away hundreds of the sheets, mostly of twenty dollar bills, and hundreds more of them were used for lighting cigars and camp-fires. He has thought of this many, very many times since, and always with regret.

Re-organization at Tupelo.--

The losses at Shiloh had been so severe and the

term of enlistment of so many of the soldiers had expired, that a re-organization took place at Tupelo, Miss., July 8, 1862. Company B of Williamson County and Company G of Maury County were consolidated into Company G, and Capt. Billington, having resigned on account of ill health, Samuel E. Shannon was elected Captain of the consolidated Company. Lieut. Wm. M. Shires, of Rally Hill, also resigned at this time. Of the Duck River Riflemen, I find that four had been discharged for disability, three for wounds received at Shiloh, also four who were too young, and seven who were too old, for military duty. Sergt. John E. Hardeman was discharged but soon re-enlisted, and though sick much of the time, remained to the end.

A Famous Fiddler.--

Among the other losses sustained by the Company, the discharge of Lieut. Frank Rowlett for ill health was one of the most keenly felt. He was the famous fiddler the Carlo Patti of the Duck River Riflemen and the monotony and drudgery of camp life had been greatly relieved by his wonderful playing. Whenever he turned his instrument the soldiers from other Commands would flock to the quarters of the 24th and when he resigned it was the regret of the whole Brigade. Rowlett moved to the Kentucky Purchase, and is now living in Arkansas.

The two companies from Hickman County were so reduced that they were also consolidated in one, and J.

A. Holmes was elected Captain.

From an undated roll, shortly afterward, the following were the new Company officers:

Captain, Sam E. Shannon

1st Lieut. J. Lon Secrest

2nd Lieut. R. N. Herbert

2nd Lieut. Brevet Joel S. Hardison

1st Sergt. David M. Hardison

2nd Sergt. R. W. Cunningham

3rd Sergt. Ira Shires

4th Sergt. S. J. McMurray

5th Sergt. Calvin M. Cheek

1st Corp. J. B. Copeland

2nd Corp. J. R. Beasley

3rd Corp. Wm. A. Collins

4th Corp. J. H. Roberts

In the changes in the Regimental officers in this

reorganization Col. Allison had resigned and formed the Allison Squadron of Cavalry as mentioned before. Lieut. Col. Thomas H. Peebles had also resigned, and Hugh Lawson White Bratton , of DeKalb County, had been advanced from a subaltern office to the Lieut. Colonelcy, and was placed in Command of the 24th. Major Jack J. Williams of Hickman County, also retired because of wounds at Shiloh and was succeeded by John. A. Wilson, who had been captain of the company from Rutherford County, and who later was Colonel of the 24th. Brig. Gen. Alex O. P. Stewart commanded the Second Brigade and Maj. Gen. B. Frank Cheatham the division, while the Soldier-Priest, Maj. Gen. Leonidas Polk, commanded the Left Wing.

Bragg and Buells Foot Race in Kentucky.--

Under this organization the Regiment took part in the Kentucky campaign under Bragg, which was without special interest in connection with this sketch until the battle of Perryville, Oct. 8th, 1862. Here Lieut. J. Lon Secrest was shot through the body and died on the field. Sergt. Ira Shires had his thigh shattered rendering amputation necessary, from which he died. G. F. Davis was wounded and sent to Atlanta Hospital. Wm. D. Hardison was detailed as nurse for Sergt Ira Shires and others, and was captured later. Major Shires, Tom Harmon, and other members of the Riflemen have told me that Col. Bratton's horse received seventeen wounds in this fight, all of them very slight, but Col. Bratton himself escaped without a scratch. And yet in less than three months, horse and rider were both killed by the same shell at Murfreesboro. Col Bratton was promoted to the full Colonelcy of the 24th and Samuel E. Shannon commissioned Major. The Confederate army retired leisurely out of Kentucky through East Tennessee, bringing a wagon train of supplies forty miles long, it advanced towards Nashville, taking position around Murfreesboro in the Autumn of 1862.

A Close Call for a Rifleman.--

While encamped at Murfreesboro, one of the Duck River Riflemen was arraigned on a charge of desertion after the Shiloh battle. It seems that he had been given a leave of absence for several days. And that the time had been extended by Col. Allison, who was then in command of the regiment. Nothing was thought or done about this for some months, but at Murfreesboro the matter was called up and a court martial was ordered to try his case. On this hasty military trail the proof could not be produced of the extension of his leave of absence, as Col. Allison was in a different command then. Greatly to the surprise of all he was found guilty and under Bragg's idea of strict discipline, he was sentenced to be shot the second day afterwards. As is customary in military execution, the firing detail is made from the company and regiment of the condemned man, and W. M. Shires, Chris Shires, George Rummage, and Sam Daimwood, of the Duck River Riflemen, were of this detail to shoot their companion. The execution was to take place at four o'clock in the afternoon, the grave had been dug, the troops of the Brigade and Division were all in position on the conventional three sides of a hollow square; the wagon had driven up with the man seated on his coffin; the firing squad had taken position ten paces in front of the doomed victim., who had been blindfolded and placed at the grave, when an officer dashed up, his horse in a foam of sweat, with a reprieve from General Polk.

Nat Reynolds had heard of this strange trial and sentence at his home in Maury County the night before. He had been and Enrolling Officer with the regiment in Mississippi at the time the leave of absence had been extended, and knowing this man's innocence of the charge, he had ridden all right and well up in the day, nearly killing his horse in the effort to reach Murfreesboro. He had barely time to make his statement to General Polk and for the General to send a staff officer with the reprieve. The sentence of the court martial was reversed, and an honorable discharge granted, and today he is living near Kedron, in Maury County, a highly respected man in the community. He says he knows exactly how a dead men feels for he considered himself a dead man. (Robert Brown was his name).

The Battle of Murfreesboro.—

The Regiment went into the Battle of Murfreesboro

on the last of Dec. 1862, remaining in line until the 4th of Jan., and was one of the last commands to be withdrawn on the retreat to Tullahoma, It entered the fight with 31 commissioned officers and 313 men, taking a total of 344 effectives; it lost 3 officers and 6 men killed, and 5 officers and 39 men wounded.

Lieut. Joel Hardison was shot in the face and killed in the first day's fight. Willis A. Jones was killed on the 3rd of Jan. Wm. T. Lee was wounded in the collar bone and sent home. John Davis was slightly wounded.

Death of Col. Bratton.--

Col. N. L. W. Bratton had his left leg shattered by a piece of shell, or grape shot, which passed on through the horse, killing it, and sounding the colonel in the right leg. The limb was amputated and on the retreat he was left at Murfreesboro, where he died soon after. Bratton was the idol of the regiment, and had he lived, would undoubtedly had attained high rank. Gen. Stewart paid him a deserved compliment in the official report of the battle, ending his encomium by calling him a 'Knight without fear and without reproach.' Major Samuel E. Shannon assumed command of the regiment, the Lieut. Colonel being seriously wounded.

On the 3rd of Oct. 1863, an order was issued from the Adjutant and Inspector General's office at Richmond, which , after explaining that the delay in procuring medals and badges of distinction had been unavoidable promulgated.

The Confederate Roll of Honor.--

This was ordered to be read on Dress Parade at the head of every regiment in the Confederate service, and on it was placed the name of Willis A. Jones, of Company B, 24th Tenn, Volunteers, for Conspicuous Bravery at the Battle of Murfreesboro. Some of his comrades and his two brothers now living in Maury County have told me of this conduct in this battle. Although he had been wounded in the ankle by a piece of shell in the first day's fight, and sent to the hospital, yet on the third day he hobbled back to the line; while handing his gun, a grape shot struck the lock, driving the hammer through his lung with fatal effect.

A Brave Yankee Colonel.--

A peculiar incident occurred in this fight in the cedarbrake, the like of which tends to soften the horrors of war, and strongly illustrates the respect that the true soldier has for bravery and gallantry, even if exhibited by and enemy.

Col. George W. Roberts of the 42nd Illinois was in command of the 3rd Brigade which, with the other troops, under the command of Gen. Phil H. Sheridan, had been routed. Colonel Roberts tried in vain to stop the break in the Federal ranks caused by the charge of the Tennessee troops, and made effort after effort to reform and to restore the broken lines. He was everywhere conspicuous for his bravery and daring, and about eleven o'clock he fell, killed by a minie ball, This Colonel Roberts was the Federal officer who had given the Confederates such an April Fool nine months before at Island No. 10 on the Mississippi River. With a few small boats and about fifty picked men, he slipped down the river after dark in a furious storm, keeping concealed in the brush till near midnight, then they crawled over the parapet of the first fort, overpowered the sentinels, spiked the six huge 84 pounders, and by daylight had escaped up the river to the Federal fleets. For this daring act he was nominated by the Secretary of War as a Brevet Brigadier General the next day, April 3rd. After the battle of Shiloh, in all the various operations in North Alabama and Middle Tennessee, his Command and always under strict discipline, and conspicuous for never plundering of 'Turchinizing' the people.

Touching Tribute from his Enemies.--

Little wonder it is then that the Confederate have him a soldiers funeral. After the lull in the fight, his late enemies dug a grave among the rocks and cedars. Major Luke W. Finlay, of Gen. Stewart's staff, wrapped him in his own military cloak and read the impressive service of the dead over his remains; the military salute was fired; 'taps' sounded by the bugler and all seemed over. But the private soldiers, especially of the 11th Tennessee, wanted to show their respect. Their Colonel George W. Gordon had been dangerously wounded, and their Brigade Commander and former Colonel, the noble Gen. James E. Rains, had been killed, both of them in that same furious fight in the cedar-brake. So they brought a large smooth stone and placed it on Colonel Roberts- grave, and on this stone they had laboriously scratched and chipped an inscription with a bayonet. This courtesy to Colonel Roberts probably influenced Gen. Rosecrans to permit the remains of Gen. Rains and Gen. Roger W. Handon to be removed to Nashville a week later, but these were denied a military, or even a public funeral.

The Retreat to Chattanooga.--

On April 1st 1863, in the reorganization of the army, before the Tullahoma Chattanooga Ringgold campaign, John A. Wilson as Colonel of the 24th; Col. O.F. Strahl commanded Stewart's Brigade; Maj. B. B. Cheatham still commanded the Division, and Lt. Gen. Leonidas Polk was Corps Commander. Before the opening of the campaign. And while the 24th was stationed at Shelbyville, Sidney Black of the Duck River Riflemen was discharged for disability. The command participated in the various minor engagements incident to the withdrawal of the Confederate forces from Middle Tennessee, without suffering and losses killed or seriously wounded. Although actibely engaged at Chickamauga, none of the Riflemen were killed and only two wounded; Martin V. Hardison, who was struck in the foot by a piece of shell, and T. Anderson Daniel slightly.

An Interesting document.--

Before me lies the muster Roll and Pay Roll of this company, made March 1st, 1864. Capt. Tindall has carefully preserved this Roll for forty years, and in a memorandum by him it is stated that this was the last roll made for the Company.

Both rolls are on one large sheet of paper, 23 by 35 inches, of a quality that would now be regarded as a good grade of wrapping paper, and the printing and ruling are good, and the printing, considering the facilities then possessed in the Confederacy.

The Company Officers were then:

Captain R. N. Herbert

1st Lieut. David M. Hardison, absent on furlough

2nd Lieut. F. M. Hill

2nd Lieut. Brevet R. W. Tindall

1st Sergt. T.H. Burk

2nd Sergt. R. W. Cunningham

3rd Sergt. J. R. Beasley

4th Sergt. George W. Rummage

5th Sergt. Jasper N. Dillehay

1st Corp. J. A. Dougherty

2nd Corp. John E. Hardeman

3rd Corp. Wm A. Collins

4th Corp. J. H. Roberts

Colonel John A. Wilson Commanded the Regiment.

The Roll shows that all the foregoing were enlisted at Camp Trousdale Aug. 24, 1861 for the original period of ten months. There were a total present and absent of 56 officers and privates at this time, which included those that had been added under the Conscript Act.

Had No Money.--

The pay roll shows that the soldiers were about four months in arrears for pay. The privates were due eleven dollars a month, in confederate money, that was then greatly depreciated, the United States soldiers were paid thirteen dollars and later sixteen in green backs. There were five, R. D. Clark, John H. Derryberry, George W. Hardison, B. F. Roberts, and H. D. P. Hogan, who were in hospital, and entitled to commutation for clothing, averaging about one hundred and twenty dollars each. Four privates were entitled to a bounty of fifty dollars each for re-enlistment; the various State and Government bounties in the North were from five hundred to one thousand dollars for re-enlistment.

Missionary Ridge.--

This was the next great battle of the campaign. Although the 24th was hotly engaged in the fight, none of the Company were killed, but George W. Pinkleton was missing and never heard of afterwards. Hazard C. Tindall was wounded in the heel, and died in hospital Feb, 29th 1864, from the scourge more to be dreaded than bullets, gangrene. B. F. Roberts was slightly wounded. Tom Harmon, Jacob B. Shires, Wm. H. Shires, John Caldwell, W. H. Fox, and J. A. Vernon were captured. Martin V. Hardison who had been wounded in the ankle at Chickamauga, went through this battle on a crutch.

On Dec. 14th, 1863, the field returns show that the 24th then had an effective force of 244; total present 257 number of arms, 148 with 40 rounds of ammunition per man, During the Ringgold Campaign the 24th lost 3 killed, 5 wounded, and 45 missing , but as is generally the case in the official record of the War of the Rebellion; the lists of names are omitted.

On the Resaca-Dalton Campaign, the field returns of April 30th shows that Lt. Col. Sam E. Shannon commanded the Regiment, Gen. O. F. Strahl the Brigade; Maj. Gen. B. F. Cheatham the Division Lt. Gen. W. J. Hardee the Corps and Old Joe Johnston is our Commander in the words of a favorite camp song.

A Picket Duel.--

On May 15th on the picket line at Resaca, occurred an incident that it seems strange, was of not uncommon occurrence during the Civil War. Calvin M. Cheek spied the Federal picket a short distance off, and took a shot a t him, which was also returned in due time by the Federal. These two soldiers kept this up until about twenty shots were exchanged, neither taking two shots to the other's one, or as the soldiers called it, they 'took shot about,' This duel did not end with the usual salutation, 'Good bye, Yank, ' and 'Good bye, Reb,' for the 'Yank' had the last shot, which stuck young Cheek in the bowels, from which he died the next day. Cheek had just attained manhood, and was a great favorite with the whole regiment as well as with the Duck River Riflemen. John F. Barham was also wounded in the arm while a vidette at Resaca, George G Daimwood was captured July 5th, and remained in prison until July 1865, Sergt. Sam W. Daimwood was wounded in July.

Hood Supplants Johnston.--

On July 17th Hood was commissioned a full General over the head of Hardee, and on the next day Joe Johnston was removed by President Davis, and Hood was placed in command of this army. This was one of the most unpopular acts of President Davis whole administration, especially with the rank and file of the western army. In that wonderful retreat from Dalton to Atlanta, the greatest display of military strategy that the Civil War presented. Johnstons methods had impressed the soldiers so highly with his abilities, as a great general, that the certain change of the Fabian policy into an entirely different system of tactics nearly demoralized that army and ony the fine discipline of these troops prevent almost an open mutiny. And, yet the soldiers had the greatest respect fro Hoods fighting qualities, which had never been doubted, and for his personal gallantry in action, But he had as yet had opportunity of showing his ability as Commander of an independent army in the field, and Beauregards appointment soon after as Department commander of the two armies in the West (Hoods and Dick Taylors) as practically only advisory.

The Personal Side of Gen. Hood.--

Just a line of two about Hood himself may not be too far out of place in this sketch of a local company. Hood was a Kentuckian and a West Pointer, graduation in 1853 in the same class with his present foes, Schofield and McPherson. He was a lieutenant in the famous Second Cavalry a regiment that had been organized by Jeff Davis when the latter was Secretary of War under Franklin Pierce of this regiment. Albert Sidney Johnston as Colonel, Robert E. Lee Lieutenant Colonel, and Wm. J. Hardee and George H. Thomas were the Majors, it also had many other officers of less rank who became famous in the Civil War. Hood was Adjutant to Major George H. Thomas Old Slow Trot: as Thomas was then called when in Texas; and U. S. Grant was Quartermaster of his Dragoons when in California. Hood had been appointed Chief of Cavalry at West Point in the fall of 1860, but declined not wishing to be hampered in case Kentucky should secede. In April 1861 finding that Kentucky was too slow in deciding what course she would pursue he offered his services to the Provisional Government at Montgomery, enlisting from Texas. Under the laws of the new Confederacy, he was given the same rank he had held in the U. S. Army, First Lieutenant, and reporting to Lee in Richmond. And was immediately assigned to duty under Magruder and soon rose rapidly in rank. In and Indian ambuscade some years before, Hoods left hand had been crippled; at Gettysburg one arm had been mangled, from which he had not recovered when at Chickamauga he lost the right leg, but in spite of these mutilations he managed a horse so well that he never required a ambulance.

Hood Takes the Offensive.--

Hood lost no time in changing Joe Johnstons Fabian policy, and in less than a week he fought two great battles for Atlanta, in both of which he suffered severely without gaining any corresponding advantage. Hardee was relieved from duty with the Army of Tennessee, and the President assigned him to the Command of the Department of South Carolina and Florida. In the battle on July 22nd, Sergt. George W. Rummage, of the Duck River Riflemen, was shot through the head and instantly killed in the charge on a fort just east of Atlanta. Wm. D. Hardison was captured in the next fight, on the 24th, and sent to Camp Chase. This was the second time he experienced a Federal prison, for it will be remembered that he had been detailed at Perryville for hospital duty, and in the retreat from Kentucky he had been ordered to remain in care of the wounded.

Soldiers Cried for Old Joe Johnston.--

The discontent of the soldiers increased to such an extent the President Davis visited the army, July 26th, and made patriotic talks to the troops. While passing down the line in review, some of the soldiers cried out, Give us back Old Joe Johnston much to the mortification of the officers. After the operations around Atlanta, Hood moved off to the North of Shermans line of communication; Sherman followed him back near to Rome, still leaving Atlanta strongly garrisoned. And then the novel spectacle was presented in war, of both armies running away from each other Sherman on his famous March to the Sea, and Hood on his ill-fated Raid into Tennessee. The late Gen. Francis A. Shoupe, of the Female Institute, who had been Joe Johnstons chief of Artillery, was Hoods Chief of Staff throughout his Campaign, and I am indebted to him for much of the information here detailed.

Hoods Raid.--

The failure of Hoods expeditions into Tennessee was almost assured by being delayed at Tuscumbia and Florence three weeks before completing the crossing of the Tennessee River. This delay was caused by the want of supplies and the absence of Forrests Cavalry in West Tennessee, in the famous movement which resulted in the destruction of so many millions of dollars worth of Federal stores at Johnsonville. Hood finished crossing the river on the 21st of November, with an admitted effective force of 30, 600 men, which was larger than was then available to Gen. George H. Thomas. Hoods plan was to get between Nashville and the Federal forces at Pulaski, Athens and Decatur, while Thomass object was to delay him south of Duck River until re-enforcement could be brought from Missouri and the north.

In Hoods Official Report he complains of the want of an accurate map of the country and in the march from Florence, with Columbia as an objective point. Stewarts and Lees two corps took the old Military road through Lawrenceburg, while Cheathams corps started by Waynesboro and Henryville. The day after the march began, snow fell, and then rain, making the movement very arduous; on Cheathams road the mud and hills were so bad that sometimes two regiments were detailed to help the artillery over the worst places. The Federal cavalry under Hatch and Capron also harassed the movement by constant skirmishing and obstructing the roads and stream crossing.

But by night fall on the 23rd, the advance of the Confederate infantry was in the Central Basin, on good roads, seventeen or eighteen miles southwest of Columbia, and by eight or nine oclock that night, Caprons Cavalry was being driven out of Mt. Pleasant by Forrests advance, led by Col. (now Rev.) David C. Kelley, who is so well known and loved in Columbia. Hatchs cavalry had also been driven from the old Military road, and had withdrawn east to Campbellsville.

The Race for Columbia.--

The Federal Army had retired north from Pulaski and most of it had been moved that afternoon around Lynnville, about 18 miles south of Columbia, but Gen. Jacob D. Coxs had been pushed on over the Elk Ridge and was encamped that night at McCains, seven miles south of Columbia on the Pulaski Pike. So it was to be a race between the two armies for Columbia, which a brigade of Rugers Division, in all about 800 men. These occupied Fort Mizner on Mount Parnassus, and had begun fortifying the town bridge and ford, and the railroad bridge.

The couriers bearing dispatches of Caprons disaster at Mt. Pleasant, did not reach Lynnville until about one oclock the next morning (the 24th) As soon as Schofield knew that the advance of the Confederate Infantry had got off the Highland Rim, and that Capron had been driven out of Mt. Pleasant, he sounded the reveille, and in about an hour his jaded troops were on a force march for Columbia, the artillery park and wagon trains leaving a little later. Schofield also at once dispatched a courier to Gen. Cox who was 11 miles nearer to Columbia, to march immediately; the troops were awakened, and by four oclock these were also on the march for Columbia.

When within three miles of town, Cox moved his column to the west. Taking the Pond Bridge road and going through the woods and fields, as most of the fences had been destroyed. By seven or eight oclock he was on the Mt. Pleasant pike, on the est side of Little Bigby, and immediately began making barricades of rails and timber to protect the bridge. And he was just in time, for in a short while Caprons Cavalry came rushing down the pike from Ashwood, closely pressed by Forrest, but the Confederate advance was checked by Coxs infantry and had to retire, after which the bridge was destroyed. Gen. Stanley says in his official report that Coxs rapid march to Little Bigby Creek saved Caprons command from annihilation, and probably Columbia from being captured by Forrest.

Death of Col. W. A. Dawson.--

In this pursuit, the gallant Col. W. A. Dawson of the 15th Tennessee Cavalry was killed while leading the command. He had galloped ahead of his men, and after emptying his revolver he rode up to the color bearer of one of Caprons regiment; while trying to wrest the flag from the Federal soldiers grasp, he was shot and killed in his hand-to-hand fight. Gen. Cox made his headquarters at the Martin place (now A. N. Akins) and as fast as the troops came up, they began making entrenchment, timber barricades, and rifle pits on the east side of the creek, The beautiful grove at Mrs. Wilsons, now E. H. Hatchers, and most of the other trees across the Mt. Pleasant pike were spared, but the lawns had rifle pits covering the entrenched works on the hills east of the Garnett Rainey place. The Confederates planted some artillery on the bluff on the west bank of the creek; north of the old fair grounds, which did but little damage.

The Fortifications at Columbia.--

The Federal forces from Lynnville reached Columbia about noon of the 24th. Gen. Schofield making army headquarters at the Athenaeum. As fast as the troops reached the hills about a mile south of town, they began constructing breastworks, aided by all the Contrabands: they could impress for the soldiers were broken down by the forced marches and loss of sleep. This line crossed the Pulaski Pike where the creamery is now, and the Campbellsville Pike just west, at the James place. From there it continued over the hills west nearly to the pike at the crossing of the Mt. Pleasant railroad, By the night of the 25th, these outer entrenchments and the detached works were sufficiently strong to resist any infantry attack, and it was not to be supposed that the Confederates would use artillery, with the city in the rear of the Federal line.

It began raining that Friday night (the 25th) and all day Saturday it was a hard, steady downpour, But the Federals and Contrabands had commenced building other works on the interior line, one beginning about half a mile below the railroad bridge connecting the Holland Mill and Fort Mizner, with detached words east to the river, This was to protect the river crossing, and placed most of the town between the two lines, and if the outer line should be taken, the Federals could ball back to the Fort and the interior line, and the battle would be fought from the streets and houses.

About fifty yards form the top of Mount Parnassus another entrenchment was made of rocks and dirt, almost encircling the Fort. What timber that remained on The Knob was cut down as close to the ground as possible, so as to prevent even a stump being used by a Confederate sharpshooter. The logs were used to strengthen this encircling line of breastworks and an abates made of the lines; this chevaux de frise or shiver and freeze as it was called in the cold weather, was made with the outward points sharpened, and all were fastened together with telegraph wire, making an obstruction that it seemed impossible to get over.

Telegraph Wire Spiked.--

I have heard but do not myself remember that the telegraph wire was spiked from stump to stump so as to trip any advancing troops; this was a Yankee Invention that had been first used at Knoxville just a year before, and which saved that city from capture by Longstreet and Hood. In 1862 the Federals under Gen. Negley had made a small entrenchment on West Market Street at the corner of the Female Institute lot, which was only intended to be sufficient fro attacks from Dunc. Coopers and other similar bodies of Cavalry. This was now enlarged into a strong redoubt, occupying part of the lot afterwards sold to George L. Thomas, and right on the bed of the Old Military Road to Florence. A smaller entrenchment was made just across the street where G. T. Hughes now lives, and about fifty feet west the street was cut and entrenched, leaving the usual turn out for vehicles; these works were connected with Fort Mizner by rifle pits and abatis. The artillery in this redoubt commanded the street west to the junction of the Mt. Pleasant and Hampshire Pikes, as well as the Old Military Road. Good approaches were prepared for the pontoon bridge at the Santa Fe Pike, and the railroad bridge was floored over for the passage of troops and teams.

Entrenchments at Riverside,--

The Federals and impressed Negroes also dug strong entrenchments and rifle pits in the peninsula where Riverside is now, especially to guard the town ford and bridge. But there was still so much timber there, and the peninsular being commanded by the bluffs on the south side of the river from above Ashtons Mills down to Whites Spring, that another and stronger line was built by Gen. Cox on the higher ground about a mile north of town, which the Brown residence was near the center.

The rain and cold did not stop this work, night or day, and those soldiers and darkies worked on in the rain and mud like beavers; the soldiers with guns stacked close at hand ready to return to the entrenchments in case of an attack, and the Negroes badly scared at the prospect of a battle. Time has obliterated many things connected with the Civil War, but some of these entrenchments yet remain and are silent reminders of the times that tried mens souls. Fort Mizner, with its underground magazines, which was considered impregnable from any direct assault, has given way to the reservoir which supplies the city with water. But the redoubt near the Mooresville pike east of the present Fair Grounds, the breastworks on the hills south; the entrenchments at Col. Allen Browns; the fort at the railroad bridge these and many others, are still plainly visible.

The Confederates Invest Columbia.--

Owing to the hard rains and the conditions of the roads, it was the 27th before the Confederate forces were all in position in front of Columbia. On that day Cheathams Corps was sent east to the right win, his headquarters being moved from E. H. Hatchers to John M. Francis; Stewarts headquarters at Nimrod Porters (now Mrs. Major Joe Dobbins) while Army headquarters had been moved by

Hood from Andrew J. Polk, at Ashwood, to Mrs. Cornelia Warfields.

The Federals Evacuate.--

Most of the Federal forces had been withdrawn to the interior line in Columbia on the night of the 26th, leaving however a strong force of infantry and some artillery in the outer works. On Sunday night, the 27th, all were placed on the north side of the river, the outer line being quietly abandoned by the Federals after midnight. The Fort and Magazine were then fired but the destruction was only partial; The pontoons were taken up or scuttled, and the town bridge burned; the railroad bridge was fired at both ends, but like the magazine in the fort, was not entirely destroyed.

Burning of Citizens Houses.--

That Sunday afternoon under orders from Gen. George D. Wagner, the homes of Col. Trotter and Col. Sanford, at the intersection of the Campbellsville Pike and Shun Street, and the residence of Rev. Jon F. Hughes and Judge Wm. S. Fleming, between the Pulaski Pike and Campbellsville Pike, were burned. These were large prominent houses between the picket lines, and their destruction was deemed a military necessity by the Federals. The officers notified these people an hour or so previously, and permitted the families to remove such of the contents of the houses as they could, but with no conveyances at hand and none of the men at home, but little was saved. The whole community suffered in the loss of Judge Flemings library and historical data.

Confederates Pillage Columbia.--

Before daylight of the 28th, the Confederate pickets discovered that the outer works were abandoned and Col. W. R. Butlers Tennessee troops pressed in, hoping to secure the ford and bridge, but were repulsed by the Federals on the north bank of the river, In a few hours swarms of Maj. Gen. Carter L. Stevensons command were in town, and the stores and many residences were looted by our own troops more than had occurred during the war. Gen. Hoods headquarters were three miles south of town, and as soon as he heard that Columbia had been wantonly and disgracefully plundered, he issued orders which soon restored discipline.

Hoods Famous Flank Movement.--

The Federal position was so strong and the possibility of a direct attack in front was so apparent, that Hood decided to flank it on the east. The Sappers and Miners were sent up the river to Davis Ford on the 28th, and made good approaches on both banks for the pontoon bridges, which were successfully laid that evening and night without interruption by the Federal cavalry pickets at Hueys Mill, two or three miles below. Some of Forrests cavalry had crossed at Davis Ford, but most of them had been sent further up the river, and had affected a crossing on the 28th, securing a lodgement on the Lewisburg and Franklin Pike. Caprons Brigade of Federal cavalry was guarding the approaches at Hardisons Mills and the fords in the vicinity, holding the peninsula south from Orrs Cross Roads. By some mishap this force was allowed to escape north up the pike, although the Confederates had them as it were in a cul de sac, with nothing to do but pull the string and bag them. The escape of this command had a depressing effect on the Confederates and the Federals were correspondingly elated next day on the retreat to Franklin.

Confederates Cross the River.--

Leaving Stephen D. Lee with a port of his corps to make demonstrations and feints at Columbia, and thus help conceal the flank movement, Hood moved to the right early on the morning of the 29th. He deemed this movement of such importance that he had crossed the river about daylight with his staff and was in personal command. Cheathams corps was in the advance, followed by Stewarts and a division from Lees corps, all in the lightest possible marching order, with only one battery of artillery to the corps. These crossed Duck River on the pontoon bridges near Davis Ford, the small body of accompanying cavalry fording or swimming the river, and by nine of half past nine oclock, this entire force was across Duck River without discovery or interruption by the Federals.

Following the Old Davis Ford Road north, the command pressed rapidly on, moving by the right flank, the column occupying the road and the woods and fields adjoining, for there were precious few fences left to Maury County. The weather had turned warm, the day was bright and sunny, and the troops were in good spirits. The Duck River Riflemen were pressing on in the advance with Strahl and Cleburne, and passing through a country that was home; yet none dropped out of ranks, although short furloughs had been given to most of the troops from this section but all seemed animated with the desire of the command to complete this movement.

Schofield Was Awake.--

The hills east of the Nashville Pike and west of the Davis Ford Road, it was thought, would partly screen this movement from the observation of the Federals, and with Lees feints and assaults at Columbia, would prevent them from moving until their line of communication could be cut in the rear. But Schofield was far to experienced a soldier to be caught napping quite that badly, and Posts Federal Brigade being sent up what is now the Bear Creek Pike to reconnoiter, reported the movement of infantry in force. The Federals immediately began evacuating the peninsula north of Columbia early in the afternoon, and another race this time to Spring Hill or Franklin was on.

Lee Crosses Duck River.--

Lees order was at Columbia were that as soon as the enemy showed signs of retreating, to cross the river and press him north. He had posted Col. J. M. Dedmans Alabama regiment on the bluffs up the river about the lime kiln, while Greenwood Cemetery and the bluff where the jail is now, fairly swarmed with sharpshooter. Col. R. F. Beckham, Gen. Lees Chief of Artillery, superintended the planting of the batteries on the bluff, and was mortally wounded on the 29th, lingering until the 10th of December. He lies in an honored grave in historic St. Johns churchyard at Ashwood, where so many of his gallant brother officers were buried after the battle of Franklin.

The Grape-Vine Pontoon Train.--

But Lee had to lay a pontoon bridge before the infantry could cross. And when that reserve pontoon train came into town, it was followed by scores of boys who were attracted by the novelty of the sight, and such a sight it was. Those huge canoes probably 25 feet long, only one on each ramshackle wagon, with load after load of bridge timbers on a little better wagons, drawn by the first (and poorest) long-horned Texas steers ever seen here, and instead of leather or ropes or chains to draw the wagons grape vines. One of these pontoon boats had been sent down to the river in advance, and although the men in charge of it were being constantly fired on, they pushed it into the river, and commenced carrying the soldiers over. After the boat had been launched, the troops that were being carried over were comparatively safe, the north bank of the river protecting them from the fire of the rifle pits. After getting to the northside these troops remained under the bank until a great many loads had been charged with a rebel yell, driving the remaining Federals back to the line of works of the Brown house. The pontoon bridge was then laid in a few hours. The last of the Federal soldiers retired from the works after dark and began that perilous night march to Spring Hill and Franklin.

Gen. Hoods Guide.--

Nearly every old citizen knows Mr. J. S. R. Gregory, who although in his 76th year, bears his age well, and his memory in unimpaired. Uncle Sol as he is familiarly called, has told me many of his personal recollections of these and other local events. He was a member of Capt. Groves

Company in Biffles Cavalry and had been detailed to act as a guide to Gen. Hood in this flank movement. About ten oclock on the morning of the 29th, Hood, Cleburne, and some other officers made special inquiries of him about the Davis Ford Road they were then on, as Hoods map, which had been furnished by the Richmond authorities, differed materially from the information then obtained. Mr. Gregory drew a rough sketch on the ground, showing the relative distance and location of the roads, explaining it at some length to the officers. Mr. Jim Smith, who now lives about two miles southwest of town, was there as guide to Gen. (now Senator) W. B. Bate and Gen. Pat Cleburne, and corroborated Gregorys information. Cleburne made a copy on a piece of paper of Gregorys map or ground plan and said that having known Gregory when the latter lived in Arkansas, and this information being confirmed by Jim Smith, that he had more confidence in it than in the map which Hood was complaining of as being so imperfect. Hood and Cleburne had quite a discussion on this matter, and the conclusion seemed to Gregory to be that it would require great effort to get to where they intended going by the time they wanted to be there.

Gregory was sent alone to the Eph. Davis hill and from there he saw a Federal line of battle formed on the Beasley place south and southeast of the present location of Mount Olivet Church, the line was facing south down the small ravine from the Beasley spring; this a Posts brigade, which had been sent out to reconnoitre. Gregory returned to Hood; who by that time was at the Amos place at the former site of Old Asbury Church, and reported this fact. At that time there was much timber on the hills between Beasley and Amos places and Hood said that these would help the woods and muddy fields parallel with the Davis Ford Road, even wading Rutherford Creek a few hours later.

Hood at the Loftin Mill.--

When the column crossed the Murfreesboro Road just west of Center Star, Hood rode off a short distance on the Loftin Hill just east, and had his big Dutchman (as Jim Smith calls him) help him off his horse; here he sat down on a log and consulted with some officers and his staff, making frequent references to his map, and inquiries from the guides as to the three (?) roads; if he was not impressed with the view, one of the most beautiful in Maury County, he must have felt elated at the success so far of this brilliant flank movement. Eight miles south of west, the prominent figure in the landscape was Fort Mizner, from which the Confederate flag now floated; while between and beyond lay the fertile valley of Duck River, a country worth fighting for, or dying for, as was remarked by one of the officers.

Lees Artillery Helped.--

The booming of artillery at Columbia could be plainly heard, showing that Lee was keeping the attention of the enemy engaged in his feints and demonstrations of crossing. Almost at their feet were passing column after column of the veterans of the Confederate army, all in high spirits and elated with the idea of getting in the rear of the enemy for the object of this rapid march was now apparent to even the common soldier. Hood remained here some little while, then his big Dutchman helped him on his horse and he again rode forward to the head of the column.

Hood, Cleburne and Granberry Quarrel.--

They halted for dinner at a late hour just south of Blantons Chapel, when there was some more misunderstanding between Hood, Cleburne, and Granberry. Gregory overheard it all but did not pay much attention to it; his present impression is that there were some words between them, as to Cleburne or Granberry being put in the extreme advance and some chafing and dissatisfaction because some of the troops were so slow in coming up.

The Great Blunder Occurs. --

About sundown Cleburne had got his infantry up to the pike about a mile south of Spring Hill, and there was a sharp skirmish with the Federal forces marching north on the pike, which lasted till after dark. The Duck River Riflemen were with their command in the advance, and the forward movement of the 24th was stoped by a staff officer. The regiment remained in position near McCutcheons creek, throughout the night, eagerly expecting the order to resume the advance and cut the train in retreat on the pike but the order never came.

That Fatal Tuesday, Night, Nov. 29, 1864.

Hood made army headquarters that night at Capt. Thompsons two miles and a half South of Spring Hill. Almost as soon as headquarters were established, Hood come out of the house and sat on a log some two hundred yards from the house, near the fishpond. Gregory was there in attendance, and saw couriers frequently come, and from what he overheard, then reports were that the enemy were giving way. Granberry was there on the log with Hood for quite a while, but Gregorys impression is that Cleburne did not come up until the skirmish was over, by which time Hood had returned to the house, after a long conference with Gen. Stewart, who had arrived about dark.

Confederate Generals Were Drinking.--

Capt. Thompsons folks spread a big feast that Tuesday evening for these officers and as they were constantly coming and going, it was between eleven and twelve oclock before it was over. There had been much drinking and hilarity among the officers (and some of the men) that day. Uncle Sol says that Hood and Governor Isham G. Harris had not been drinking, or if they had, they showed no effects of it. Gen. Cheatham was much under the influence of spirits; Walthall, Cleburne and Granberry had also been toasting rather freely, but were not at all drunk.

Stewarts Incompetent Guide.--

Gen. Stewart was given a guide (who proved very incompetent) and told to continue north on the Spring Hill and Rally Hill Pike, connect with Cheathams right, and take position on the pike at or near Spring Hill. After marching north on the pike to where it bends west in the suburbs of Spring Hill his guide took him east up the private pike leading to Col. R. W. McLemores residence; he kept this road probably half a mile, then struck out across the country, and about eleven oclock bivouacked in the woods and fields near the road on the Military Reservation line.

Whole Federal Army Passed by Unchallenged.--

That night the Confederate Army remained close to the Columbia Pike, in easy hailing distance of the Federal forces that with trains 15 miles long were crowding the pike in the hurried retreat to Franklin and Nashville. One of the Federal officers said that in riding up and down the line they had to remain close to the column to keep from riding over the Confederate pickets. A single column thrown across the road would in all probability have routed Schofields entire command, and that would have given Middle Tennessee, and probably Kentucky, to the Confederacy.

The Failure at Spring Hill.--

But it is useless in this sketch to moralize on The Failure at Spring Hill, which has been so much discussed (and cussed) for nearly forty years. No satisfactory explanation of it has ever been made but the fact remains that the Commanding General was on the ground in person, and if his orders were not delivered or executed, he should have led the movement himself Or fixed the responsibility of the failure on his subordinate. But if the world does not know the cause of this failure, it does know that through some blunder worse then criminal, the opportunity lost that night the greatest offered in the Civil War caused the frightful useless butchery the next evening at Franklin, which brought desolation to so many thousand southern homes.

Hood awoke the next morning to find that there were no Federals south of Spring Hill on the Columbia Pike, and not believing it possible that they all could have escaped up that pike, he sent Forrest to the Carters Creek and Franklin pike to intercept them.

The Pursuit to Franklin.--

That night march of the Federals was one of the most trying experiences of the war. These soldiers had been on hard duty for some days and nights; they had marched from Lynnville to Columbia by night less than a week and frequently with scanty food and fuel. And now to be again on the retreat by night, with the prospect of a night attack by the Confederates to position and flank with a strong force to say nothing of Lee crowding them in the rear was extremely trying.

Coxs Division led the retreat to Franklin, as it had done from Lynnville to Columbia; arriving at Franklin about sunrise on the morning of the 30th, his broken down soldiers were allowed one hour for rest and breakfast, and them immediately began work on the line of entrenchments on the Columbia Pike at the Carter house and the old gin. As the other commands arrived, they too, were put to work on the fortifications, which were already strong from long occupation by the Federals as an outpost of Nashville. By three oclock these works were in good order, and Schofields trains were across Harpeth River and well on the way to Nashville.

By the time the Confederate forces in pursuit came in sight and commenced deploying. Schofield did not think that Hood would attack another flank movement, which would be comparatively easy, with the river fordable almost anywhere, But in this he was mistaken, for Hood at once began to prepare for battle. He evidently was chafing under the disappointment and the blunder of the night before at Spring Hill, and he probably had thought all day of the storm of criticism Schofields escape would provide throughout the country. And then, possibly he had heard mutterings from the men of his army that day and he determined to retrieve everything by defeating Schofield in open battle.

An Inspiring Scene.--

The history of the world presents few scenes more thrilling than the one at Franklin that beautiful autumn evening. The advance of the Confederate host in battle array to the martial music of the bands, with flags flying, the generals and their staffs mounted, and the regimental officers as carefully dressing the lines as if on parade. In thee near distance directly in front, this the horizon line was the strong fortifications, under whose head logs projected the gleaming rifles which foretold the useless butchery about to take place. At Fort Roper on the northeast the Federal artillery kept up a constant fire on the reforming and advancing lines, but it was not until within close musket range that the carnage was so great, for all other battles this was one principally of infantry and infantry, where the other branches of the service, the cavalry and artillery, played a comparatively unimportant part.

I notice that in the last installment published of the Duck River Riflemen, that I omitted some facts related by Mr. Gregory of that Tuesday night, Nov. 29, 1864, as the Confederate officers were enjoying Capt. Thompsons hospitality near Spring Hill. The Federals were under the impression that Mr. McMeens house, about half a mile south of Capt. Thompsons was the Confederate headquarters for the night; they fired their artillery on it, which set it on fire, and it burned to the ground just about dark, This was after the Duck River Riflemen and Strahls advance was in position just east of the Columbia pike, and after the skirmish there had been.

Gen. Forrest had a son, a mere boy who was wounded that afternoon in the calf of his leg by a minie ball, and who had been sent to Capt. Thompsons for surgical attention. But Forrest himself had pressed on north with his cavalry and had crossed the pike, burning several wagons and loads of supplies on the pike and at Thompsons Station a few miles further north.

About midnight Forrest came back to Capt. Thompsons to see how seriously his boy was wounded and how he was getting on. As he rode up he seemed astounded at the drinking and carousing going on among the higher officers, and at once asked for Gen. Hood, who with Governor Isham G. Harris, had retired. On being shown to the room by Mr. Gregory, Forrest told Hood that the Yankees were getting through on the pike, and suggested and urged in his emphatic way that a force of infantry be thrown forward immediately and cut the retreating column on the Columbia Pike. He told him of his burning the wagons and the stampede of the teamsters and guards, a few miles up the pike near the Duck River Ridge, and of his success at Thompsons Station a few hours previously. Gregory says that Hood was not at all excited nor had been that evening when the skirmish was going on, and he heard him remark to Forrest in his calm, unmoved way, that hed find the Yankees in the morning. After this interview with Hood, Forrest went out to where his wounded boy was laying, muttering to himself such a rush of expletives that might show what a task it was for his preacher-colonel the Rev. David C. Kelley to convert him into the utmost Christian he finally became.

In the battle of Franklin the 24th Regiment was on the left of Strahls Brigade, in the supporting line, following the advance of Vaughans Brigade, at a distance of about 200 yards just west of the Columbia Pike, and directly south of Carters brick house, where the Federals breastworks were very high and unusually strong. Wagners Federal division had built a hasty barricade of rails on the pike in front of the main line of works, and with more bravery that discretion held this until the Confederates were right on them; and when they retired, the Federals and Confederates were so intermixed that the Federal fire was withheld from the mass of blue and gray that crowed pell mell through the turn out gap in the pike, and over the breastworks at the Carter house. The Confederates captured the artillery stationed at this point and turned it against the late comers. It was at this critical moment for the Federals that Colonel Emerson Opdyke of the 115th Ohio advanced his reserve line from the north side of the Carter house and regained possession of the breastworks, captured nearly 400 of the confederates who were inside and recovered possession of the artillery which had been lost a few minutes previously. Many of

Wagners men were captured by the Confederates in the rush on the outer barricades, and twelve members of the consolidated company of which the Duck River Riflemen formed a part, sent these prisoners to the rear. The four commissioned officers and the remaining 24 privates pressed on with the rest of the command to the Federal line, but their advance was retarded by and abatis about twenty yards in the front of the fortifications. In going over this obstruction, Lieut. Tindall had four bullet holes put through his hat. When these men got on top of this high Federal breastworks, Lieut. Tindall says that right in front were four lines of Federal infantry, standing with fixed bayonets glistening in the setting sun, and the rifle barrels seemed big enough to crawl in. A Confederate Captain, who was conspicuous from having on a brand-new uniform ran from near the pike on top of the works, down to the position of the 24th, and urged the men to come on and get on the inside. A Federal soldier immediately stopped his jaw by bayoneting him in the cheek; the irate Captain called to some of the men in the ditch on the berm, Give me a gun this kill this _____ yankee rascal. Tindall handed him a sword with which he slashed at the Ohio soldier, and in doing so, the unknown Captain fell among the enemy. The Federal line having by this time been restored, just east of the pike and gin-house, Strahl was subjected to a heavy enfilading fire, in which the artillery in the fort across Harpeth River joined; and of this consolidated company, now consisting of four officers and 24 men, three of the officers and 22 of the privates were killed or wounded.

Charley Nicholson was shot seven or eight times, dying on the Federal breastworks near Gen. Strahl. The brave boys remains were brought home a few day late by Humphrey

Hardison and buried with military honors in the family graveyard near Rock Spring by Capt. Fount Scott and an accompanying escort. The day before he was killed, he passed in sight of his home while making the march along the Davis Ford road, and despite the entreaties of his family (and sweetheart) to take his furlough and stop, he went on with the command. Sergt. Jasper W. Dillehay, George W. Hardison and Martin V. Hardison were so badly wounded that they had to be left at home on Hoods retreat. This was the third time that Martin V. Hardison had been wounded in battle, yet he is still living. Lt. Col. Sam E. Shannon was wounded in the neck and the next morning at three oclock was carried by some of the Riflemen to his sisters in Franklin. Col. John A. Wilson was wounded in the shoulder and the 24th Regiment was commanded by a Second Lieutenant all the higher officers being killed or wounded. Even an outline of this unique battle would require a separate article but some idea of the useless butchery (as Gen. Joe Johnston called it) may be formed from a few facts:

The Confederate deploying and advance was over a large open plain, where every movement was easily seen, until the smoke of battle and the evening haze soon settled like a pall over the field. Almost the whole of this advance was subject to the fire from the breastworks, as well as Fort Roper. The Confederates had only three batteries of artillery, and these could be used but sparingly, on account of the town being in the rear of the Federal lines. The Fourth Army Corps (Federal) used one hundred wagon loads of ammunition in this short battle. In proportion to the forces engaged, and the short duration of the fight, it was the bloodiest battle in the Civil War. Hood admits a loss of about 4,500 but Thomas makes the total 6.252; the Federal loss was not nearly so great, being protected by the fortification. The proportionate loss of the Commissioned Officers in the attacking lines was probably never equalled not even at Bunker Hill. Generals Cleburne, Adams, Strahl, and Granberry were killed; Generals Brown, Carter, Manigault, Quarles, Cockrell, and Scott were wounded; and Gen. Gordon was captured.

Granberrys Brigade consisted of these regiments: 5th and 6th Texas, 5th Conf. Regulars, 7th Texas, 10th Texas, 35th Tenn,. 17th and 18th Texas Cavalry, besides Nutts Louisiana Cavalry Company. At the close of the fight the Brigade was commanded by a Captain. In Quarles Brigade of Walthalls Division every staff officer was killed, and the highest officer in command was a Captain. This Brigade had only six regiments and lost three of the regimental flags, the color bearers having been killed or wounded within the Federal interior line. Col. Ellison Capers of the 24th South Carolina (now the Episcopal Bishop of S. C.) was wounded for the third time in the same leg. A year ago he visited his son here, Rev. W. B. Capers, Rectory of St. Peters Church, and together they went over the battlefield, He reports that every staff officer of Gen. Gist was killed except one, and that this brigade was also commanded by a captain. Capt. Robert D. Smith who was Ordnance Officer of Gen. Walthalls Staff had every Ordnance Officer under him killed on the field.

The 24th Tennessee Regiment of which the Duck River Riflemen formed a part, had the colonel, Lieut. Colonel, Major, Adjutant, and every Captain and First Lieutenant, killed or wounded, the ranking officer being a Second

Lieutenant. The third day after the fight I want over the battlefield, and the impression made on my boyish memory by the hundreds ad hundreds of dead men in every conceivable position still remaining unburied upon the field have never been effaced. The Charge of the Light Brigade in the Crimean War in 1854 is noted as being one of the most celebrated in history. Poets have sung it and painters have pictured it in the most glowing colors; the British government granted pensions to the survivors and heaped honors on those who fell, And what hosts of school boys on Public Fridays for nearly 50 years have recited Tennysons stirring poem of ~

Half a league, half a league

Half a league onward

All in the valley of Death rode the Six Hundred.

As a matter of act, there were 673 horsemen in this Charge, but poetic license reduced the number to 600. Yet in this Death Charge a Balaklava, as our British cousins like to call it, the total casualties were only 247 or some writers place them a 280 and some of them were very slightly wounded; which included the 12 officers killed and 11 wounded.

Now does this compare with the record of this local command, which lost over half its number in killed and wounded at Shiloh and at Franklin and had only three men unhurt out of 28. It is a far cry from Englands Poet Laureate and the Crimean War to the impromptu camp rhymster in our own late unpleasantness, but as the old adage says there it is but one step from the sublime to the ridiculous, here is a sample verse of camp song that soon became very popular with the Southern soldier:

You talk about your Beauregard, And boast of R. E. Lee

But J. B. Hood of Texas, he played hell in Tennessee.

Another curious item about the battle of Franklin is that although Schofield was present, his position across the river left the management of the battle to Stanley. In the first rush of the Confederates, the worse on the Columbia Pike were carried. Federals and Confederates crowding through the gap in a continued mass. Stanley was wounded at this time and the command developing on Cox, he drove the Confederates back, except about 400 who were captured within the lines, and regained possession of part of the breastworks. It was Cox who had led the advance of the march the night before and had thrown up these works, Cox practically fought this battle and yet his name was not even mentioned in Gen. Thomas official report. After the war, Cox was elected Governor of Ohio and President Grant gave him a seat in his cabinet as Secretary of the Interior. While filling the latter office his family spent part of a season with us at the Athenaeum hoping that the change of climate would prove beneficial to his son Kenyon Cox. who has become world famous as an artist.

The Field Returns November 6th shows Stewarts Army Corps to have 8,708 total effectives resent, and Cheathams Corps, 10,519. The next field return is December 10th (after the Franklin fight and before the Battle of Nashville) when the figures are respectively 5,321 and 7,272, showing a loss of over one-third.

Hoods Bravado Advance on Nashville.--On the 10th of December, in the trenches in front of Nashville, where the fires behind the breastworks sillohoutted the troops., into emptying targets from Federal bullets, a sort of reorganization was made, by which the remains of the 19th, 24th, and 41st Tennessee Regiments were consolidated and place under the command of Captain Daniel A. Kennedy, Strahls Brigade, was commanded By Col. Andrew J. Kellar, the noted editor of Memphis.

The Battle of Nashville, December 15th and 16th was the finishing blow for Hoods army, routing it until Duck River was placed between it and the pursuing Federals and it was not much after that. John L. Biggers and Jacob Bennett of the Duck River Riflemen were captured at Nashville, the other members going with the escaping Confederates.

Hoods Memorable Retreat.--

Hoods Retreat out of Tennessee that December was one of the most horrible episodes of the Civil War. On the morning of the 18th it began raining. It stormed all day of the 19th, stopping about night and beginning again the next afternoon, winding up with a heavy snow and sleet on the 21st. The weather had turned intensely cold, and it was a mud, mud everywhere with a frozen crust on top, through which men, horses, and wheels continually broke. The previous movements of the armies had cut the roads and adjoining fields into a state that can hardly be imagined; the bridges were all destroyed, and even the culverts were in most cases torn up or damaged. The conditions of the fords and approaches to the pontoon bridges defy description with the mud knee-deep, and dead horses and mules making stepping places for the soldiers.

Probably a third of the Confederate infantry had no shoes and every stop was marched in bleeding feet cut by the frozen ground and ice. These men would tie strings around the bottom of their trousers just at the ankle as the mud and ice would wear this into a fringe and break off. They would tie higher up, and many had the strings so high that with their bare legs below the knee they looked like Highlanders. And for rations, well, there were almost none issued regularly, and few citizens had any to give. Fuel had become extremely scarce, and may people had to cut dawn the shade trees near their homes, as there were no teams to haul wood with. Hoods army was routed, demoralized, and had entirely lost faith in him, and yet, in spite of all the bare-footed veterans plodding along, cracking jokes, singing, and often cursing, in a jolly good-natured way.

Forrest to the Rescue.--

Forrest had been hastily recalled from the right wing where he was operating against the Nashville and Chattanooga railroad. He began retreating on the 16th crossing a good part of his command at Lillards Mills next day, but the waters rose so rapidly that he had to come down the north bank of the river to Columbia to avail himself of the pontoon bridge,

The Confederates finished crossing Duck River on the 19th of Dec. during a hard storm, and immediately took up the pontoon bridge and moved out of town on the Pulaski Pike, after which the rain ceased. Three of the cannon that could not be put across were spiked ad pitched into the river and were afterwards fished out by the Federals. Forrest remained in town until all the infantry had gone out, deploying skirmishers from about Ashtons Mills to Greenwood Cemetery until this was completed.

Forrest and Hatch Meet at the River--

After these troops had withdrawn from town the Federal advance which had finally succeeded in getting over Rutherford Creek, appeared across the river, and a battery was placed at the Brown house, which shelled the town. Forrest rode back to Columbia with an escort, carrying a flag of truce, and went to the bridge abutment. Gen. Hatch and an escort soon came to the north side with a flag of truce, in answer, when Forrest told him that the city had been evacuated by the Confederates, and Hatch promised that he would stop the shelling which he did.

The escape of the entire Confederate army from its perilous situation north of the Duck River was permitted, or at least greatly assisted by one of the most ludicrous mistakes in military annals. But as this incident was not especially connected with the subject of this sketch, it will be reserved for another article.

The Famous Rear Guard.--

Hood made army headquarters at the Nathan Vaught place (now R. G. Sparrows) from the 18th to the morning of the 20th of December 1864, when he left for Pulaski. On that morning Forrest was placed in command of the rear guard of the army, and Walthall was ordered to support him with eight brigades of picked infantry. These eight brigades gave him an effective force of 1900 men of whom about 400 were without shoes, and many more were practically barefooted. Such was the picked infantry of the famous rear guard! Two of these brigades, Maneys and Strahls were commanded by the gallant Col. Hume R. Field, and the field returns next day show a total of only 113 effectives for both brigades. Among them was the wreck of the Duck River Riflemen, which had now become so absorbed in these reorganizations and consolidations that it lost all semblance of existence as a separate organization. Yet these few were true and faithful soldiers unto the end and followed the waning star of the Lost Cause until it sank never more to rise.

The Last Consolidation.--

In North Carolina, March 21st, 1865, in the final death gasp of the Confederacy, the Third Tennessee Consolidated Regiment was organized; it was composed of the 4th, 5th, 19th, 31st, 33rd, 35th, 38th, and 41st, Regiments of which James D. Tillman was commissioned Colonel in the Brigade of Brig. Gen. Joseph B. Palmers. Maj. Gen. B. F. Cheathams Division, Lt. Gen. W. J. Hardees Corps, and Gen. Joseph E. Johnston, Commander. The whole of the 24th Regiment was used to help make up Company K of the new Third Tennessee

Consolidated, and the following members of the Duck River Riflemen were among the officers for the new company just before the surrender in April 1865:

R. W. Tindall, Capt.

John E. Hardeman, 2d Lieut.

Sam W. Daimwood, Orderly Sergt.

Spun Cotton as Money after the Surrender.--

In the return home from North Carolina the Confederate money even if the soldiers had been paid would have been worthless to defray the expenses. It was impracticable to furnish food and transportation for it was over the mountains to Tennessee even if the food and transportation had been available. But there was a good supply of spun cotton yarns on hand and with raw cotton worth over a dollar a pound in good money this spun cotton was a valuable currency easily carried, and this was what was given to the soldiers to trade with citizens on the road for food. One wagon and team was allowed to each large command to haul the cotton yarns, and incidentally to help such of the men as should be broken down on the trip. And so, with heavy hearts these soldiers began their homeward march.

The Last Charge--

John H. Derryberry had suffered with chronic diarrhea in the army and on the march over the mountains this was complicated with pneumonia. The few retiring members of his company remained with him at a widows house about ten mile east of Greeneville, Tennessee, and gave him al the attention that they could, but he died in a few days, There was not means enough among his comrades to bury him, and as he was now a civilian since the surrender, they wanted to put him in a coffin, So a council of war was held, and after much deliberation it was decided to make one more charge. That night four of the Riflemen led by Anderson Daniel made the charge on the combined commissary, Quartermaster, Paymaster, and Ordnance Train which was the one headquarters wagon carrying the spun cotton yarns, and captured four bales. With three of these, a coffin was procured from Greeneville and the other bale was given to the widow for her attention to John H. Derryberry and for a grave for him in her apple orchard. This was the last official act of the Duck River Riflemen.

A Glorious Record.--

Here is a summary of this Company, compiled from the best information now available; it is necessarily incomplete, yet any changes would only show an increased loss. It is a record that was equalled by few companies in the Civil War- -a record of which the members and families of the Duck River Riflemen, and all Maury Countians, can well be proud.

2 commissioned officers and 15 men killed in battle.

4 mortally wounded.

3 missing, never heard of afterwards

1 died on the way home after the surrender

4 died from sickness

31 wounded in battle, some more than once.

7 wounded and discharged, or left at home

10 discharged for ill health.

9 otherwise discharged too young, or too old.

8 captured

1 name placed on the Confederate Roll of Honor at Richmond for conspicuous Bravery in the Battle of Murfressboro.

Something of Capt. Tindall.--

Before closing this sketch let me add a line or two about Capt. Robert W. Tindall, the last Captain of the Company, and one of the best of the many good citizens of Maury County. He was like so many others, a strong Union man and opposed to secession, yet when Tennessee cast her lot with the Southern Confederacy, he enlisted as a private in the Duck River Riflemen. His comrades tell me that he was in every battle and skirmish in which the command participated, was never wounded or captured, never had a furlough, and never shirked any military duty. And he tells me that he surrendered at Greensboro (formerly known as Guilford Court House) where he was born, and that the pay he received at the close of the war was one dollar and twenty-five cents in silver. He paid the dollar for a marriage license, and has kept the quarter on which two generations of children have cut their teeth.

A Tribute to the Riflemen.--

And a final paragraph about the personnel of the Company. These men belonged to that God fearing, law abiding, hard working class that fulfilled the Biblical command of earning a living by the sweat of the brow. Not a tenth of them over owned a slave of had any personal interest in preserving the peculiar Institution except in so far as it affected the general interest of the community, and nearly all of them were Union men until President Lincoln issued his call of 75.000 men to suppress insurrection. Returning to their desolate homes at the close of the war to encounter the horrors of the Reconstruction period, berefit of all save honor, disfranchised, the Duck River Riflemen were types of the Confederate soldiers, who, accepting the logic of events, went to work and succeeded in that wonderful development and rehabilitation of the South which has made it the most important factor in the present prosperity of the United States a result which is the wonder of the political economist and will be the admiration of the future historian.

Columbia, Tenn., March 1904

Frank H. Smith

First Hand Account

A Civil War Filler:

INCIDENT OF THE WAR--Maury Democrat, 12 August 1897

August 5. -- Today is the anniversary of a war incident that is indelibly impressed on the minds of at least several of Franklins citizens. It was just 35 years ago today that Gen. John M. Palmer, commanding the Federal troops, retreated through this place (Franklin) on his way to Nashville. During the retreat Gen. Palmer had been greatly annoyed by Confederates firing on his men, and, anticipating further trouble at Holly Tree Gap, five miles north of here, the General arrested 11 citizens of this place and took them along with him as hostages. The troops were not molested on the march, and after passing Holly Tree Gap, the citizens were allowed to return home.

After a lapse of 35 years, almost an average life-time, seven of those citizens are still alive. They are Messrs. James Karr, Ed. G. Sherman, Henry P. Fowlkes, Mack Craig, O. C. Owen, of Columbia, Thos, L. Owen and Rev. John W. Hanner, of Bellbuckle. The dead are Charley Crouch, Robert Brown, William Ragsdale, and Dick Gault.

First Hand Account [14]

The Twenty~Fourth Tennessee Regiment

By Rev. H. D. Hogan, Rosedale, Kans.

The 24th Tennessee Regiment was organized at Camp Trousdale, near LaVergne, Tenn., in 1861. Don Allison was elected colonel, and Thomas H. Peebles, lieutenant colonel. The regiment had an organization of ten companies, with something like a thousand men. Without mentioning certain historical events- going into winter quarters at Bowling Green, Ky., the fall of Fort Donelson, and our hasty retreat to Corinth, Miss., to checkmate Grant's concentration of troops at Pittsburg Landing--I will pass on to what was one of the bloodiest battles of the war; known as the battle of Shiloh.

Sunday morning, April 6, 1862, found us in mortal combat with the blue. Colonel Allison being incapacitated, it devolved on the intrepid Peebles to lead the regiment to victory. With his horse shot from under him, a stubborn foe in the open-now with uplifted sword flashing in the sunlight of that beautiful Sunday morning- we still hear the stentorian voice rising above the din of battle: Forward! Forward! Forward, boys! Forward!" which gave inspiration that led to victory. That stentorian voice appealed to General Prentice; who after capture; asked: "who commanded that regiment with the big voice!"

---

[14] From the Confederate Veteran pg 85,86.

Sunday evening, at the hour that General Johnston fell, the enemy had been driven from the field in wild disorder. If Beauregard had pressed the rout, he would have captured Grant's entire army.

At the organization of the regiment at Camp Trousdale, the ladies of Nashville presented the 24th with one of the most beautiful battle flags, which was soon to be a leading factor in a great battle. As the ordnance department had not provided a more suitable flag for service- a smaller flag that could be carried through brush without hindrance-our highly prized flag was destined to be a central figure in the victorious onslaught of the first day's battle.

The 7th opened up bright and cheery. The night had been followed by a heavy rainfull, which extinguished the many fires that caused much suffering to the wounded and dispelled the terrible stench incident to such a bloody battle. We engaged the enemy only to be forced back to Buells' fresh troops to a line parallel to the old Shiloh Church.

The two lines were in close proximity, and we fought in the open. Jack Reece, our gallant color bearer, unflinchingly stood with the colors unfurled to the morning breeze, which was a great inspiration at this tense moment. Under the folds of those colors, I was severely wounded, as well as the color bearer. Here the curtain falls, and I am next found at Corinth nursing a wound.

At first dress parade after the battle, the regiment unanimously presented the old bullet-scarred battle flag to

Colonel Peebles, as a mark of high appreciation of his gallantry on the field of battle; and these colors are sacredly held by T. H. Peebles, Jr. who will take this loved relic to Dallas next May.

First Hand Account [15]

Last Surviving Officer.

The following comes from Rev. Henry D. Hogan, of Rosedale, Kans., as a tribute to an old comrade and friend, Col. J. A. Wilson, only surviving officer of the 24th Tennessee Regiment, who is now living at Bowie, Tex., in his eighty seventh year. Comrade Hogan says:

"As a member of the 24th Tennessee Regiment and chaplain of same for three years or more and one of the few members who remain to tell the story and one who was in camp and in battle often, I wish to pay a tribute of respect and to make honorable mention of my highly esteemed old friend, Col. John A. Wilson, who was captain of Company D, 24th Regiment, Tennessee Volunteers. He was promoted major of the regiment in July, 1862. After his return fro the hospital he was made colonel of the regiment, January, 1863.

"He succeeded the brave, intrepid Hugh L. W. Bratton, who fell mortally wounded at Stone's River, December 31, 1862. He was also severely wounded in that bloodiest battle of the war at Franklin, Tenn., between Hood and Thomas. Colonel Wilson not only led his command at Chickamauga, Missionary Ridge, but also that long-drawn and continuous fighting with Sherman's hordes from near Dalton, Ga., to the

---

[15] Confederate Veteran~XXXII p. 452

right of Atlanta, Ga., July, 1864. When this hard fought battle was in full swing, Colonel Wilson was severely wounded within ten feet of me when he fell. He called to me and said: "Henry, get me away from here, or I will be killed." I pressed into service three men who were behind trees. I rolled him on a large blanket that I swiped from the Yanks at City Point, Va., April, 1863. (By the way, I was captured at Stone's River, and sent to Camp Morton, Ind.) Now with this hastily improvised stretcher, we bore him to a place of safety.

"I was appointed chaplain of the regiment by the Colonel; he forbade my bearing arms, which order I violated providentially in the fearful charge; when he fell I was at his side; the Colonel claims I saved his life.

"The most important factor in the Colonel's life was his Christlike demeanor, which was in evidence daily. He was loved by his men who confidingly followed him in battle."

One Man Company & Regimental Flag

The Rev. Henry D. Hogan, 89, of Kansas City, chaplain of the Twenty-fourth Tennessee Regiment in the Confederate Army and only surviving member of Company B, who marched in the Confederate parade at Little Rock, is visiting his sister, Mrs. William Drumwright of Nashville. He was born near the custom house at Nashville.

He is shown with his regimental flag which was shot to pieces in the battle of Shiloh and was presented to Col. T.H. Peebles by Gen. Cleburne. The flag is now in possession of Col. Peeble's son at Clarendon, TX.

Mr. Hogan had the peculiar fortune to minister on the field of battle to three famous officers of the Confederate army- to Col. L. C. Bratton, who was mortally wounded at Murfreesboro; to Col. John A. Wilson at Atlanta; and to Lieut. Col. S. E. Shannon at Franklin. A tribute to Mr. Hogan is on file with many other papers pertaining to his record of courage and gallantry in the state department of archives under John Trotwood Moore. Col. John A. Wilson of the Twenty-fourth Regiment has written to the department of archives in this regard, and his letter reads in part:

"His last battle of the civil war was fought just in front of Nashville, Dec. 16, 1864. Hood's army was routed by overwhelming numbers; Hogan, being conversant with the topography of this section, conducted Col. Tighlman, now in command of Strahl's brigade, with hundreds of comrades, over the crest of those knobs; from near the Granny White Pike to Brentwood, the Franklin and Granny White pikes having been already invested by the enemy; this was the only way out of capture.

On Hood's retreat Hogan was on the firing line, with his old command to the Tennessee River, after which about Jan. 15, 1865. Hood's army fell back to Tupelo, Miss., at which place the Rev. Hogan asked for a transfer to Baxter's battery, now stationed at Macon, Ga., for the following reasons" "I am the only one of my original company who is left. The balance have all been killed or captured; I have but one, my youngest brother in the service, and he is a member of Baxter's Battery, and I wish to be with him."

"One-Man Company and Regimental Flag"

Chaplain Henry D. Hogan / 24th TN Inf. Co. B

First Hand Account [16]

Chaplaincy Of The 24th Tennessee Regiment.

Statement by Rev. H. D. Hogan, Rosedale, Kans.

REV. H. D. HOGAN.

---

[16] Confederate Veteran~XXVIII p. 278.

On April 29, 1861, I celebrated my twenty-first birthday by casting my lot with the destiny of my State. Rev. J. W. Cullom, a traveling preacher of the Tennessee Conference and I, a local preacher, enlisted at the same time in Company B, 24th Tennessee Regiment. At the organization Rev. J. W. Cullom was elected chaplain of the regiment, which office he faithfully filled until his resignation, some two years later. After his resignation it devolved on me to look after the spiritual interest of the regiment. I was exempt from military service and could have returned home, but the "love of Christ constrained me" to remain with those with whom I had cast my lot.

A number of strange and sad coincidences followed me. Colonel Bratton, who fell mortally wounded at Murfreesboro and whom I assisted off the field of battle, implored me not to leave him. He died in peace; "he found the Christ," Assisted by several of my captors, we buried him with his head to the east against that old snarled maple at the south door of the old Methodist church. I was made prisoner and sent to Camp Morton. When released the following April I found my command south of Murfreesboro. I held a most wonderful meeting; scores of souls were brought to Christ. In speaking of this meeting Mrs. Snyder's "History of the Civil War" says: "Rev. H. D. Hogan, a private soldier, held a fine revival in his regiment, the 24th Tennessee."

The following April we commenced and held over a great revival till in May; scores were converted. Colonel Wilson in that charge of the enemy's works on the 22d of July right off Atlanta was wounded seriously. I saw him through a rain of shot and shell to a place of safely. In that fearful charge of the enemy's second line of works at Franklin on November 30, 1864, I assisted in removing them to the Carter house, where they received temporary emergency treatment.

At the Reunion in Nashville soon after the war I was elected Chaplain of the 24th Regiment. I have honored my appointment by looking after my charge by correspondence and otherwise.

Now, I modestly make the above statements in vindication of my right to the honors of the chaplaincy of the 24th Tennessee Regiment as a historical fact and append the following in corroboration:

"Bowie, Tex., July 18, 1919.

"This is to certify that the 24th Tennessee Regiment being without a chaplain after the resignation of Rev. J. W. Cullom, the Rev. H. D. Hogan; a private of Company B; was the only recognized chaplain till the close of the war; then having no legal successor to Rev. J. W. Cullom. He also carried me off the field of battle at Atlanta, Ga., on the 22d of July, 1864; hence it is due to him that I survive.

John A. Wilson,

Colonel 24th Tennessee Regiment."

"Touching the above statement of the chaplaincy of Rev. H. D. Hogan, of the 24th Tennessee Regiment, it is correct.

S. E. Shannon,

Lieutenant Colonel 24th Tennessee Regiment."

First Hand Account [17]

Comrades True

Devoted friends are Col. John A. Wilson, now living at Bowie, Tex., and who commanded the 24th Tennessee Regiment, and Rev. Henry D. Hogan, of Rosedale Kans., who served with that regiment. Their pictures show them as they are today. Colonel Wilson in his eighty-eigth year. A sketch of him in the Veteran for December, 1924, stated that he was first captain of Company D, was promoted to major in July, 1862, and was made colonel of the regiment in January, 1863. This was just after the battle of Stone's River, where he was wounded.

Comrade Hogan enlisted in Company B, of the 24th Tennessee Regiment, on April 29, 1861, saying to the boys: "*I am with you to stay*" He served as a private for the first two years, drilling, on guard and picket duty, and also leading the religious services. He was first under fire at the battle Shiloh, April 7, 1862, also at Stones' River in December of that year, and after that battle he was detailed to remain and care for Colonel Bratton, who had been mortally wounded there. He was thus a prisoner and was sent to Camp Morton and exchanged the following April. He found his regiment at Dug Gap, Tenn., and then began his ministrations as the chaplain, which he accepted, thinking his influence would be stronger with the boys. At the battle Atlanta, on July 22, 1864, Colonel Wilson fell desperately wounded, and

---

[17] Confederate Veteran~XXXIII p.365

Chaplain Hogan helped him to a place of safety. *"It is due to him that I survive today,"* wrote Colonel Wilson. He was also at the bloody battle of Franklin, where Lieutenant Colonel Shannon was wounded, and Comrade Hogan remained with him through that awful night of November 20, 1864, until he could be removed to the Carter house for treatment. His last battle was at Nashville, and, being familiar with that section, he helped Colonel Tillman, of Strahl's Brigade, and many comrades to escape by conducting them over the hills toward Brentwood-the only way to escape capture.

On Hood's retreat, Comrade Hogan was on the firing line with his old command to the Tennessee River, and when the army fell back to Tupelo, Miss., along in January, 1865, he asked for a transfer to Baxter's Battery, then stationed at Macon, Ga., stating that he was the only one of his original company left, and his youngest brother was a member of Baxter's Battery, and he wanted to be with him. So the transfer was granted, and with that command he served to the end, stacking his gun at Greensboro, N. C., on April 29, 1865, just four years to a day since he entered the army. He was the only one of his original company who surrendered there.

After the war, at the reorganization of the 24th Tennessee Regiment, Rev. H. D. Hogan was elected its chaplain. His later life was as a minister of the gospel, until his retirement some years ago.

Though these old friends are so widely separated, they keep in touch by correspondence. Colonel Wilson is the only surviving officer of the regiment.

JOHN ROY.

OLDEST AND YOUNGEST SOLDIERS.

John Roy was born in Roanoke County, Va., March 2, 1785. He had three uncles in the Continental army, who fought under Greene and Morgan at King's Mountain and at Guilford Court House; Va. He came fom Virginia to

Tennessee in 1809, and settled near Nashville, He enlisted under "Old Hickory" for the Creek war. He had seven teeth shot out at Talladega, and was within a few feet of Maj. Montgomery when he was killed in the battle of the Horseshoe.

Again, when Jackson called for troops to go to New Orleans, Roy's desire to go was so great that he gave a horse and one hundred Spanish silver dollars for the place of a man who drew the lucky number to go. In the battle on January 8, 1815, he was near a British officer, Maj. Renne; who exhibited great courage and was killed in that battle.

After that war he married, and settled near Brentwood, Tenn., and reared a family of three daughters and two sons. Three grandsons took part in the civil war; J. G. and W. H. Moody, of Comany D, First Tennessee Infantry, and John Roy (born May 5, 1848), who enlisted in Company L, First Tennessee Infantry, in November 1861, and was killed October 8, 1862 at the battle of Perryville. This picture was taken at nine years of age.

John Roy, Sr., enlisted in Company B, Twenty-fourth Tennessee Infantry, at the age of seventy-six years and four months; but his service was brief, because of afflictions. He died November 6, 1868.

Confederate Veteran V, p. 407

JOHN ROY, JR.

B. F. Roberts, Jr.

B. F. Roberts, Jr., was born January 8, 1844, in Williamson County, Tenn.; and died November 20, 1912, at his home in Franklin.

At the age of seventeen he enlisted in Company B, 24th Tennessee Infantry, which served much in Strahl's Brigade, Cheatham's Division, Army of Tennessee, He participated with his regiment in the battle Murfressboro and in all of the war. Frequently during the Atlanta campaign he volunteered for scout service within the enemy's lines, performing his duty with intellignece, fidelity, and promptness, He was wounded at Missionary Ridge and again in an effort to scale the Federal main line of warks at Franklin. He was paroled during the spring of 1865. The testimony by an officer of his regiment is that he never shirked a duty nor failed a comrade.

He was a charter member of McEwen Bivoac, at one time its President, and continued in good standing unitl his death. He was ever dilignet to entertain of serve a comrade. In civil life he took an active interest in the affairs of his country, State, and communtiy, He was for more than twenty years a member of the County Court and at one period its presiding officer. As a soldier and citizen loyalty to principle, devation to high ideals, and uncompromising opposition to wrong were his commanding characteritics.

Confederate Veteran XXI, p.88

RICHARD RANSOM.

Judge Richard Ransom

Capt. Richard Beard, of Murfreesboro, pays tribute: "Comrade Richard Ransom was born at Versailles, Ruterford County, Tenn., July 3, 1835; and died at his home in Murfreesboro February 4, 1903, in his sixty-eighth year. His entire life was spent in this county, except while away at school, and the four years of his young manhood in the Confederate army.

"In the spring, or early summer , of 1861 he enlisted in

the Twenty-Fourth Tennessee Infantry as a private, but was afterwards promoted to a lietuenancy, which rank he held at the close of his service in the army. He was a faithful and gallant soldier, and came home with a parole in his pocket. His consciousness of having done his duty well was a n inspiration from the day of his return to the day of his death. And this , my comrades, should an inspriation to us all, as no prouder heritage can we leave to our children than the memory of having done our duty faithfully during those stormy years of that great war.

On returning home, Comrade Ransom took up the business of farming, and was successful. He was three times elected sheriff of the county, and as such served with credit to himslf ad the county. For years he was a member of the County court and for seven successive terms was elected and served at its chairman. He was one of the charter members of J. B. Palmer Bivouac, and was for one or more terms its president, and at one time was vice president of the State Association.

Never was a call made upon the Bivouac that he was not ready to shoulder his part of the burden. He was an upright man, good and true, with a great deal more of the sunshine of life in his nature than is ordinarily found in men. He was faithful to every trust that was imposed upon him."

Confederate Veteran XI p.177

LEWIS E. SIMPSON.

ACTIVE SERVICE AND PRISON

Lewis E. Simpson, of Alexandria, Tenn., who has been an interested patron of the veteran from its beginnings, entered the Confederate service in his nineteenth year, in February, 1861, becoming a member of Company, F, 24th Tennessee Infantry. This regiment was formed at Murfreesboro and went from that place to Bowling Green, Ky., then to Corinth, Miss, in 1862. After taking part in the battle of Shiloh, it went back to Corinth and was in the battle there, going thence to Tupelo for a while and then on raid with General Bragg by Atlanta, Birmingham, and Nashville, into Kentucky, taking part in the battle of Perryville. It was then sent to Camp Dick Robinson and from there, by way of Cumberland Gap, back to Tennessee and was in the fight at Murfreesboro. Going next to Chattamooga, the regiment took part in the battle of Chickamauga and was then at Missionary Ridge, where Comrade Simpson was taken prisoner in front of Bragg's headquarters. He was sent to Nashville and placed in the Zollicoffer Barracks; from there he was sent to Rock Island, where he stayed for fifteen months. During the time he was so afflicted with rheumatism that his release was at last obtained by special petition to President Lincoln, and he returned home in March, 1865. He was slightly wounded by a shell during his service.

Confederate Veteran XXIV p.185

Col. R. D. Allison

Allison's Tennessee Cavalry Squadron [18]

Allison's Tennessee Cavalry Squadron was raised March 1862, at Alexandria, TN., by Col. R. D. Allison, John S. Reece, and Robert V. Wright. Col. Allison and John Reece had previously served with the 24th Tennessee Infantry but had been discharged due to their age.

. . . The three companies that made up Allison's were mostly men from DeKalb Co. TN with a few from the surrounding counties. It was one of the few DeKalb units that actually fought in there home area. During the first half of 1863 it was involved in several small battles and skirmishes in and around Alexandria and Liberty.

---

[18] http://www.tennessee-scv.org/Camp1513/allison.htm

HARDISON, David Mark 2/18/1831-4/23/1931 s/o Wiliam Joshua Hardison & Martha G Patsy Long - Sgt then Lt, Co B 24th TN Inf - "Duck River Riflemen". Shot in right arm at Shiloh. Captured 6/20/1864 till end of war. [Mil]

" . . . I will give the names of my best soldier friends who stood by me in the struggle: Capt S L Hardison, Eff Hardison, Orin Cheek, E Journey, John Barham, Same Clymore, J H Clymore, Bill Lee. All soldiers were considered as friends but I believe those mentioned would have divided the last crumb with me, even died for me. I lost some of my best friends in battle: W T Lee, Dick Mills, Van Johnson, James Kinnard, H Cranford. All of those mentioned on this page were my mess mates from time to time. 8 in a mess, as one was lost we would add another." (Historic Maury, Vol 13, 1977 p 167 - Hardison & Allied Families by Fred L Hawkins & Dorothy Westmoreland Gilliam, Columbia, TN 1922 p 250) "General: My scouts on the Shelbyville road have reported that they ran on to a small squad of the enemy, supposed to be Sam Hardison's guerrilla band. . . The country is full of guerrillas. . . Very Respectfully, Horace Capron, Col . . . " (The War of the Rebellion, Official Records, Seires I, Vol 45, Part I p 1097 - Hardison & Allied Families by Fred L Hawkins & Dorothy Westmoreland Gilliam, Columbia, TN 1922 p250) 1st Sergt David M Hardison, shot at Shiloh, flesh of right arm; captured 6/20/1864; remained in prison till end of war; living on the county line of Marshall, 1 mile west of Berlin. Co G opened fight at Shiloh, about sunrise on Sunday morning. All casualties at the time except Dave Hardison later. Eight men died in line and sixteen wounded in first fire before the riflemen fired a shot. (Hitory of Maury Co, TN, Frank H Smith, 1969, pp 269, 273,274 - Hardison & Allied Families by Fred L Hawkins & Dorothy Westmoreland Gilliam, Columbia, TN 1922 p268)

[Source: Confederate Veteran]
TWENTY-FOURTH REGIMENT

J.H. CLARK, of Lubbock, Tex., would like to hear from any of the old comrades of the 24th regiment, Tennessee Volunteers, Co H. The colonel of this regiment was R.D. ALLISON. The captain of Co. H was C.W. BEAL and his first sergeant was H.C. CAMPBELL. Company H was afterwards consolidated and became Co. I. The second first sergeant was JOE HOLMES and J.H. CLARK was the third first sergeant. He enlisted at Nashville on July 22, 1861. [written 1899]

TENNESSEE CONFEDERATE PHYSICIANS : PART 5 (RICE - YANDELL)
http://www.state.tn.us/sos/statelib/pubsvs/doctor5.htm
Wellborn, Wm. Thomas (AS) p. 269 ? 24th TN Regt.

Black Southerners In Gray, Index To Tennessee Confederate Pension Applications:
[2] William Easley/24th TN Infantry/#10/Hickman County.
http://www.37thtexas.org/html/HistRef4.html

The following White County soldiers responded to a questionnaire posed by the State of Tennessee after the War. The complete questionnaires can be found in the published source.
Source: Index to Questionnaires of Civil War Veterans
Manuscript Section Archives Division
Tennessee State Library and Archives
Nashville, TN 1962
Confederates
Johnson, J. O. - 24th TN Inf Co. A

Field Staff and Band

Colonels:

- Robert D. Allison
- Hugh L. W. Bratton
- John A. Wilson

COL. JOHN A. WILSON.

Courtesy Tennessee State Archives.

Lieutenant Colonels:

Thomas H. Peebles

Samuel E. Shannon

COL. S. E. SHANNON.

[Source: *Confederate Veteran*]

COL. S.E. SHANNON, born March 12, 1838, died Sept. 7, 1921, at his home in Williamson County, Tenn.

In his early manhood he was a beloved and successful teacher. When the tocsin of war sounded, calling for the best and bravest, S.E. SHANNON answered the call and enlisted in Co. B, 24th Tennessee Infantry. When T.H. PEEBLES, captain of the company, was elected colonel of the regiment, S.E. SHANNON was made captain. At the battle of Shiloh, April 6 and 7, 1862, he handled his company with such dautless courage and distinguished skill as to receive the praise of his superior officers and the love and devotion of his men. At the reorganization at Corinth, he was made major of the regiment, and was with it at the battle of Perryville, Ky. At the battle of Stones River, Jan. 3, 1863, Colonel BRATTON was killed and SHANNON was made lieutenant colonel.

He was in the battle of Chickamauga, Missionary Ridge and all the engagements from Dalton to Atlanta. On July 22, on the right of Atlanta, COLONEL WILSON was severely wounded and COLONEL SHANNON took command of the regiment. At Jonesboro, in making a charge, the color bearer was shot down. Col. SHANNON seized the flag and led the regiment through the fight. When HOOD came into Tennessee, Col. SHANNON led his regiment in that fearful charge at Franklin and was shot down within ten feet of the enemy's works. He was supposed to be mortally wounded, but survived to the good old age of 83. As a cool, gallant, and fearless soldier he may have had equals, but no superior.

After the war he married MISS ELIZABETH H. ROBERTS, a daughter of one of the most prominent and respected farmers of Williamson County. As a citizen, he was honored and respected by everyone who knew him.

We deplore his loss, for his place can never be filled.

John J. Williams

Major:

- William C. Fielding

Company A

Allison, Alfred J. - Rank in Private. Rank out Private.

Allison, Andrew J. - Rank in Private. Rank out Private.

Arbuckle, C.T.L. - Rank in Private. Rank out Sergeant.

Arnold, Henry - Rank in Corporal. Rank out Private.

Bauland, J.P. - Rank in Private. Rank out Private.

Benton, James C. - Rank in Private. Rank out Private.

Boyce, A. - Rank in Private. Rank out Private.

Brown, E. G. - Rank in Private. Rank out Corporal.

Brown, W.J. - Rank in Private. Rank out Private.

Carlton, D.O. - Rank in Private. Rank out Private.

Carlton, J.M. - Rank in Sergeant. Rank out Sergeant.

Carlton, J.N. - Rank in Private. Rank out Private.

Carlton, W.J. - Rank in Private. Rank out Private.

Carsen, J.M. - Rank in Private. Rank out Private.

Carsen, R.G. - Rank in Private. Rank out Sergeant.

Carson, J.M. - Rank in Private. Rank out Private.

Carson, James M. - Rank in Private. Rank out Private.

Carson, R.G. - Rank in Private. Rank out Sergeant.

Carson, R.J. - Rank in Private. Rank out Sergeant.

Carson, W.H.H. - Rank in Private. Rank out Private.

Carson, William H.H. - Rank in Private. Rank out Private.

Castleman (Casleman), J.J. - Rank in Private. Rank out Private.

Cleveland (Clieveland), F.G. - Rank in Private. Rank out Private.

Cole, A.W. - Rank in Private. Rank out Private.

Collins (Collens), M.(W.) J. - Rank in Private. Rank out Private.

Cook, J. K. - Rank in Private. Rank out Private.

Cook, J. P. - Rank in Private. Rank out Private.

Cosey, W.L. - Rank in Private. Rank out Private.

Coursey, J.B. - Rank in Private. Rank out Private.

Coursey, Joseph - Rank in Private. Rank out First Sergeant.

Coursey, T.H. - Rank in Private. Rank out Sergeant.

Coursey, W.L. - Rank in Private. Rank out Private.

Coursey, William - Rank in Private. Rank out Private.

Cousey, W.L. - Rank in Private. Rank out Private.

Davis, S.T. - Rank in Private. Rank out Private.

Davis, W.E. - Rank in First Sergeant. Rank out Second Lieutenant.

Denny, B.R. - Rank in Private. Rank out Private.

Dickens, J.A. - Rank in Private. Rank out Private.

Dickens, W.T. - Rank in Private. Rank out Private.

Dunn, C.W. - Rank in Private. Rank out Private.

Dunn, E.F. - Rank in Private. Rank out Private.

Dunn, W.D. - Rank in Private. Rank out Private.

Fain, T.J. - Rank in Private. Rank out Private.

Fain, W.G. - Rank in Private. Rank out Private.

Fain, William W. - Rank in Private. Rank out Private.

Fain Jr., R.W. - Rank in Private. Rank out First Lieutenant.

Faris, J.W. - Rank in Second Lieutenant. Rank out Second Lieutenant.

Faris, Richard W. - Rank in Private. Rank out Private.

Faris, William J.S. - Rank in Private. Rank out Private.

Farris, John W. - Rank in Second Lieutenant. Rank out Second Lieutenant.

Farris, R.W. - Rank in Private. Rank out Private.

Farris, W.J.S. - Rank in Private. Rank out Private.

Featherston, Calvin - Rank in Private. Rank out Private.

Fergerson, J.C. - Rank in Private. Rank out Private.

Fetherston, Calvin - Rank in Private. Rank out Private.

Furgerson, J.C. - Rank in Private. Rank out Private.

Garrett, T.W. - Rank in Private. Rank out Sergeant.

Garrett, W.H. - Rank in Private. Rank out Private.

Gentry, W.H. - Rank in Private. Rank out Private.

Gregory, Abraham - Rank in Private. Rank out Private.

Grigory, Abraham - Rank in Private. Rank out Private.

Grinadge, J.R. - Rank in Private. Rank out Private.

Halstead, J.O. - Rank in Private. Rank out Private.

Halstead, J.P. - Rank in Private. Rank out Private.

Halsted, J.O. - Rank in Private. Rank out Private.

Haris, W.N. - Rank in Private. Rank out Private.

Harris, J.W. - Rank in Second Lieutenant. Rank out Second Lieutenant.

Harris, W.N. - Rank in Private. Rank out Private.

Haskings, Samuel B. - Rank in Private. Rank out Corporal.

Haynes, J.H. - Rank in Private. Rank out Private.

Haynes, T.H. - Rank in Private. Rank out Private.

Heath, David - Rank in Private. Rank out Private.

Heath, J.W. - Rank in Private. Rank out Private.

Hendrix, Jr., E.W. - Rank in Private. Rank out Private.

Holden, George W. - Rank in Private. Rank out Private.

Holden, J.H. - Rank in Private. Rank out Private.

Holden, J.M. - Rank in Private. Rank out Private.

Holder, J.A. - Rank in Private. Rank out Private.

Holder, James A. - Rank in Private. Rank out Private.

Holdon, George W. - Rank in Private. Rank out Private.

Hoskins, Samuel B. - Rank in Private. Rank out Corporal.

Hudson, John C. - Rank in Private. Rank out Private.

Hutcherson, John S. - Rank in Private. Rank out Private.

Hutchinson, J.S. - Rank in Private. Rank out Private.

Jackson, D.C. - Rank in Sergeant. Rank out Sergeant.

Jackson, F.M. - Rank in First Lieutenant. Rank out Captain.

Jackson, J.C. - Rank in Captain. Rank out Captain.

Jackson, John L. - Rank in Private. Rank out Corporal.

Jackson, M.R. - Rank in Private. Rank out Private.

Jackson, W.H.H. - Rank in Private. Rank out Private.

Jackson, William - Rank in Private. Rank out Private.

Jackson, Sr., W.H. - Rank in Private. Rank out Private.

James, W.C. - Rank in Private. Rank out Private.

Johnson, J.R. - Rank in Private. Rank out Sergeant.

Johnson, James R. - Rank in Private. Rank out Sergeant.

Jones, B.A. - Rank in Private. Rank out Private.

Jones, Cornelius - Rank in Private. Rank out Private.

Jones, D.A. - Rank in Private. Rank out Private.

Jones, David A. - Rank in Private. Rank out Private.

Jones, E.D. - Rank in Private. Rank out Private.

Jones, Edward D. - Rank in Private. Rank out Private.

Jones, J.C. - Rank in Private. Rank out Private.

Jones, John J. - Rank in Private. Rank out Private.

Jones, R.H. - Rank in Private. Rank out Private.

Kidian, Henry - Rank in Private. Rank out Private.

Kimens, J.E. - Rank in Sergeant. Rank out Brevet Second Lieutenant.

Kimmins, J.E. - Rank in Sergeant. Rank out Brevet Second Lieutenant.

King, J.J. - Rank in Private. Rank out Private.

King, James - Rank in Private. Rank out Private.

King, R.W. - Rank in Private. Rank out Private.

Lamb, N.H. - Rank in Private. Rank out Private.

Lamb, William M. - Rank in Private. Rank out Private.

Leverett, Robert - Rank in Private. Rank out Private.

Lewis, B.W. - Rank in Private. Rank out Private.

Lewis, J.W. - Rank in Private. Rank out Private.

Maddox, F.F. - Rank in Private. Rank out Private.

Maddox, T.F. - Rank in Private. Rank out Private.

Mangram, Jesse - Rank in Private. Rank out Private.

Mangrum, J.W. - Rank in Private. Rank out Private.

Mangrum, Jesse - Rank in Private. Rank out Private.

Mangrun, Jesse - Rank in Private. Rank out Private.

Manire, A.W. - Rank in Private. Rank out Private.

Manire, D.C. - Rank in Private. Rank out Private.

Manire, Lemuel - Rank in Private. Rank out Private.

Manire, Leonard - Rank in Private. Rank out Private.

Maxwell, J.A. - Rank in Private. Rank out Private.

McDowell, William - Rank in Private. Rank out Private.

McGowan, T.M. - Rank in Private. Rank out Private.

McGowen, T.M. - Rank in Private. Rank out Private.

McGowin, M. - Rank in Private. Rank out Private.

Moseley, Henry - Rank in Private. Rank out Private.

Mosely, Henry - Rank in Private. Rank out Private.

Mosley, Henry - Rank in Private. Rank out Private.

Murfrey, E.M. - Rank in Private. Rank out Corporal.

Nance, Benjamin F. - Rank in Private. Rank out Private.

Nance, John W. - Rank in Third Lieutenant. Rank out Adjutant.

Norval, C.B. - Rank in Private. Rank out Private.

Norval, D.G. - Rank in Private. Rank out Private.

Norvell, D.G. - Rank in Private. Rank out Private.

Norvell, Daniel G. - Rank in Private. Rank out Private.

Norville, D.G. - Rank in Private. Rank out Private.

Norville, D.Z. - Rank in Private. Rank out Private.

Owen, James H. - Rank in Private. Rank out Private.

Parsley, J.W. - Rank in Private. Rank out Private.

Pope, Ezell - Rank in Private. Rank out Private.

Pope, F.M. - Rank in Corporal. Rank out Private.

Pope, Francis M. - Rank in Corporal. Rank out Private.

Pope, John K. - Rank in Private. Rank out Private.

Ransom, Richard - Rank in Private. Rank out Second Lieutenant.

Ray, N.J. - Rank in Private. Rank out Private.

Robertson, W.D. - Rank in Private. Rank out Private.

Roland, James K. - Rank in Private. Rank out Private.

Rolland, James K. - Rank in Private. Rank out Private.

Rowland, J.K.P. - Rank in Private. Rank out Private.

Rowland, James K. - Rank in Private. Rank out Private.

Russell, William - Rank in Private. Rank out Private.

Rutledge, W.C. - Rank in Private. Rank out Private.

Savage, William - Rank in Private. Rank out Private.

Smith, T.B. - Rank in Private. Rank out Private.

Smith, T.P. - Rank in Private. Rank out Private.

Smith, Thomas P. - Rank in Private. Rank out Private.

Smith, W.L. - Rank in Private. Rank out Private.

Smitherland, J. - Rank in Private. Rank out Private.

Smotherman, Barton - Rank in Private. Rank out Private.

Smotherman, C.C. - Rank in Private. Rank out Private.

Smotherman, Calvin C. - Rank in Private. Rank out Private.

Smotherman, D.D. - Rank in Private. Rank out Private.

Smotherman, J.T. - Rank in Private. Rank out Private.

Smotherman, J.W. - Rank in Private. Rank out Private.

Smotherman, John W. - Rank in Private. Rank out Private.

Smotherman, Joseph - Rank in Private. Rank out Private.

Smotherman, William - Rank in Private. Rank out Private.

Smuthermon, Barton - Rank in Private. Rank out Private.

Smuthermon, C.C. - Rank in Private. Rank out Private.

Smuthermon, D.D. - Rank in Private. Rank out Private.

Smuthermon, J.W. - Rank in Private. Rank out Private.

Smuthermon, Joseph - Rank in Private. Rank out Private.

Smuthermon, William - Rank in Private. Rank out Private.

Spence, Francis - Rank in Corporal. Rank out Private.

Spence, Francis M. - Rank in Corporal. Rank out Private.

Spence, Francis N. - Rank in Corporal. Rank out Private.

Spencer, F.V. - Rank in Corporal. Rank out Private.

Stegall, John G. - Rank in Private. Rank out Private.

Stegall, W.J. - Rank in Private. Rank out Private.

Stem, J.E. - Rank in Private. Rank out Private.

Stigall, J.G. - Rank in Private. Rank out Private.

Stigall, W.G. - Rank in Private. Rank out Private.

Stigall, W.J. - Rank in Private. Rank out Private.

Stone, James R. - Rank in Private. Rank out Private.

Stugall, J.G. - Rank in Private. Rank out Private.

Stugall, W.G. - Rank in Private. Rank out Private.

Stull, J.E. - Rank in Private. Rank out Private.

Tanner, Robert - Rank in Private. Rank out Private.

Taylor, C.P. - Rank in Private. Rank out Private.

Taylor, Charles P. - Rank in Private. Rank out Private.

Taylor, J.A. - Rank in Private. Rank out First Lieutenant.

Toliver, Henry - Rank in Private. Rank out Private.

Tolliver, Henry - Rank in Private. Rank out Private.

Turner, Robert - Rank in Private. Rank out Private.

Underwood, Atariah - Rank in Private. Rank out .

Underwood, J. E. - Rank in Private. Rank out Private.

Underwood, John - Rank in Private. Rank out Private.

Underwood, W. A. - Rank in Private. Rank out Private.

Underwood, William - Rank in Private. Rank out Private.

Vernon, W. T. - Rank in Private. Rank out Private.

Vickrey, Burnett - Rank in Private. Rank out Private.

Vicory, Burnet - Rank in Private. Rank out Private.

Vincent, Moses - Rank in Private. Rank out Private.

Vincent, W.A. - Rank in Private. Rank out Private.

Vinson, W. - Rank in Private. Rank out Private.

Ward, B.B. - Rank in Private. Rank out Private.

Whites (Whitts / Whitice / Whiteas), Robert L. - Rank in Private. Rank out Corporal.

Winn, L.A. - Rank in Private. Rank out Private.

Wright, Isaac - Rank in Private. Rank out Private.

Wright, James - Rank in Private. Rank out Private.

Wright, T.W. - Rank in Private. Rank out Private.

Young, Joseph - Rank in Private. Rank out Private.

Company B

Bain, Ed. C. - Rank in Private. Rank out Private.

Barnes, John H. - Rank in Private. Rank out Private.

Barns, John A. - Rank in Private. Rank out Private.

Basdal, Jesse - Rank in Private. Rank out Private.

Basdal, John H. - Rank in Private. Rank out Private.

Basdal, William D. - Rank in Private. Rank out Private.

Bass, Daniel S. - Rank in Private. Rank out Private.

Bazdale, J.M. - Rank in Private. Rank out Private.

Bazdale, Jesse J. - Rank in Private. Rank out Private.

Bazdale, W.D. - Rank in Private. Rank out Private.

Bazell, George W. - Rank in Private. Rank out Private.

Bazell, William D. - Rank in Private. Rank out Private.

Bazen, William D. - Rank in Private. Rank out Private.

Bazzell, G.M. - Rank in Private. Rank out Private.

Bazzell, James M. - Rank in Private. Rank out Private.

Bazzell, Jesse J. - Rank in Private. Rank out Private.

Bazzell, John H. - Rank in Private. Rank out Private.

Beard, A.P. - Rank in Corporal. Rank out Private.

Beasley, James R. - Rank in Private. Rank out Sergeant.

Beasley, James R. - Rank in Private. Rank out Sergeant.

Beasly, James R. - Rank in Private. Rank out Sergeant.

Beech, R.T. - Rank in Private. Rank out Private.

Beech, Richard - Rank in Private. Rank out Private.

Beech, William - Rank in Private. Rank out Private.

Beeck, R.T. - Rank in Private. Rank out Private.

Bennett, Jacob - Rank in Private. Rank out Private.

Bennett, Thomas A. - Rank in Private. Rank out Private.

Berge, J.P. - Rank in Private. Rank out Private.

Berge, William A. - Rank in Private. Rank out Private.

Bezell, William D. - Rank in Private. Rank out Private.

Biggers, J.L. - Rank in Private. Rank out Private.

Biggers, John L. - Rank in Private. Rank out Private.

Black, D.S. - Rank in Private. Rank out Private.

Black, David - Rank in Private. Rank out Private.

Black, S. S. - Rank in Private. Rank out Private.

Black, William F. - Rank in Private. Rank out Private.

Bosdol, James M. - Rank in Private. Rank out Private.

Bozzell, J.H. - Rank in Private. Rank out -.

Brown, Robert - Rank in Private. Rank out Private.

Burge, J.P. - Rank in Private. Rank out Private.

Burge, William - Rank in Private. Rank out Private.

Burk, N.C. - Rank in Private. Rank out Private.

Burk, T.A. - Rank in Private. Rank out First Sergeant.

Burk, Thomas H. - Rank in Private. Rank out First Sergeant.

Buzzell, J.H. - Rank in Private. Rank out .

Cacy, Fleming - Rank in Private. Rank out Private.

Caldwell, Thomas H. - Rank in Private. Rank out Private.

Cayce, Flemming S. - Rank in Private. Rank out Private.

Chadwell, Everett - Rank in Sergeant. Rank out Private.

Chadwell, John - Rank in Private. Rank out Private.

Chadwin, John - Rank in Private. Rank out Private.

Chambers, T.J. - Rank in Private. Rank out Private.

Chartwell, John - Rank in Private. Rank out Private.

Chatwell, John - Rank in Private. Rank out Private.

Clark, James S. - Rank in Private. Rank out Private.

Collins, William A. - Rank in Private. Rank out Corporal.

Copeland, J.B. - Rank in Private. Rank out Corporal.

Copeland, John - Rank in Private. Rank out Corporal.

Cowan, George W. - Rank in Private. Rank out Private.

Cowan, Jo. W. - Rank in Private. Rank out Private.

Cowen, J.W. - Rank in Private. Rank out Private.

Crockett, George B. - Rank in First Lieutenant. Rank out First Lieutenant.

Culberson, S.H. - Rank in Private. Rank out Private.

Culbertson, Sam H. - Rank in Private. Rank out Private.

Cunningham, Robert W. - Rank in Sergeant. Rank out Sergeant.

Curren, Everette P. - Rank in Private. Rank out Private.

Currin, E.P. - Rank in Private. Rank out Private.

Daimwood, G.G. - Rank in Private. Rank out Private.

Daimwood, S.W. - Rank in Private. Rank out Sergeant.

Dainwood, G.G. - Rank in Private. Rank out Private.

Dainwood, S.W. - Rank in Private. Rank out Sergeant.

Daniel, Thomas A. - Rank in Private. Rank out Private.

Danwood, George G. - Rank in Private. Rank out Private.

Darity, J.A. - Rank in Corporal. Rank out Corporal.

Darity, T.N. - Rank in Private. Rank out Private.

Darity, W.L. - Rank in Private. Rank out Private.

Darmwood, G.G. - Rank in Private. Rank out Private.

Daugherty, James A. - Rank in Corporal. Rank out Corporal.

Daughrity, James A. - Rank in Corporal. Rank out Corporal.

Daughrity, T.N. - Rank in Private. Rank out Private.

Daughrity, W.C. - Rank in Private. Rank out Private.

Daughrity, W.L. - Rank in Private. Rank out Private.

Daughrity, W.L. - Rank in Private. Rank out Private.

Davis, George F. - Rank in Private. Rank out Private.

Davis, John - Rank in Private. Rank out Teamster.

Davis, John C. - Rank in Private. Rank out Teamster.

Dellehay, J.W. - Rank in Private. Rank out Sergeant.

Derryberry, John H. - Rank in Sergeant. Rank out Private.

Dillehay, J. N. - Rank in Private. Rank out Sergeant.

Dillehay, Jasper N. - Rank in Private. Rank out Sergeant.

Dillehay, T. N. - Rank in Private. Rank out Sergeant.

Dilleyhay, J. N. - Rank in Private. Rank out Sergeant.

Dilleyhay, J. W. - Rank in Private. Rank out Sergeant.

Donwood, George G. - Rank in Private. Rank out Private.

Dorwood, George G. - Rank in Private. Rank out Private.

Dowell Sr., M.C. - Rank in Private. Rank out Private.

Edwards, Edom - Rank in Private. Rank out Private.

Edwards, William - Rank in Private. Rank out Private.

Fergerson, C.D. - Rank in Private. Rank out Private.

Fergerson, Nimrod - Rank in Private. Rank out Private.

Ferguson, A. - Rank in Private. Rank out Private.

Ferguson, C.D. - Rank in Private. Rank out Private.

Ferguson, James A. - Rank in Private. Rank out Private.

Ferguson, Nimrod - Rank in Private. Rank out Private.

Ferguson, Thomas - Rank in Private. Rank out Private.

Fields, Henry - Rank in Private. Rank out Private.

Fingerton, George W. - Rank in Private. Rank out Private.

Fox, Willis H. - Rank in Private. Rank out Private.

Furguson, H. - Rank in Private. Rank out Private.

Furguson, Thomas - Rank in Private. Rank out Private.

Gowen, Washington - Rank in Private. Rank out Private.

Graham, W.B. - Rank in Private. Rank out Private.

Green, Jo John - Rank in First Sergeant. Rank out Acting Quartermaster.

Guinn, Literel - Rank in Private. Rank out Private.

Hagan, H.D.P. - Rank in Private. Rank out Private.

Hamer, George - Rank in Private. Rank out Private.

Hampton, J.H. - Rank in Private. Rank out Private.

Hampton, Jerry - Rank in Private. Rank out Private.

Hanman, Thomas - Rank in Private. Rank out Private.

Hardaman, J.E. - Rank in Private. Rank out Second Lieutenant.

Hardeman, John E. - Rank in Private. Rank out Second Lieutenant.

Hardison, David M. - Rank in Private. Rank out First Lieutenant.

Hardison, G.W. - Rank in Private. Rank out Private.

Hardison, George - Rank in Private. Rank out Private.

Hardison, Joel S. - Rank in Second Lieutenant. Rank out Second Lieutenant.

Hardison, Martin V. - Rank in Private. Rank out Private.

Hardison, S.T. - Rank in Private. Rank out Private.

Hardison, William D. - Rank in Private. Rank out Private.

Harman, H.D. - Rank in Private. Rank out Private.

Harman, Thomas - Rank in Private. Rank out Private.

Harmen, Thomas - Rank in Private. Rank out Private.

Harmon, H.D. - Rank in Private. Rank out Private.

Harmon, Thomas - Rank in Private. Rank out Private.

Harmond, Thomas - Rank in Private. Rank out Private.

Harper, W.F. - Rank in Private. Rank out Private.

Harris, Edward - Rank in Private. Rank out Private.

Harrison, William H. - Rank in Private. Rank out Musician.

Herbert, R.H - Rank in Second Lieutenant. Rank out Captain.

Herbert, Richard N. - Rank in Second Lieutenant. Rank out Captain.

Hill, Albert - Rank in Private. Rank out Private.

Hill, Andrew D. - Rank in Private. Rank out Private.

Hill, F.M. - Rank in Sergeant. Rank out Second Lieutenant.

Hill, James A. - Rank in Private. Rank out Private.

Hill, James W.M. - Rank in Private. Rank out Private.

Hinson, Merril - Rank in Private. Rank out Private.

Hogan, H.D.P. - Rank in Private. Rank out Private.

Holland, F.A. - Rank in Private. Rank out Private.

Holland, Frank A. - Rank in Private. Rank out Private.

Horseford, William - Rank in Private. Rank out Private.

Horsford, William - Rank in Private. Rank out Private.

Hosford, Henry - Rank in Private. Rank out Private.

Hosford, William - Rank in Private. Rank out Private.

Howell, F. - Rank in Private. Rank out Private.

Howell, Harrison - Rank in Private. Rank out Private.

Howell, Lafayette - Rank in Private. Rank out Private.

Hubbard, Richard H. - Rank in Second Lieutenant. Rank out Captain.

Hughes, William - Rank in Private. Rank out Private.

Hughs, William - Rank in Private. Rank out Private.

Hurcleman, John E. - Rank in Private. Rank out Second Lieutenant.

Hurdeman, John E. - Rank in Private. Rank out Second Lieutenant.

Hurdiman, J.E. - Rank in Private. Rank out Second Lieutenant.

Huse, William - Rank in Private. Rank out Private.

Irvin, W.H. - Rank in Private. Rank out Private.

Irwin, W.H. - Rank in Private. Rank out Private.

Jackson, David - Rank in Private. Rank out Private.

Jackson, David A. - Rank in Private. Rank out Private.

Jamison, Thomas R. - Rank in Private. Rank out Private.

Jimerson, Thomas - Rank in Private. Rank out Private.

Johnson, B.D. - Rank in Private. Rank out Private.

Johnson, John A. - Rank in Sergeant. Rank out Private.

Johnson, R.A.W. - Rank in Corporal. Rank out Private.

Jones, D.S. - Rank in Private. Rank out Private.

Jones, Robert - Rank in Private. Rank out Private.

Jones, Spencer - Rank in Private. Rank out Private.

Jones, Stephen - Rank in Private. Rank out Private.

Jones, T.H. - Rank in Private. Rank out Private.

Jones, W.A. - Rank in Private. Rank out Private.

Jones, W.P. - Rank in Private. Rank out Private.

Jones, Wiley - Rank in Private. Rank out Private.

Jones, Willis - Rank in Private. Rank out Private.

King, Andrew L. - Rank in Private. Rank out Private.

Ladd, John C. - Rank in Private. Rank out Private.

Laine, W.J. - Rank in Private. Rank out Private.

Lane, William J. - Rank in Private. Rank out Private.

Lawrence, William - Rank in Private. Rank out Private.

Layne, W. J. - Rank in Private. Rank out Private.

Lee, W.T. - Rank in Private. Rank out Private.

Lovett, J.N. - Rank in Private. Rank out Private.

Lovett, N.J. - Rank in Private. Rank out Private.

Lovit, N.J. - Rank in Private. Rank out Private.

Mackey, A.B. - Rank in Private. Rank out Teamster.

Martin, B.F. - Rank in Private. Rank out Private.

Martin, J.T. - Rank in Private. Rank out Private.

Maupin, James A. - Rank in Private. Rank out Private.

Maupin, James M. - Rank in Private. Rank out Private.

Mayfield, A.P. - Rank in Private. Rank out Private.

McFadden, S.L. - Rank in Private. Rank out Private.

McFaddin, S.L. - Rank in Private. Rank out Private.

McMahan, And. A. - Rank in Private. Rank out Private.

McMahon, Andrew A. - Rank in Private. Rank out Private.

McMahon, Henry A. - Rank in Private. Rank out Private.

McMayhan, A.A. - Rank in Private. Rank out Private.

McMayhan, L.L. - Rank in Private. Rank out Private.

McMayhan, Lem L. - Rank in Private. Rank out Private.

McMurray, J.F. - Rank in . Rank out .

McMurray, S.J. - Rank in Private. Rank out Sergeant Major.

McMurry, Samuel J. - Rank in Private. Rank out Sergeant Major.

Modlin, William M. - Rank in Private. Rank out Private.

Moor, Austin - Rank in Private. Rank out Private.

Moore, A. - Rank in Private. Rank out Private.

More, Austen - Rank in Private. Rank out Private.

Morton, Green W. - Rank in Private. Rank out Private.

Neeley, Miles E. - Rank in Private. Rank out Private.

Nicholson, C.G. - Rank in Private. Rank out Private.

Nicholson, John M. - Rank in Sergeant. Rank out Private.

Owen, L.B.R. - Rank in Second Lieutenant. Rank out Second Lieutenant.

Palmore, Rob F. - Rank in Private. Rank out Private.

Peebles, Thomas H. - Rank in Captain. Rank out Lieutenant Colonel.

Pingleton, G.W. - Rank in Private. Rank out Private.

Pingleton, George W. - Rank in Private. Rank out Private.

Potts, J.S. - Rank in Private. Rank out Private.

Potts, W.M. - Rank in Private. Rank out Private.

Potts, William S. - Rank in Private. Rank out Private.

Pulley, Sly G. - Rank in Private. Rank out Private.

Pully, S.J. - Rank in Private. Rank out Private.

Pumroy, J.W. - Rank in Private. Rank out Private.

Pumroy, James P. - Rank in Private. Rank out Private.

Ray, John - Rank in Private. Rank out Private.

Rivers, J.A. - Rank in Private. Rank out Private.

Rivers, J.B. - Rank in Private. Rank out Private.

Roberts, B.F. - Rank in Private. Rank out Private.

Roberts, John H. - Rank in Corporal. Rank out Corporal.

Roberts, William T. - Rank in Private. Rank out Private.

Rucker, John E. - Rank in Private. Rank out Private.

Rumage, George - Rank in Private. Rank out Sergeant.

Rummage, George - Rank in Private. Rank out Sergeant.

Sage, Oliver - Rank in Private. Rank out Private.

Scott, William - Rank in Private. Rank out Private.

Secrest, W.H. - Rank in Private. Rank out Private.

Seward, B.R. - Rank in Private. Rank out Private.

Shannon, Samuel C. - Rank in Captain. Rank out Lieutenant Colonel.

Shiers, William - Rank in Corporal. Rank out Private.

Shires, C.N. - Rank in Private. Rank out Private.

Shires, Ira - Rank in Corporal. Rank out Sergeant.

Shires, Jacob B. - Rank in Private. Rank out Private.

Shires, Peter - Rank in Private. Rank out Private.

Shires, W.M. - Rank in Corporal. Rank out Private.

Shires, William - Rank in Corporal. Rank out Private.

Shires, William H. - Rank in Corporal. Rank out Private.

Shivers, Ira - Rank in Corporal. Rank out Sergeant.

Stephens, J.P. - Rank in Private. Rank out Private.

Stephens, Milton - Rank in Private. Rank out Private.

Stevens, John P. - Rank in Private. Rank out Private.

Stevens, Milton - Rank in Private. Rank out Private.

Stignor, J.M. - Rank in Private. Rank out Private.

Stinson, John - Rank in Private. Rank out Private.

Stinson, W.B. - Rank in Private. Rank out Private.

Thompson, James W. - Rank in Private. Rank out Private.

Thompson, Robert H. - Rank in Private. Rank out Private.

Tigner, John M. - Rank in Private. Rank out Private.

Tignor, John M. - Rank in Private. Rank out Private.

Tindall, H.C. - Rank in Private. Rank out Private.

Tindall, R.W. - Rank in Private. Rank out Captain.

Tindell, H.C. - Rank in Private. Rank out Private.

Tindell, Robert W. - Rank in Private. Rank out Captain.

Tindill, R.W. - Rank in Private. Rank out Captain.

Tisdale, F.M. - Rank in Private. Rank out Private.

Vaughn, Jerry H. - Rank in Private. Rank out Private.

Vernon, James A. - Rank in Corporal. Rank out Private.

Vernon, James Alex - Rank in Corporal. Rank out Private.

Vernon, Richard T. - Rank in Private. Rank out Private.

Walker, Henry J. - Rank in Private. Rank out Private.

Walters, Thomas L. - Rank in Private. Rank out Private.

Warren, Jesse - Rank in Private. Rank out Private.

Warren, Jesse A. - Rank in Private. Rank out Private.

Warren, John - Rank in Private. Rank out Private.

Warren, John B. - Rank in Private. Rank out Private.

Warren, John B. - Rank in Private. Rank out Private.

Warren, John M. - Rank in Private. Rank out Private.

Warren, R.M. - Rank in Private. Rank out Private.

Warren, Randle - Rank in Private. Rank out Private.

Warren, Thomas J. - Rank in Private. Rank out Private.

Warren, William - Rank in Private. Rank out Private.

Welsin, James - Rank in Private. Rank out Private.

Whitby, Richard B. - Rank in Private. Rank out Private.

Whitfield, Smith - Rank in Private. Rank out Private.

Whitley (Whitly), John - Rank in Private. Rank out Private.

Williams, Francis M. - Rank in Private. Rank out Private.

Williams, George W. - Rank in Private. Rank out Private.

Williams, Harrison A. - Rank in Private. Rank out Private.

Wilson, Jason - Rank in Private. Rank out Private.

Wilson, Joseph D. - Rank in Private. Rank out Private.

Wright, Franklin J. - Rank in Private. Rank out Private.

Wright, H.M. - Rank in Private. Rank out Private.

Company C

John M. Uhles - Captain. Wounded at Shiloh, April 6, 1862. Died of wound at a Memphis, Tennessee hospital on April 27, 1862.

Bratton, H.L.W. - Rank in Private. Rank out Colonel.

Carr, W.K. - Rank in First Lieutenant. Rank out First Lieutenant.. Discharged at reorganization, May 2, 1862.

Carr, D. A. Rank in Second Lieutenant. Rank out Third Lieutenant.

J. W. Rose- 2nd Lieutenant. Wounded at Shiloh, April 6,1862. Sent to hospital at Columbus, Mississippi. Captured at Nashville, Tennessee on December 16, 1864. Sent to Johnson's Island, Ohio. Paroled June 17, 1865.

David Anderson Carr - 2nd Lieutenant. Discharged at reorganization on May 2, 1862. Enlisted in Company E, 9th Cavalry, also see.

Burrow, J. W. - 1st Sergeant (Ordnance Sergeant). Made Captain at the reorganization on May 2, 1862. Wounded at Shiloh on April 6, 1862. Killed at Missionary Ridge on November 25, 1863.

John N. Ogles - 2nd Sergeant. Died at Atlanta, Georgia on March 24, 1864.

S. D. Adams - Rank in Private. Rank out 3rd Sergeant. Wounded at Jonesboro, Georgia on August 31, 1864. Paroled at Augusta, Georgia on May 2, 1865.

C. B. Wright - 4th Sergeant. Discharged as a non-conscript at Tupelo, Mississippi on July 16, 1862. Under age. Captured at Gallatin, Tennessee in 1864. Forced to take the Oath or go to prison.

Burrow (Barrow / Barnon / Barrows), Henry C. - Rank in Private. Rank out Corporal. Captured at Nashville, Tennessee on December 15, 1864. Sent to Camp Chase, Ohio.

Carr, Franklin W. - Rank in Sergeant. Rank out Private. Captured at Nashville, Tennessee on December 15, 1864. Sent to Camp Chase, Ohio.

Carter, Richard L. - Rank in Private. Rank out Sergeant. Wounded severely at Perryville, Kentucky on October 8, 1862. Left there when army retreated. Captured. Sent to Camp Butler, Illinois and then to City Point, Virginia. Exchanged on April 17, 1863. Captured at Dalton, Georgia on January 20, 1864.

J. A. Burrow - Rank in Corporal. Promoted to 2nd Sergeant on May 2, 1862. Rank out Private. Deserted on January 20, 1864.

Robert Davis - Corporal. 3rd Lieutenant on April 13, 1863. 1st Lieutenant on June 27, 1863. Captured at Missionary Ridge on November 25, 1863. Commanding company. Sent to Johnson's Island, Ohio.

J. M. Garrett - Corporal. Discharged as a non-conscript on July 16, 1862.

Abraham, B. Ellis - Rank in Private. Rank out Corporal. Wounded severely and captured at Perryville, Kentucky on October 8, 1862.

Claborne, William H. H. - Corporal. Captured. Took the Oath at Nashville, Tennessee. Rank in Private. Rank out Corporal.

Adams, William L. - Rank in Private. Rank out Private. Killed at Shiloh, Tennessee on April 6, 1862.

Belt, S. K. - Rank in Private. Rank out Private. Detailed as hospital nurse. Discharged on July 3, 1862, by Mental Board of Directors.

Belt, William H. - Rank in Private. Rank out Private. Discharged with disability on January 2, 1862.

Black, H. M. - Rank in Private. Rank out Private. Wounded at Shiloh, Tennessee on April 6, 1862. Died of wound in a Memphis hospital. No date given.

Bratton, Robert Wilson - Rank in Private. Rank out Private. Captured in Macon County, Tennessee on December 12, 1862. Exchanged. Shown present through December 1863.

Brown, J. G. (C.) - Rank in Private. Rank out Private. Died on January 12, 1862.

Carr (Carn), C. S. - Died at Corinth, Mississippi on May 24, 1862.

Carr, James A. - Transferred from Company H, 2nd Tennessee Infantry on April 1, 1862. Wounded and captured at Shiloh, Tennessee on April 6, 1862. Exchanged. Discharged with disability. Enlisted in Company G, 9th Tennessee Cavalry.

Carr, Mathew A. (R.) - Rank in Private. Rank out Private. Captured at Nashville, Tennessee on December 15, 1864. Sent to Camp Chase, Ohio.

Carr, Newton H. - Rank in Private. Rank out Private. Discharged with disability from Company H, 2nd Tennessee Infantry in September 1861. Enlisted in this company. Wounded at Shiloh, Tennessee on April 6, 1862. Sent to hospital at Memphis, Tennessee. Discharged with disability on June 9, 1862.

Carter, John Edward - Rank in Private. Rank out Private. Wounded at Perryville, Kentucky on October 8, 1862. Left hip badly shattered by mini ball. Left there when army retreated. Captured. Sent to Camp Butler, Illinois and then to City Point, Virginia. Exchanged. Discharged as unfit for service on January 8, 1864. Stayed with army. Home in 1865.

Cauley, John - Rank in Private. Rank out Private.

Chamberlain (Chamberland / Chamberlin / Chamlin), William F. (L.) - Sent home sick from Camp Trousdale, Tennessee. Returned to duty. Discharged with disability on July 3, 1862. Debilititis. Captured, sick at home by U.S. forces. Refused to take the Oath. Sent to Camp Chase, Ohio. Finally released on physical condition. Went home. In bed helpless for three years.

Claborne, J. W. - Wounded at Shiloh, Tennessee on April 6, 1862. Sent to hospital at Columbus, Mississippi. Enlisted in Company H, 9th Tennessee Cavalry, also see.

Claborne, W. D. - Died in hospital at Nashville, Tennessee on February 15, 1862.

Crawford, James - Rank in Private. Rank out Private.

Crawford, T. Joseph - Sick at Camp Trousdale until December 16, 1861. Captured in Perry County, Kentucky on June 6, 1863. Sent to Point Lookout, Maryland. Released after taking the Oath on April 12, 1864.

Creasey, John - Killed at Shiloh, Tennessee on April 6, 1862.

Creasey, Franklin (Frank) - Captured at Missionary Ridge, November 25, 1863. Sent to Rock Island, Illinois. Prior service in Company C, 7th Cavalry Battalion, also see.

Creasey, J. M. - Wounded severely in left thigh at Perryville, Kentucky on October 8, 1862. Wounded at Chickamauga, Georgia in left hip. Was in battles at Murfreesboro, and Missionary Ridge. Listed as deserted on January 20, 1864. He took the Oath at Chattanooga, Tennessee.

Dallas, W. M. - Given a thirty day furlough at Camp Trousdale, Tennessee on September 18, 1861. Missing.

Dearing (Deerin / Dering / Derrin), A. J. - Listed as deserted. Captured as a deserter by U.S. forces on May 11, 1863. Sent to Ft. McHenry, Maryland.

Deerwood, George G. – Name does not appear in the National Archives Index.

Dixon, J. A. - Died at Bowling Green, Kentucky on December 7, 1861.

Duke, W. J. - Transferred to Company B, 7th Cavalry Battalion on March 1, 1862, also see.

Duke, Micajah - Transferred to Company B, 7th Cavalry Battalion on March 1, 1862, also see.

Duncan, Willam Anderson, Jr. - Enlisted for ten months. Transferred to Company H, 2nd Tennessee Infantry.

Durrin, A. J. - Rank in Private. Rank out Private.

Ellis, P. P. - Died in hospital at Tupelo, Mississippi on July 20, 1862.

Ferguson (Fergusson), Wilson T. - Wounded in left thigh at Shiloh, Tennessee on April 6, 1862. Left on battlefield. Captured. Sent to Camp Chase, Ohio. Exchanged. Wounded severely at Murfreesboro, Tennessee on December 31, 1862. Left there in hospital. Died.

Fisher, William Franklin (H.) - Sergeant. 2nd Lieutenant on May 2, 1862. Detailed as wagoner at Bowling Green, Kentucky through August and September 1862. In battles at Shiloh, Tennessee; Corinth, Mississippi; Munfordville, Kentucky; Harrodsburg, Kentucky; Murfreesboro, Tennessee, and Perryville, Kentucky. Wounded at Perryville, Kentucky and captured. Sent to Ft. Delaware, Maryland and then to Johnson's Island, Ohio, then to Point Lookout, Maryland. Exchanged. Wounded at Murfreesboro, Tennessee in the right leg while fighting on crutches at Perryville, Kentucky. Discharged with disability at Fayetteville, Tennessee. Stayed with army. Paroled at Calhoun, Georgia, at the end of the war.

Ford (Foard), E. G. - Died at Bowling Green, Kentucky on November 16, 1861.

Ford (Foard), Daniel M. - Detailed as wagoner to drive officers baggage wagon. Paroled at Columbia Bridge, South Carolina on May 5, 1865.

Freeman, Richard - Corporal. Offered a medical discharge on July 3, 1862. Refused it. Wounded severely at Murfreesboro, Tennessee on December 31, 1862. Sent to hospital at Liberty, Georgia, then to Petersburg, Virginia where he was captured in hospital when Petersburg was being evacuated. Sent to Camp Butler, Illinois.

Fuqua, James C. - In battle at Perryville, Kentucky. Then wounded twice at Murfreesboro, Tennessee. A mini ball entered his groin and came out the back of his hip. Wounded by mini ball in his right shoulder. Left there when army retreating. Captured. Exchanged. Retired from active service and sent to Montgomery, Alabama where he washed dishes in a hospital for six months then detailed as watchman at the Selma, Alabama in the Navy Yard.

Gammons, Moses - Died August 20, 1861.

Goulden, J. C. - Listed as deserted on November 20, 1862. Captured at Franklin, Kentucky while on his way to Indiana. Sent to Johnson's Island, Ohio where he took the Oath on October 9, 1863. Enlisted in Company E, 7th Cavalry Battalion. Transferred to Colonel Allison's 54th Tennessee Infantry.

Gifford, Brice - Died at Bowling Green, Kentucky on October 7, 1861.

Grigg, John R. - Shown present through November 1863. He took the Oath.

Gross, Van Buren - Listed sick in a hospital at Bowling Green, Kentucky in December 1861. Transferred to Company H, 2nd Tennessee Infantry, no date given.

Haley, William - 2nd Lieutenant on July 3, 1861. Captain on May 2, 1862. Detailed as Recruiting Officer. Captured at Lafayette, Tennessee on March 14, 1863. Sent to Ft. Delaware, Maryland and then to Johnson's Island, Ohio on July 18, 1863, then to Point Lookout, Maryland on February 20, 1865.

Haynes, W. D. - Discharged with disability on July 12, 1862. Died at Bowling Green, Kentucky on November 22, 1861. Deserted on January 1, 1862.

Haynes, F. P. - Died at Bowling Green, Kentucky on November 22, 1861.

Hastings, A. J. - Listed as deserted on January 1, 1862.

Holland, John R. - Wounded in the neck at Shiloh, Tennessee on April 6, 1862. Sent to hospital at Columbus, Mississippi. Discharged as a non-conscript on July 16, 1862. Over age. Discharged at Tupelo, Mississippi.

Howell, Martin - Detailed as a Teamster at Shelbyville, Tennessee and Dalton, Georgia. Deserted on December 21, 1863.

Hughes, Joseph - Wounded in the left leg below his knee at Chickamauga, Georgia on September 19, 1863, shattering the bones. Paroled in 1865. Residence Bethpage, Tennessee.

Hutcherson, John A. - Sergeant. In hospital at Tupelo, Mississippi for three months, very seriously ill. Paroled on May 9, 1865.

Johnson, W. H. - Transferred to a Pioneer Battalion in General Cleburne's Brigade.

Johnson, J. M. - Captured at Reseca, Georgia on May 18, 1864. Sent to Rock Island, Illinois.

Johnson, J. W. - 2nd Lieutenant on May 20, 1863. Commanding the company in September 1863. Furloughed by General Order No. 227 on April 5, 1864. Resigned October 26, 1864.

Jones, J. C. - Listed as deserted on January 1, 1863.

Jones, C. J. - Died at Chattanooga, Tennessee on March 10, 1863.

Jones, J. M. - Fell at Shiloh, Tennessee on April 6, 1862, injuring leg and hip and dislocating knee. Discharged as a non-conscript on July 16, 1863. Over age.

Jones, John Wesley - Wounded in right ankle at Shiloh, Tennessee on April 6, 1862. Muscles cut. In hospital at Columbus, Mississippi and at Chattanooga, Tennessee on August 17, 1863, when Bragg's troops were in retreat. Residence Parham, Tennessee.

Jones, T. D. - Corporal. Discharged on December 11, 1861. Enlisted in the 19th / 20th Tennessee Cavalry.

Kerley, James M. - Captured at Missionary Ridge on November 25, 1863. Sent to Rock Island, Illinois.

Kerley, Robert H. - Captured at Chickamauga, Georgia on September 19, 1863. Sent to Camp Douglas, Illinois. Paroled after taking the Oath on March 16, 1865.

Leath, Thomas - Listed as deserted on January 20, 1864.

Linville, J. N. - Transferred from Company C, 30th Tennessee Infantry on March 16, 1862, also see.

Lovings, William - Died on January 20, 1862.

Markum, J. W. - Died in a hospital at Columbus, Mississippi on June 16, 1862.

Marshall, J. M. - Discharged with disability on July 5, 1862.

Meador, John A. - Deafened by concussion of a shell bursting within two feet of him while laying down in line of battle at the Battle of Murfreesboro, Tennessee on December 31, 1862. Unable for duty for four weeks. Deserted on January 20, 1864.

Meador, T. F. - Died at Bowling Green, Kentucky on November 29, 1862.

Meador, I. J. - Died in a hospital at Columbus, Mississippi on June 1, 1862.

Meador, Ira - Discharged with disability, a non-conscript, 16 years of age, July 3, 1862.

Meador, J. D. - Enlisted on August 24, 1861. No more information located.

Meador, W. J. - Listed in a hospital on February 12, 1862. Dropped from roll.

Meador, J. W. - Listed as deserted on January 20, 1864.

Meador, Pleasant G. - Paroled at the end the of war.

Mongle, D. G. - Sergeant on March 16, 1862. Deserted on March 6, 1864.

Morrison, W. E. - Shown on the roll through February 1862.

Nichols, C. W. - Died at Tupelo, Mississippi on January 20, 1862.

Oglesby, J. K. P. - Discharged as a non-conscript on July 16, 1862. Enlisted in Company H, 2nd Tennessee Infantry then in Company E, 2nd (22nd) Tennessee Cavalry. Also see these commands.

Quinn, T. B. - Born in Ireland. Deserted on April 11, 1863. Dropped from roll on April 18, 1863. Enlisted in 3rd Texas Artillery. Wounded at battle of the Wilderness, Virginia in May 1864. Took a mini ball in left groin and in left foot. Wounded by a sharpshooter. Hospital only three days. In the Stonewall Jackson Brigade. Mini ball stayed in groin for three years.

Reid, Thomas Reziah - Furloughed, sick, from Camp Trousdale, Tennessee. Enlisted in Company E, 9th Tennessee Cavalry, also see.

Reid, H. E. - Discharged as a non conscript on July 16, 1862. Enlisted in Company D, 9th Tennessee, also see.

Robinson, J. H. - Furloughed sick. Never returned.

Robinson, A. J. - Listed as deserted. Dropped from roll on May 1, 1862 by order of General Hardee. Captured as a deserter by C.S.A. forces on November 20, 1862. Deserted again on February 6, 1864.

Sanders, S. H. - Died at Bowling Green, Kentucky on October 7, 1861.

Short, J. D. - After battle of Shiloh he was listed in a hospital at Columbus, Mississippi with Rheumatism. Detailed as Ambulance driver. Then made Wagon Master. Paroled at Greensboro, North Carolina on May 1, 1865.

Smith, J. C. - Shown present to February 24, 1862.

Solomon, J. W. - Captured on December 1, 1862.

Stinson, A. A. - Deserted. Captured as a deserter by U.S. forces at Epperson Springs, Macon County, Tennessee. Removed to City Point, Virginia and then to Camp Chase, Ohio. Prior service in Company B, 7th Cavalry Battalion, also see.

Sullivan, James - Captured at Jonesboro, Georgia on August 31, 1864. He took the Oath and was released on October 30, 1864.

Sullivan, Josephus - Captured at Perryville, Kentucky on October 8, 1862. Exchanged. Wounded severely at Murfreesboro, Tennessee on December 31, 1862. Discharged with disability on January 28, 1863.

Thomas, J. H. - Killed at Shiloh, Tennessee on April 6, 1862.

Turner, F. P. - Discharged as a non-conscript on July 16, 1862. Enlisted in Company C, 9th Tennessee Cavalry, also see.

Uhles, Jacob - Killed at Shiloh, Tennessee on April 6, 1862.

White, Caleb - Discharged at Bowling Green, Kentucky on December 12, 1861. Enlisted in Company C, 9th Tennessee Cavalry, also see.

White, W. H. - Enlisted for ten months. Then enlisted in Company F, 7th Cavalry Battalion, also see.

Wix, Marshall - Wounded at Shiloh, Tennessee on April 6, 1862. Sent to hospital at Columbus, Mississippi. Died from wounds.

Wright, J. A. - Sergeant on May 2, 1862, at re-organization. Wounded at Murfreesboro, Tennessee on December 31, 1862. Discharged on February 16, 1863.

Wright, John S. - 1st Sergeant on May 2, 1862. Deserted on February 6, 1864.

Wright, P. N. - Killed at Shiloh, Tennessee on April 6, 1862.

Again notice the discharge of trained veterans and that a number of them went into other commands. Partly patriotism and partly because they could not remain at home. If discharged they were forced to take an oath of allegiance or go to prison.

Company D

Aldridge, A.J. - Rank in Private. Rank out Private.

Alldridge, A.J. - Rank in Private. Rank out Private.

Allen, H.H. - Rank in Private. Rank out Private.

Aronheart, W.A. - Rank in Private. Rank out Private.

Barham, John H. - Rank in First Lieutenant. Rank out First Lieutenant.

Biggar, John R. - Rank in Private. Rank out Private.

Bigger, John R. - Rank in Private. Rank out Private.

Bigger, L.C. - Rank in Private. Rank out Teamster.

Bigger, William L. - Rank in Private. Rank out Private.

Bond, James H. - Rank in Private. Rank out Private.

Bond, James O. - Rank in Private. Rank out Private.

Cathey, John A. - Rank in Second Lieutenant. Rank out Second Lieutenant.

Cerbett, J. - Rank in Private. Rank out Private.

Cherry, Isaac J. - Rank in Private. Rank out Private.

Chrisman, John - Rank in Private. Rank out Private.

Chrissman, John A. - Rank in Private. Rank out Private.

Chrisswell, Laban - Rank in Private. Rank out Private.

Chrisswell, Samuel D. - Rank in Private. Rank out Private.

Christopher, Alfred N. - Rank in Private. Rank out Private.

Christwell, S.D. - Rank in Private. Rank out Private.

Cook, H. C. - Rank in Private. Rank out Private.

Corbett, James - Rank in Private. Rank out Private.

Corbett, John - Rank in Private. Rank out Private.

Corbitte, James - Rank in Private. Rank out Private.

Corbitte, John R. - Rank in Private. Rank out Private.

Covington, Larkin M. - Rank in Private. Rank out Private.

Covington, M. - Rank in Private. Rank out Private.

Covington, R.M. - Rank in Private. Rank out Private.

Covington, Robert W. - Rank in Private. Rank out Private.

Covington, W.F. - Rank in Private. Rank out Private.

Covington, William - Rank in Private. Rank out Private.

Cozort, Benjamin - Rank in Private. Rank out Private.

Craftin, Jeseph - Rank in Private. Rank out Private.

Crafton, Joseph - Rank in Private. Rank out Private.

Creek, Samuel - Rank in Private. Rank out Private.

Cresswell, Thomas A. - Rank in Private. Rank out Private.

Crick, Joseph W. - Rank in Private. Rank out Private.

Crick, Samuel R. - Rank in Private. Rank out Private.

Crisswell, Thomas A. - Rank in Private. Rank out Private.

Criswell, Laban - Rank in Private. Rank out Private.

Criswell, Thomas A. - Rank in Private. Rank out Private.

Cromer, Joseph H. - Rank in Sergeant. Rank out Sergeant.

Dowdy, H.L. - Rank in Private. Rank out Private.

Dowdy, L.H. - Rank in Private. Rank out Private.

Dowdy, Robert J. - Rank in Private. Rank out Sergeant.

Dowley, R.J. - Rank in Private. Rank out Sergeant.

Dowly, L.H. - Rank in Private. Rank out Private.

Earnheart, William A - Rank in Private. Rank out Private.

Eassonheart, W.A. - Rank in Private. Rank out Private.

Edminson, R.C. - Rank in Private. Rank out Bass Drummer.

Edmonds, J.T. - Rank in Private. Rank out Drummer.

Edmonds, Joseph H. - Rank in Private. Rank out Drummer.

Edmonds, Joseph S. - Rank in Private. Rank out Drummer.

Edmondson, R.C. - Rank in Private. Rank out Bass Drummer.

Edmons, J.S. - Rank in Private. Rank out Drummer.

Edmons, Joseph T. - Rank in Private. Rank out Drummer.

Edmonson, R.C. - Rank in Private. Rank out Bass Drummer.

Elmer, Henry - Rank in Private. Rank out Private.

Elmore, Henry - Rank in Private. Rank out Private.

Elmore, P.H. - Rank in Private. Rank out Private.

Elmore, W.H. - Rank in Private. Rank out Private.

Farrar, William A. - Rank in Private. Rank out Private.

Floyd, Drury A. - Rank in Private. Rank out Private.

Floyd, J.A. - Rank in Private. Rank out Private.

Floyd, Joshua - Rank in Private. Rank out Private.

Floyd, Monroe - Rank in Private. Rank out Sergeant.

Floyd, R.M. - Rank in Private. Rank out Sergeant.

Floyd, W.J. - Rank in Private. Rank out Private.

Frey, James B. - Rank in Private. Rank out Drummer.

Fry, James B. - Rank in Private. Rank out Drummer.

Garrett, James W. - Rank in Private. Rank out Private.

Gilaspie, J. S. - Rank in Private. Rank out Private.

Gillespie, J. S. - Rank in Private. Rank out Private.

Gillespie, James J. - Rank in Private. Rank out Private.

Gillispee, J. S. - Rank in Private. Rank out Private.

Graham, William - Rank in Private. Rank out Private.

Gray, Daniel J. - Rank in Private. Rank out Private.

Grey, D.J. - Rank in Private. Rank out Private.

Haines, John A. - Rank in Private. Rank out Private.

Hampton, P. - Rank in Private. Rank out Private.

Hampton, Smith - Rank in Private. Rank out Private.

Hampton, T. - Rank in Private. Rank out Private.

Hanes, John A. - Rank in Private. Rank out Private.

Hanson, H.C. - Rank in Private. Rank out Private.

Harris, Richard A. - Rank in Private. Rank out Private.

Hartley, Washington - Rank in Private. Rank out Private.

Hartley, William - Rank in Private. Rank out Private.

Hartly, W. - Rank in Private. Rank out Private.

Hasley, Wash - Rank in Private. Rank out Private.

Haynes, A.J. - Rank in Private. Rank out Private.

Haynes, John A. - Rank in Private. Rank out Private.

Heartley, W. - Rank in Private. Rank out Private.

Hemphill, George R. - Rank in First Sergeant. Rank out First Sergeant.

Hendricks, Francis J. - Rank in Private. Rank out Private.

Hendricks, Isaac H. - Rank in Private. Rank out Private.

Hendrix, F.J. - Rank in Private. Rank out Private.

Hendrix, Isaac H. - Rank in Private. Rank out Private.

Hendrix, John G. - Rank in Private. Rank out Sergeant.

Hendrix, W.F. - Rank in Private. Rank out Private.

Hendrucks, J. - Rank in Private. Rank out Private.

Hicks, John M. - Rank in Private. Rank out Private.

Hinson, H.C. - Rank in Private. Rank out Private.

Hinson, John - Rank in Private. Rank out Private.

Hinson, M.C. - Rank in Private. Rank out Private.

Holdon, J.R. - Rank in Private. Rank out Private.

Holland, W.C. - Rank in Private. Rank out Private.

Holton, John R. - Rank in Private. Rank out Private.

Hurley, Washington - Rank in Private. Rank out Private.

Johnson, Joshua - Rank in Private. Rank out Private.

Johnson, Samuel C. - Rank in Private. Rank out Private.

Johnson, W.F. - Rank in Private. Rank out Private.

Johnson, W.T. - Rank in Private. Rank out Private.

Jordan, John A. - Rank in Private. Rank out Private.

Jordan, W.A. - Rank in Private. Rank out Private.

Jordan, William A. - Rank in Private. Rank out Private.

Kelley, Enoch B. - Rank in Sergeant. Rank out Sergeant.

Kelly, Enoch Beal - Rank in Sergeant. Rank out Sergeant.

Kelly, S.B. - Rank in Sergeant. Rank out Sergeant.

Laflin, William H.H. - Rank in Private. Rank out Sergeant.

Lamb, Nicholas H. - Rank in First Lieutenant. Rank out Captain.

Lamb, W.H. - Rank in Private. Rank out Private.

Lamb, Wilis - Rank in Private. Rank out Private.

Laptin, William H.H. - Rank in Private. Rank out Sergeant.

Lillard, M.C. - Rank in Private. Rank out Private.

Loftin, William H.H. - Rank in Private. Rank out Sergeant.

Lofton, N.H.H. - Rank in Private. Rank out Sergeant.

Marshall, W.J. - Rank in Private. Rank out Private.

Marshall, William S. - Rank in Private. Rank out Private.

Maupen, G.W. - Rank in Private. Rank out Private.

McLaron, A.J. - Rank in Private. Rank out Private.

Mclaron, A.J. - Rank in Private. Rank out Private.

Moore, Thomas - Rank in Private. Rank out Private.

Moppin, George W. - Rank in Private. Rank out Private.

Morgan, James W. - Rank in Corporal. Rank out Private.

Morgan, Thomas D. - Rank in Private. Rank out Private.

Morgin, J.W. - Rank in Corporal. Rank out Private.

Mosely, William C. - Rank in Corporal. Rank out Corporal.

Mosley, William C. - Rank in Corporal. Rank out Corporal.

Murphrey, E.M. - Rank in Private. Rank out Corporal.

O'Briant, W.C. - Rank in Private. Rank out Private.

O'Bryane, W.C. - Rank in Private. Rank out Private.

Olldridge, A.J. - Rank in Private. Rank out Private.

Parsley, G.H. - Rank in Private. Rank out Private.

Parsley, Newton J. - Rank in Private. Rank out Private.

Pyram, W.H. - Rank in Private. Rank out Private.

Pyrin, W.H. - Rank in Private. Rank out Private.

Pyron, W.H. - Rank in Private. Rank out Private.

Riley, John A. - Rank in Private. Rank out Private.

Robertson, N.J. - Rank in Private. Rank out Private.

Robinson, Newton J. - Rank in Private. Rank out Private.

Russell, W.J. - Rank in Private. Rank out Fifer.

Russell, William S. - Rank in Private. Rank out Private.

Ryan, W.M.P. - Rank in Private. Rank out Private.

Ryan, William P. - Rank in Private. Rank out Private.

Ryley, John A. - Rank in Private. Rank out Private.

Rylie, John A. - Rank in Private. Rank out Private.

Scales, Pleasant D. - Rank in Private. Rank out Commissary Sergeant.

Sharber, M.R. - Rank in Private. Rank out Private.

Sharbro, M.R. - Rank in Private. Rank out Private.

Smith, John A. - Rank in Corporal. Rank out Corporal.

Smith, T.P. - Rank in Private. Rank out Private.

Smith, Thomas J. - Rank in Private. Rank out Private.

Smith, W.F. - Rank in Private. Rank out Private.

Snell, John S. - Rank in Private. Rank out Private.

Taylor, Edward E. - Rank in Private. Rank out Private.

Taylor, R.H. (A.) - Rank in Private. Rank out Corporal.

Turner, S. H. - Rank in Private. Rank out Private.

Turner, Stephen - Rank in Private. Rank out Private.

White, David - Rank in Private. Rank out Private.

White, Joseph S. - Rank in Private. Rank out Private.

White, Thomas - Rank in Corporal. Rank out Corporal.

White, W.H. - Rank in Private. Rank out Private.

White, William A. - Rank in Private. Rank out Private.

White, William J. - Rank in Third Lieutenant. Rank out First Lieutenant.

Williamson, John Arch - Rank in Private. Rank out Private.

Wilson, Henry R. - Rank in Private. Rank out Private.

Wilson, James B. - Rank in Private. Rank out Private.

Wilson, John A. - Rank in Captain. Rank out Colonel.

Wilson, Lafayette - Rank in Private. Rank out Third Lieutenant.

Wilson, M.L. - Rank in Private. Rank out Third Lieutenant.

Wilson, William A. - Rank in Sergeant. Rank out Sergeant.

Wilson, Zacheus M. - Rank in Private. Rank out Private.

Windrow, I.N. - Rank in Private. Rank out Private.

Company E

Albright, J.W. - Rank in Private. Rank out Sergeant.

Anderson, C.H. - Rank in Private. Rank out Private.

Austin, H.M. - Rank in Private. Rank out Captain.

Austin, Henry M. - Rank in Private. Rank out Captain.

Auston, H.M. - Rank in Private. Rank out Captain.

Baskerville, John A. - Rank in Captain. Rank out Captain.

Baskerville, Richard K. - Rank in Private. Rank out Private.

Bertrand, R.B. - Rank in Private. Rank out Private.

Blackman, Joseph - Rank in Private. Rank out Private.

Branham, J. R. - Rank in Private. Rank out Private.

Bromley, James P. - Rank in Private. Rank out Private.

Brumley, J.P. - Rank in Private. Rank out Private.

Brumley, T.S. - Rank in Private. Rank out Private.

Brumley, W.J. - Rank in Private. Rank out Private.

Burns, C.B. - Rank in Private. Rank out Private.

Burtrand, R.B. - Rank in Private. Rank out Private.

Byrnes, C.B. - Rank in Private. Rank out Private.

Cambell, James - Rank in Second Lieutenant. Rank out Second Lieutenant.

Campbell, James - Rank in Second Lieutenant. Rank out Second Lieutenant.

Carter, J.W. - Rank in Private. Rank out Sergeant.

Cissoms, J.M. - Rank in Private. Rank out Private.

Clara, J.H.T. - Rank in Private. Rank out Private.

Cloar, J.H.T. - Rank in Private. Rank out Private.

Coal, J.M. - Rank in Private. Rank out Private.

Cole, J.M. - Rank in Private. Rank out Private.

Cox, Henry - Rank in First Sergeant. Rank out Private.

Crenshaw, N.D. - Rank in Private. Rank out Private.

Dalbins, J.A. - Rank in Corporal. Rank out Second Lieutenant.

Dalbins, W.H. - Rank in Sergeant. Rank out Private.

Day, E. - Rank in Private. Rank out Private.

Dickens, J.H. - Rank in Private. Rank out Private.

Dickerson, M. T. - Rank in Private. Rank out Private.

Dinkins, J. H. - Rank in Private. Rank out Private.

Dobbins, F. D. - Rank in Private. Rank out Private.

Dobbins, F. L. - Rank in Private. Rank out Private.

Dobbins, Foster - Rank in Private. Rank out Private.

Dobbins, J. A. - Rank in Corporal. Rank out Second Lieutenant.

Dobbins, W. H. - Rank in Sergeant. Rank out Private.

Dobbins, William - Rank in Sergeant. Rank out Private.

Dobbs, H. S. - Rank in Private. Rank out Private.

Dorris, W.A. - Rank in Private. Rank out Private.

Dutton, Wiley - Rank in Private. Rank out Private.

Etheridge, G.W. - Rank in Private. Rank out Private.

Grandham, Lewis - Rank in Private. Rank out Private.

Grantham, Lewis - Rank in Private. Rank out Private.

Granthan, Lewis - Rank in Private. Rank out Private.

Graves, B.H. - Rank in Sergeant. Rank out First Sergeant.

Graves, B.M. - Rank in Private. Rank out Private.

Graves, Bannister M. - Rank in Private. Rank out Private.

Gregory, A. - Rank in Private. Rank out Private.

Gregory, J.L. - Rank in Private. Rank out Private.

Gregory, William - Rank in Private. Rank out Private.

Gregory, William A. - Rank in Private. Rank out Private.

Grigg, John - Rank in Private. Rank out Private.

Grigors, Willim A. - Rank in Private. Rank out Private.

Grigory, William - Rank in Private. Rank out Private.

Guinn, Jesse - Rank in Second Lieutenant. Rank out Captain.

Guthrie, W.P. - Rank in Corporal. Rank out Corporal.

Gwin, Jesse - Rank in Second Lieutenant. Rank out Captain.

Harrell, R.F. - Rank in Private. Rank out Private.

Harrison, W.H. - Rank in Private. Rank out Private.

Harroll, R.T. - Rank in Private. Rank out Private.

Harshaw, Benjamin - Rank in Private. Rank out Private.

Henry, Jo E. - Rank in Private. Rank out Private.

Henry, Owen - Rank in Corporal. Rank out Private.

Hibbett, A.J. - Rank in Private. Rank out Private.

Hill, J.B. - Rank in Private. Rank out Private.

Hill, R.G. - Rank in Private. Rank out Private.

Hill, W.H. - Rank in Private. Rank out Private.

Holland, T.J. - Rank in Private. Rank out Private.

Holt, J.S. - Rank in Private. Rank out Private.

Holt, James - Rank in Private. Rank out Private.

House, M.P. - Rank in Private. Rank out Private.

Hunt, J.S. - Rank in Private. Rank out Private.

Hunt, J.W. - Rank in Private. Rank out Private.

Hunt, James - Rank in Private. Rank out Private.

Hunter, D.L. - Rank in Private. Rank out Sergeant.

Hunter, F.M. - Rank in Private. Rank out Sergeant.

Jarden, William - Rank in Private. Rank out Private.

Johnson, Thomas P. - Rank in Private. Rank out Corporal.

Jones, J.W. - Rank in Private. Rank out Private.

Jordan, William - Rank in Private. Rank out Private.

Kerley, D.W. - Rank in Private. Rank out Private.

Key, C.P. - Rank in Private. Rank out Corporal.

Key, W.T. - Rank in Private. Rank out Private.

Kirly, D.W. - Rank in Private. Rank out Private.

Levingston, Robert - Rank in Private. Rank out Private.

Livingston, J.F. - Rank in Private. Rank out Private.

Livingston, R.N. - Rank in Private. Rank out Private.

Livingston, Robert - Rank in Private. Rank out Private.

Martin, J.F. - Rank in Private. Rank out Private.

McGee, Robert - Rank in Private. Rank out Private.

McNeely, R.D. - Rank in Private. Rank out Private.

McWhirter, J.S. - Rank in Private. Rank out Private.

McWhirter, James - Rank in Private. Rank out Private.

Meador, J.I. - Rank in Private. Rank out Private.

Meador, W.J. - Rank in Private. Rank out Private.

Megee, Robert - Rank in Private. Rank out Private.

Moncrief, C.T. - Rank in Private. Rank out Private.

Moncrief, T.J. - Rank in Private. Rank out Private.

Moncrief, Thomas J. - Rank in Private. Rank out Private.

Moris, J.H. - Rank in Private. Rank out Private.

Morris, J.W. - Rank in Private. Rank out Private.

Morris, James H. - Rank in Private. Rank out Private.

Morris, John W. - Rank in Private. Rank out Private.

Morris, Joseph H. - Rank in Private. Rank out Private.

Myrick, Russell - Rank in Private. Rank out Private.

Neal, W.H. - Rank in Private. Rank out Assistant Surgeon.

Neel, W.H. - Rank in Private. Rank out Assistant Surgeon.

Overton, J.W. - Rank in Private. Rank out Private.

Perry, S.M. - Rank in Private. Rank out Private.

Phelps, J.H. - Rank in Private. Rank out Private.

Redchick, James P. - Rank in Private. Rank out Private.

Reddick, J.P. - Rank in Private. Rank out Private.

Reddick, James P. - Rank in Private. Rank out Private.

Reeves, R.C. - Rank in Private. Rank out Private.

Retelick, James P. - Rank in Private. Rank out Private.

Rice, T.P. - Rank in Private. Rank out Private.

Rice, William B. - Rank in Sergeant. Rank out Brevet Second Lieutenant.

Richardson, Jesse - Rank in Private. Rank out Private.

Rives, R.C. - Rank in Private. Rank out Private.

Robberts, C.W. - Rank in Private. Rank out Private.

Roberts, C.W. - Rank in Private. Rank out Private.

Roberts, Cyrus W. - Rank in Private. Rank out Private.

Sanford, J.R. - Rank in Private. Rank out Corporal.

Simmons, J.A. - Rank in Private. Rank out Private.

Sissom, J.M. - Rank in Private. Rank out Private.

Sissom, James - Rank in Private. Rank out Private.

Sisson, James - Rank in Private. Rank out Private.

Sisson, Joseph - Rank in Private. Rank out Private.

Smith, Samuel - Rank in Private. Rank out Private.

Smith, William - Rank in Private. Rank out Private.

Spradlin, A.L. - Rank in Private. Rank out Second Lieutenant.

Spradlin, J.B. - Rank in Private. Rank out Sergeant.

Spradm, A.L. - Rank in Private. Rank out Second Lieutenant.

Stephens, James S. - Rank in Private. Rank out Private.

Stryedlin, A.L. - Rank in Private. Rank out Second Lieutenant.

Templeton, E.G. - Rank in Private. Rank out Private.

Templeton, E.J. - Rank in Private. Rank out Private.

Templeton, L. - Rank in Private. Rank out Private.

Webb, Frank - Rank in Private. Rank out Private.

West, A. J. - Rank in Private. Rank out Private.

White, T.J. - Rank in Private. Rank out Corporal.

Williams, Daniel G. - Rank in Private. Rank out Corporal.

Wilson, John Miller - Rank in Private. Rank out Private.

Wix, Robert - Rank in Private. Rank out Private.

Wright, John V. - Rank in Corporal. Rank out Corporal.

Company F

Capt. R. D. Allison's company F, Twenty-Fourth Tennessee Infantry, was raised at Alexandria (Dekalb County) in 1861. Allison was elected colonel and H. P. Dowell captain. Allison resigned in 1862 and organized a cavalry battalion at Alexandria, with J. S. Reese, who had been discharged from the Twenty-Fourth because of his age.

OFFICERS:

Colonel: R. D. Allison
Captain: H. P. Dowell
1st Lieutenant: J. F. Luckey
2nd Lieutenant: W. S. Patey

3rd Lieutenant: W. D. Fielding

ENLISTED:

Sergeants: James A. Barnett, M. D. Braswell, Lewis E. Simpson, J. W. Jaques

Corporals: C. Scott, G. W. Gordon, J. A. Clark, A. Rollands

Adams, P.L. - Rank in Corporal. Rank out Corporal.

Allen, D.L. - Rank in Private. Rank out Corporal.

Allen, David L. - Rank in Private. Rank out Corporal.

Allison, James – Died December 24, 1861. Name does not appear on the National Archives index.

Allison, Joseph - Rank in Private. Rank out Private.

Allison, R.D. - Rank in Captain. Rank out Colonel.

Allison, Robert - Rank in Private. Rank out Private.

Allman, John - Rank in Private. Rank out Private.

Allmon, J.A. - Rank in Private. Rank out Private.

Askew, J.T. - Rank in Private. Rank out Private.

Baker, L.B. - Rank in Private. Rank out Private.

Baker, L.R. - Rank in Private. Rank out Private.

Baker, Luther B. - Rank in Private. Rank out Private.

Barbee, E.A. - Rank in Private. Rank out Private.

Barbee, Ealumonson A. - Rank in Private. Rank out Private.

Barbee, Eanderson - Rank in Private. Rank out Private.

Barrett, James A. - Rank in Ordnance Sergeant. Rank out Second Lieutenant.

Batey, James K. - Rank in Private. Rank out Private.

Baw, James - Rank in Private. Rank out Private.

Beadle, R.O. - Rank in Private. Rank out Private.

Beadle, Richard O. - Rank in Private. Rank out Private.

Beatty, James K. - Rank in Private. Rank out Private.

Beedle, R.O. - Rank in Private. Rank out Private.

Bennett, W.P. - Rank in Private. Rank out Private.

Betts, E.W. - Rank in Private. Rank out Private.

Betty, James K. - Rank in Private. Rank out Private.

Betty, James R. - Rank in Private. Rank out Private.

Bowers, G.L. - Rank in Private. Rank out Private.

Bowers, George M. - Rank in Private. Rank out Private.

Bradford, A.J. - Rank in Private. Rank out Private.

Bradley, Thomas F. - Rank in Private. Rank out Private.

Braswell, John - Rank in Private. Rank out Private.

Braswell, M.D. - Rank in Sergeant. Rank out First Lieutenant.

Braswell, Mathew D. - Rank in Sergeant. Rank out Lieutenant.

Braswell, Sampson - Rank in Private. Rank out Private. Died January 4, 1862.

Briggs, Samuel - Rank in Private. Rank out Private.

Britton, Abraham - Rank in Private. Rank out Captain.

Brown, Thomas B. - Rank in Private. Rank out Private.

Brown, Thomas F. - Rank in Private. Rank out Private.

Butts, Elijah W. - Rank in Private. Rank out Private.

Cappee, Henry M. - Rank in Private. Rank out Private.

Cappee, Robert - Rank in Private. Rank out Private.

Carnes, W.D.G. - Rank in Private. Rank out Private.

Carter, W.B. - Rank in Private. Rank out Private. Killed January 10, 1862.

Chandler, T.M. - Rank in Private. Rank out Private.

Chandler, Thomas - Rank in Private. Rank out Private.

Clark, J.A. - Rank in Corporal. Rank out Private.

Cochran, R.A. - Rank in Private. Rank out Private.

Cochrhan, R.A. - Rank in Private. Rank out Private.

Cockrhan, R.A. - Rank in Private. Rank out Private.

Coffee, H.M. - Rank in Private. Rank out Private.

Coffee, Henry M. - Rank in Private. Rank out Private.

Coffee, R.D. - Rank in Private. Rank out Private.

Coffee, Robert - Rank in Private. Rank out Private.

Conger, Josiah - Rank in Private. Rank out Private.

Congo, Josiah - Rank in Private. Rank out Private.

Cooper, Isaac - Rank in Private. Rank out Private.

Corley, Nathan - Rank in Private. Rank out Private.

Corly, Nathan - Rank in Private. Rank out Private.

Covington, M.J. - Rank in Private. Rank out Private.

Craddock, J.C.J. - Rank in Private. Rank out Ordnance Sergeant. Killed at Perryville.

Craddock, N.L. - Rank in Private. Rank out Private.

Crouder, Alex. - Rank in Private. Rank out Private.

Crouch (Cwowder), A. P. Killed at Perryville. Name appears as Crowder in the National Archives index.

Curtis, William C. - Rank in Private. Rank out Private. Killed at Shiloh.

Cutler (Cutter), John J. - Rank in Private. Rank out Private.

Davis, R.G. - Rank in Private. Rank out Private.

Davis, R.James - Rank in Private. Rank out First Lieutenant.

Davis, Robert J. - Rank in Private. Rank out First Lieutenant.

Davis, W.C. - Rank in Private. Rank out Private.

Deney, W.B. - Rank in Private. Rank out Private.

Denney, W.B. - Rank in Private. Rank out Private.

Dennie, W.B. - Rank in Private. Rank out Private.

Doss, M.F. - Rank in Private. Rank out Private.

Dowell, A.P. - Rank in Captain. Rank out Captain.

Dowell, H.P. - Rank in Captain. Rank out Captain.

Estes, J.D. - Rank in Private. Rank out Private.

Estis, J.D. - Rank in Private. Rank out Private.

Ferrell, C. - Rank in Private. Rank out Private.

Fielding, William C. - Rank in Second Lieutenant. Rank out Major.

Fite, L.H. - Rank in Private. Rank out Private.

Fouch, John C. - Rank in Private. Rank out Second Lieutenant.

Fowler, Lawrence - Rank in Private. Rank out Private.

Fumel (Furrel), C. - Rank in Private. Rank out Private. Killed at Murfreesboro.

Gaultney (Galtny), J.F. - Rank in Private. Rank out Private. Killed

Glen, Joseph S. - Rank in Private. Rank out Private.

Glen, Josiah S. - Rank in Private. Rank out Private.

Gold, J.P. - Rank in Private. Rank out Private.

Gold, James E. - Rank in Private. Rank out Second Lieutenant.

Gold, John E. - Rank in Private. Rank out Second Lieutenant.

Gordon, G.W. - Rank in Corporal. Rank out Private.

Gould, J.E. - Rank in Private. Rank out Second Lieutenant.

Gould, J.P. - Rank in Private. Rank out Private.

Green, Jo John - Rank in First Sergeant. Rank out Acting Quartermaster.

Gregory, John A. - Rank in Private. Rank out Private.

Grigory, John A. - Rank in Private. Rank out Private.

Gualtney, J.F. - Rank in Private. Rank out Private.

Guinn, James - Rank in Private. Rank out Private.

Gwaltney, J.F. - Rank in Private. Rank out Private.

Hale, G.W. - Rank in Private. Rank out Private.

Hale, J.R. - Rank in Private. Rank out Private.

Hall, B.F. - Rank in Private. Rank out Musician.

Hall, Benjamin - Rank in Private. Rank out Musician.

Hall, G.W. - Rank in Private. Rank out Private. Killed at Perryville.

Hall, J.P. - Rank in Private. Rank out Private.

Hall, P.A. - Rank in Private. Rank out Private.

Harp, William H. - Rank in Private. Rank out Corporal.

Hawe, G.W. - Rank in Private. Rank out Private.

Hayes, William H. - Rank in Private. Rank out Corporal.

Hays, William H. - Rank in Private. Rank out Corporal.

Heflin, Jonathan - Rank in Private. Rank out Private.

Heftin, Jonathan - Rank in Private. Rank out Private.

Hellmentoller, Arch D. - Rank in Private. Rank out Private.

Helmantallow, A.D. - Rank in Private. Rank out Private.

Helmintaller, A.D. - Rank in Private. Rank out Private.

Helmontaller, A.D. - Rank in Private. Rank out Private.

Hibbett, J.L. - Rank in First Lieutenant. Rank out Assistant Surgeon.

Hoges, William H. - Rank in Private. Rank out Corporal.

Hubbard, J.M. - Rank in Private. Rank out Private.

Hubboard, J.M. - Rank in Private. Rank out Private.

Hubbord, J.M. - Rank in Private. Rank out Private.

Hudson, D.D. - Rank in Private. Rank out Private.

Hudson, John D. - Rank in Private. Rank out Private.

Hudson, John T. - Rank in Private. Rank out Private.

Hutton, W.M. - Rank in Surgeon. Rank out Surgeon.

Jacques, W. Isaac - Rank in Sergeant. Rank out Second Lieutenant.

Jaquees, J.W. - Rank in Sergeant. Rank out Second Lieutenant.

Jaquess, Isaac W. - Rank in Sergeant. Rank out Second Lieutenant.

Johnson, T.L. - Rank in Private. Rank out Private.

Johnston, E.M. - Rank in Private. Rank out Private.

Jones, Thomas E. - Rank in Private. Rank out Hospital Steward.

Jones, W.P. - Rank in Private. Rank out Sergeant.

Jones, W.T. - Rank in Private. Rank out Sergeant.

King, J.A. - Rank in Private. Rank out Private. Killed at Murfreesboro.

King, Sampsom J. - Rank in Private. Rank out Private.

King, W.R. - Rank in Private. Rank out Private.

Kirk, John H. - Rank in Private. Rank out Private.

Knight, Robert - Rank in Private. Rank out Private.

Knight, W.J. - Rank in Private. Rank out Private. Killed at Murfreesboro.

Lawrence, A.H. - Rank in Private. Rank out Hospital Steward.

Lawrence, Augustus H. - Rank in Private. Rank out Hospital Steward.

Lawrence, J.L. - Rank in Private. Rank out Private.

Lee, James M. - Rank in Private. Rank out Private.

Lincoln, W.H. - Rank in Private. Rank out Captain.

Llyon, F.E.P. - Rank in Private. Rank out Private.

Luckey, J.C. - Rank in First Lieutenant. Rank out First Lieutenant.

Luckey, John F. - Rank in First Lieutenant. Rank out First Lieutenant.

Luckey, S.C. - Rank in Private. Rank out Private.

Luckey, Samuel - Rank in Private. Rank out Private.

Luckey, W.H. - Rank in Private. Rank out Private.

Luckey, William - Rank in Private. Rank out Private.

Lynch, W.S. - Rank in Private. Rank out Private.

Lynch, W.T. - Rank in Private. Rank out Private.

Lyon, F. P. – Killed at Shiloh.

Marks (Markes), Bailey (Baily) - Rank in Private. Rank out Private. Killed at Perryville.

Martin, C.C. - Rank in Private. Rank out Private.

McCutchan (McCucheon / McCutchen / McCutcheon), John T. (F.) - Rank in Chaplain. Rank out Chaplain.

McLanahan, A.H. - Rank in Private. Rank out Private.

Mooneyham (Moneyhan / Moonigham / Mooningham), J. A. - Rank in Private. Rank out Private. Killed at Perryville.

Mooneyham (Moneyhan / Moonigham / Mooningham), Joel - Rank in Private. Rank out Private. Killed at Perryville.

Mooningham, James A. - Rank in Private. Rank out Private.

Mosear (Mosher / Mosiar / Mosier), Amzi M. - Rank in Private. Rank out Private.

Mott, W.H. - Rank in Private. Rank out Adjutant. Died at Alexandria after having been wounded at Murfreesboro.

Neal, Wilson S. - Rank in Private. Rank out Private.

Nolen, J.F. - Rank in Private. Rank out Private.

Nolen, Joseph - Rank in Private. Rank out Private.

Oliver, John H. - Rank in Second Lieutenant. Rank out Captain.

Owens, Jasper - Rank in Private. Rank out Private.

Parrett, Lewis - Rank in Private. Rank out Private.

Patterson, W.W. - Rank in Private. Rank out Private.

Paty, William Smith - Rank in Lieutenant. Rank out Second Lieutenant.

Petry (Pettriss), Amos - Rank in Private. Rank out Private. Killed at Perryville.

Powell, John H. - Rank in Private. Rank out Private.

Powell, Samuel A. - Rank in Private. Rank out Private.

Prentice, W.B. - Rank in Private. Rank out Corporal.

Prentis, W.B. - Rank in Private. Rank out Corporal.

Prentis, W.D. - Rank in Private. Rank out Corporal.

Preston, W.C. - Rank in Private. Rank out Private.

Preston, William C. - Rank in Private. Rank out Private.

Pretcher, James C. - Rank in Private. Rank out Sergeant.

Prichard, J.C. - Rank in Private. Rank out Sergeant.

Prichard, James C. - Rank in Private. Rank out Sergeant.

Pritchard, James C. - Rank in Private. Rank out Sergeant.

Prowell, J.H. - Rank in Private. Rank out Private.

Prowell, John H. - Rank in Private. Rank out Private.

Ragan, J.B. - Rank in Private. Rank out Private.

Rainey, Joseph - Rank in Private. Rank out Private.

Raney, Joseph - Rank in Private. Rank out Private.

Reagan, J.B. - Rank in Private. Rank out Private.

Reany, Joseph - Rank in Private. Rank out Private.

Reece, E.P. - Rank in Private. Rank out Private.

Reece, J.S. - Rank in Private. Rank out Sergeant.

Renney, Joseph - Rank in Private. Rank out Private.

Rennie, Joseph - Rank in Private. Rank out Private.

Rollands, Amon - Rank in Corporal. Rank out Private.

Rollands, L.A. - Rank in Private. Rank out Private.

Rollins, Amon - Rank in Corporal. Rank out Private.

Rollins, L.A. - Rank in Private. Rank out Private.

Rollins, Leonidas A. - Rank in Private. Rank out Private.

Rutherford, T.F. - Rank in Sergeant. Rank out Sergeant.

Scott, Charles - Rank in Corporal. Rank out Private.

Sephen, A.J. - Rank in Private. Rank out Private.

Shaver, J.T. - Rank in Private. Rank out Private.

Shaver, John - Rank in Private. Rank out Private.

Shaver, John T. - Rank in Private. Rank out Private.

Shavers, John - Rank in Private. Rank out Private.

Simpson, Lewis E. - Rank in Sergeant. Rank out Sergeant.

Simpson, Luke - Rank in Sergeant. Rank out Sergeant.

Simpson, S.E. - Rank in Sergeant. Rank out Sergeant.

Smith, John - Rank in Private. Rank out Private.

Stephens, A.J. - Rank in Private. Rank out Private.

Stepns, Andrew - Rank in Private. Rank out Private.

Stevens, A.J. - Rank in Private. Rank out Private.

Steward, Alexander - Rank in Private. Rank out Sergeant.

Stewart, Alexander - Rank in Private. Rank out Sergeant.

Stewart, Alexander L. - Rank in Private. Rank out Sergeant.

Stewart, Andrew - Rank in Private. Rank out Private.

Stewart, J.W. - Rank in Private. Rank out Private. Killed at Chickamauga.

Stoaks, Absalom - Rank in Private. Rank out Private.

Stokes, Absalom - Rank in Private. Rank out Private.

Stooks, Absalom - Rank in Private. Rank out Private.

Stuart, Alexander - Rank in Private. Rank out Sergeant.

Stuart, Andrew - Rank in Private. Rank out Private.

Stuart, J.A. - Rank in Private. Rank out Private.

Stuart, J.W. - Rank in Private. Rank out Private.

Thomas, W.H. - Rank in Private. Rank out Private.

Thomas, William H. - Rank in Private. Rank out Private.

Timberlake, W.M. - Rank in Private. Rank out Acting Quartermaster.

Tracy, D.R. - Rank in Private. Rank out Private.

Turner, Ed P. - Rank in Commissary of Subsistence. Rank out Commissary of Subsistence.

Vantreas, G. W. - Rank in Private. Rank out Private.

Vantrease, Nicholas D. - Rank in Private. Rank out Private.

Vantrees, Nicholas - Rank in Private. Rank out Private.

Vantrees, Wash. - Rank in Private. Rank out Private.

Warren, A. - Rank in Private. Rank out Private.

Washburn, J.L. - Rank in Private. Rank out Private.

Washburn, Lewis - Rank in Private. Rank out Private.

Whitley, J.W. - Rank in Private. Rank out Private.

Whitmore, Richard S. - Rank in Private. Rank out Private.

Whittemore, R.S. - Rank in Private. Rank out Private.

Whittemore, Richard - Rank in Private. Rank out Private.

Whittemore, Richard - Rank in Private. Rank out Private.

Williams, W.E. - Rank in Private. Rank out Private.

Williams, William E.L. - Rank in Private. Rank out Private.

Winfree, B.C. - Rank in Private. Rank out Private.

Winfree, Bennett C. - Rank in Private. Rank out Private.

Winfree, J.A. - Rank in Private. Rank out Private.

Winfree, J.T. - Rank in Private. Rank out First Sergeant.

Winfree, James T. - Rank in Private. Rank out First Sergeant.

Winfrey, Bemont - Rank in Private. Rank out Private.

Winfrey, J.A. - Rank in Private. Rank out Private.

Winfrey, J.T. - Rank in Private. Rank out First Sergeant.

Winfrey (Winfrie / Winfry), John A.(H.) - Rank in Private. Rank out Private.

Winfry, J.T. - Rank in Private. Rank out First Sergeant.

Wing, S.K. - Rank in Private. Rank out Private.

Woolen, J. C. Killed at Shiloh.

Wyman, John - Rank in Private. Rank out Private.

Company G

These men hailed from the eastern part of Maury & western part of Marshall Counties of Middle Tennessee & fought bravely for the Southern states during the war of Northern aggression 1861-1865. Much of the surviving information on this unit was taken largely from a series of newspaper articles published in Columbia Tennessee's "Daily Herald" April 8, 15, 23, May 6, and 13th of 1904. Judge Frank H. Smith published these articles based on the recollections of friend Capt. R. W. Tindall 2nd Sergt. Co. G who possessed an original roster of the unit made at the end of the war in 1865 but without access to the Muster Rolls of the previous four years.

The Company was organized at the old "Napier Hole" a noted place on Flat Creek just north of the Bear Creek Pike. Here they met regularly for drill under Capt. Billington and here they were sworn in by Dr. J. H. Parks. The Company originally numbered 112 men but no record is now available giving all the names. Commanded by Capt. Jas. M. Billington, the Company marched to Columbia, taking cars here for Nashville and Murfreesboro and at the latter place went into quarters at Camp Anderson, three miles from town. The regiment organization was made in July 1861 and completed at Camp Trousdale August 23, 1861.

The final summary of this company compiled from the best information now available is as follows:

R. W. Tindall, Capt.
John E. Hardeman. 2nd Lieut.

Sam W. Daimwood, Orderly Sergt.
2 commissioned officers & 15 men killed
4 mortally wounded
3 missing
1 died on way home
4 died of sickness
31 wounded some more than once
7 wounded & discharged or left at home
10 discharged for ill health
9 otherwise discharged (too young/old)
8 captured
1 name placed on the Confederate Roll of Honor at Richmond for Conspicuous Bravery in the Battle of Murfressboro. Willis A. Jones was his name.

Aldridge (Aldrige), S.B. - Rank in Private. Rank out Private.

Allison, Joseph A. - Rank in Private. Rank out Private.

Anderson, A.S. - Rank in Private. Rank out Private.

Anderson, Alex P. - Rank in Private. Rank out Private.

Anderson, George N. - Rank in Private. Rank out Sergeant.

Anderson, George W. - Rank in Private. Rank out Sergeant.

Anderson, James - Rank in Private. Rank out Private.

Anderson, T.W. - Rank in Private. Rank out Sergeant.

Arnold, John B. - Rank in Corporal. Rank out First Lieutenant.

Auldredg, S.B. - Rank in Private. Rank out Private.

Bain, F.M. - Rank in Private. Rank out Private.

Bane, F.M. - Rank in Private. Rank out Private.

Barham, John F. - Rank in Private. Rank out Private.

Beggers, John L. - Rank in Private. Rank out Private.

Bennett, W.M. - Rank in Private. Rank out Captain.

Biggers, J.L. - Rank in Private. Rank out Private.

Biggers, John L. - Rank in Private. Rank out Private.

Billington, James M. - Rank in Captain. Rank out Captain.

Black, D.S. - Rank in Private. Rank out Private.

Black, David - Rank in Private. Rank out Private.

Black, S. S. - Rank in Private. Rank out Private.

Borroughs, G.G. - Rank in Private. Rank out Private.

Brixey, Samuel H. - Rank in Private. Rank out Private.

Brown, Robert - Rank in Private. Rank out Private.

Burrows, George G. - Rank in Private. Rank out Private.

Charles, John O. - Rank in Private. Rank out Private.

Cheek, C.M. - Rank in Private. Rank out Private.

Clark, Joseph - Rank in Private. Rank out Private.

Clark, R.D. - Rank in Private. Rank out Private.

Clark, Robert D. - Rank in Private. Rank out Private.

Clark, Thomas W. - Rank in Private. Rank out Private.

Collines, W.A. - Rank in Private. Rank out Corporal.

Collins, William A. - Rank in Private. Rank out Corporal.

Crest, I.L.C. - Rank in First Lieutenant. Rank out First Lieutenant.

Crownover, C.B. - Rank in Private. Rank out Private.

Crownover, Charles P. - Rank in Private. Rank out Private.

Daimwood, G.G. - Rank in Private. Rank out Private.

Dainwood, G.G. - Rank in Private. Rank out Private.

Daniel, Thomas A. - Rank in Private. Rank out Private.

Danwood, George G. - Rank in Private. Rank out Private.

Darity, J.A. - Rank in Corporal. Rank out Corporal.

Darity, W.L. - Rank in Private. Rank out Private.

Darmwood, G.G. - Rank in Private. Rank out Private.

Daughrity, James A. - Rank in Corporal. Rank out Corporal.

Daughrity, W.C. - Rank in Private. Rank out Private.

Daughrity, W.L. - Rank in Private. Rank out Private.

Daughrity, W.L. - Rank in Private. Rank out Private.

Davis, John - Rank in Private. Rank out Teamster.

Davis, John C. - Rank in Private. Rank out Teamster.

Dawrighty, J.A. - Rank in Corporal. Rank out Corporal.

Dean, J.W. - Rank in Private. Rank out Private.

Deen, J.W. - Rank in Private. Rank out Private.

Dellehay, J.W. - Rank in Private. Rank out Sergeant.

Derryberry, A.J. - Rank in Private. Rank out Private.

Derryberry, J.H. - Rank in Private. Rank out Private.

Derryberry, John H. - Rank in Sergeant. Rank out Private.

Dillehay, J. N. - Rank in Private. Rank out Sergeant.

Dillehay, Jasper N. - Rank in Private. Rank out Sergeant.

Dillehay, T. N. - Rank in Private. Rank out Sergeant.

Dilleyhay, J. N. - Rank in Private. Rank out Sergeant.

Dilleyhay, J. W. - Rank in Private. Rank out Sergeant.

Donwood, George G. - Rank in Private. Rank out Private.

Dotson, William C. - Rank in Private. Rank out Private.

Dougherty, James H. - Rank in Corporal. Rank out Corporal.

Dowell Jr., M.C. - Rank in Private. Rank out Private.

Dowell Sr., M.C. - Rank in Private. Rank out Private.

Edwards, Edom - Rank in Private. Rank out Private.

Edwards, William - Rank in Private. Rank out Private.

Ellison, Joseph - Rank in Private. Rank out Private.

Evans, James - Rank in Private. Rank out Private.

Evans, Sidney - Rank in Private. Rank out Private.

Evins, J. - Rank in Private. Rank out Private.

Evins, S. - Rank in Private. Rank out Private.

Farris, William G. - Rank in Private. Rank out Private.

Fingerton, George W. - Rank in Private. Rank out Private.

Finney, John L. - Rank in Private. Rank out Private.

Finney, John T. - Rank in Private. Rank out Private.

Finney, Patton A. - Rank in Private. Rank out Private.

Finney, Patton P. - Rank in Private. Rank out Private.

Finney, Preston P. - Rank in Private. Rank out Private.

Finney, William J. - Rank in Private. Rank out Private.

Finny, John T. - Rank in Private. Rank out Private.

Fitzgerals, J.A. - Rank in Private. Rank out Private.

Fuller, J.H. - Rank in Private. Rank out Private.

Fuller, J.W. - Rank in Private. Rank out Private.

Gilliam, G. J. - Rank in Corporal. Rank out Private.

Gilliam, William - Rank in Private. Rank out Private.

Graham, W.B. - Rank in Private. Rank out Private.

Gwinn, James - Rank in Private. Rank out Private.

Hardison, Martin V. - Rank in Private. Rank out Private.

Hardison, W.J. - Rank in Private. Rank out Private.

Harman, H.D. - Rank in Private. Rank out Private.

Harmon, H.D. - Rank in Private. Rank out Private.

Hime, William J. - Rank in Private. Rank out Private.

Hinson, Merril - Rank in Private. Rank out Private.

Horseford, William - Rank in Private. Rank out Private.

Horsford, T. - Rank in Private. Rank out Private.

Horsford, William - Rank in Private. Rank out Private.

Hosford, Thomas - Rank in Private. Rank out Private.

Hosford, William - Rank in Private. Rank out Private.

Howard, John J.P. - Rank in Private. Rank out Private.

Howe, William W. - Rank in Private. Rank out Private.

Ivines, J. - Rank in Private. Rank out Private.

Ivines, S. - Rank in Private. Rank out Private.

Jackson, David - Rank in Private. Rank out Private.

Jackson, David A. - Rank in Private. Rank out Private.

Jenkins, Jesse J. - Rank in Private. Rank out Private.

Jenkins, William H. - Rank in Private. Rank out Private.

Johnson, John A. - Rank in Sergeant. Rank out Private.

Jones, D.S. - Rank in Private. Rank out Private.

Jones, John M. - Rank in Private. Rank out Sergeant.

Jones, Robert - Rank in Private. Rank out Private.

Jones, Samuel - Rank in Private. Rank out Private.

Jones, T.H. - Rank in Private. Rank out Private.

Jones, Willis - Rank in Private. Rank out Private.

King, N.K. - Rank in Private. Rank out Private.

Lee, Andrew J. - Rank in Corporal. Rank out Corporal.

Lee, Henry J. - Rank in Corporal. Rank out Corporal.

Long, A. Samuel - Rank in Private. Rank out Private.

Long, J.P.K. - Rank in Private. Rank out Private.

Long, James K.P. - Rank in Private. Rank out Private.

Long, James P. - Rank in Private. Rank out Private.

Lynch, William - Rank in Private. Rank out Private.

Mackey, A.B. - Rank in Private. Rank out Teamster.

Martin, John C. - Rank in Private. Rank out Private.

Mash, Albert D. - Rank in Private. Rank out Sergeant.

May, William W. - Rank in Captain. Rank out Captain.

Mayfield, A.P. - Rank in Private. Rank out Private.

McFadden, S.L. - Rank in Private. Rank out Private.

McFaddin, S.L. - Rank in Private. Rank out Private.

McMillen, A.J. - Rank in Private. Rank out Private.

McMillin, A.J. - Rank in Private. Rank out Private.

Meaders, W.C. - Rank in Private. Rank out First Lieutenant.

Meadows, W.C. - Rank in Private. Rank out First Lieutenant.

Medders, William C. - Rank in Private. Rank out First Lieutenant.

Moor, Austin - Rank in Private. Rank out Private.

Moore, A. - Rank in Private. Rank out Private.

More, Austen - Rank in Private. Rank out Private.

Moreton, James C. - Rank in Private. Rank out Private.

Morton, James C. - Rank in Private. Rank out Private.

Neathery, J.J. - Rank in Private. Rank out Private.

Nethery, J. J. - Rank in Private. Rank out Private.

Nevels, John S. - Rank in Private. Rank out Corporal.

Nevill, John L. - Rank in Private. Rank out Corporal.

Newman, Isham B. - Rank in Private. Rank out Private.

Newsom, Andrew J. - Rank in Private. Rank out Private.

Nicholson, C.G. - Rank in Private. Rank out Private.

Nicholson, John M. - Rank in Sergeant. Rank out Private.

Oliver, John H. - Rank in Second Lieutenant. Rank out Captain.

Orr, T.A. - Rank in Corporal. Rank out Corporal.

Partin, F.M. - Rank in Private. Rank out Private.

Parton, Francis M. - Rank in Private. Rank out Private.

Pearson, Farrar - Rank in Private. Rank out Private.

Penn, Joshua H. - Rank in Private. Rank out Private.

Perry, William P. - Rank in Private. Rank out Private.

Persons, Farrar - Rank in Private. Rank out Private.

Pingleton, G.W. - Rank in Private. Rank out Private.

Pingleton, George W. - Rank in Private. Rank out Private.

Pinn, Joshua H. - Rank in Private. Rank out Private.

Pool, James - Rank in Private. Rank out Private.

Price, Ewel C. - Rank in Private. Rank out Sergeant.

Purdie, Thomas J. - Rank in Private. Rank out Private.

Purdy, Thomas J. - Rank in Private. Rank out Private.

Purdy, Thomas R. - Rank in Private. Rank out Private.

Quinn, Hugh - Rank in Private. Rank out Private.

Read, Eldridge H. - Rank in Private. Rank out Private.

Read, N.B. - Rank in Private. Rank out Private.

Reed, E.H. - Rank in Private. Rank out Private.

Reed, N.B. - Rank in Private. Rank out Private.

Rice, Septimus C. - Rank in Private. Rank out Private.

Rice, Steaphen C. - Rank in Private. Rank out Private.

Rice, William A. - Rank in Private. Rank out First Lieutenant/Adjutant.

Riley, John H. - Rank in Private. Rank out Private.

Roberts, Isaac T. - Rank in First Lieutenant. Rank out Captain.

Roddy, Benjamin F. - Rank in Private. Rank out Private.

Roddy, Joseph G. - Rank in Private. Rank out Second Lieutenant.

Roulett, B.F. - Rank in Second Lieutenant. Rank out Second Lieutenant.

Rowlett, B.F. - Rank in Second Lieutenant. Rank out Second Lieutenant.

Rumage, George - Rank in Private. Rank out Sergeant.

Rummage, George - Rank in Private. Rank out Sergeant.

Rutherford, A. Sidney - Rank in Private. Rank out Private.

Rutherford, Elliott - Rank in Private. Rank out Private.

Sansom, Green F. - Rank in Private. Rank out Sergeant.

Scully, Charles - Rank in Private. Rank out Private.

Scully, Thomas - Rank in Private. Rank out Private.

Secres, W.S. - Rank in Private. Rank out Private.

Secrest, Dock - Rank in Private. Rank out Private.

Secrest, I.S. - Rank in First Lieutenant. Rank out First Lieutenant.

Secrest, S.W. - Rank in Private. Rank out Private.

Secrest, W.H. - Rank in Private. Rank out Private.

Sharp, Thomas A. - Rank in Private. Rank out Private.

Sharp, William A. - Rank in Private. Rank out Private.

Shiers, William - Rank in Corporal. Rank out Private.

Shires, C.N. - Rank in Private. Rank out Private.

Shires, Ira - Rank in Corporal. Rank out Sergeant.

Shires, Jacob B. - Rank in Private. Rank out Private.

Shires, Peter - Rank in Private. Rank out Private.

Shires, W.H. - Rank in First Sergeant. Rank out First Lieutenant.

Shires, W.M. - Rank in Corporal. Rank out Private.

Shires, William - Rank in Corporal. Rank out Private.

Shires, William H. - Rank in Corporal. Rank out Private.

Shivers, Ira - Rank in Corporal. Rank out Sergeant.

Stephens, Anther N. - Rank in Private. Rank out Private.

Stewart, J.J. - Rank in Private. Rank out Private.

Sutton, H.J. - Rank in Private. Rank out Private.

Taylor, James A. - Rank in Private. Rank out Private.

Taylor, William A. - Rank in Private. Rank out Private.

Thacker, E. Newton - Rank in Private. Rank out Private.

Thomas, Alexander C. - Rank in Private. Rank out Private.

Thomas, Freeman H. - Rank in Sergeant. Rank out Private.

Thomas, Joseph W. - Rank in Private. Rank out Second Lieutenant.

Thomas, William J. - Rank in Private. Rank out Private.

Thompson, B.J. - Rank in Private. Rank out Private.

Thompson, Benjamin B. - Rank in Sergeant. Rank out Private.

Tindall, H.C. - Rank in Private. Rank out Private.

Tindall, R.W. - Rank in Private. Rank out Captain.

Tindell, H.C. - Rank in Private. Rank out Private.

Tindell, Robert W. - Rank in Private. Rank out Captain.

Tindill, R.W. - Rank in Private. Rank out Captain.

Townsend, A.J. - Rank in Private. Rank out Private.

Townsend, Andre' J. - Rank in Private. Rank out Private.

Townsend, F.M. - Rank in Private. Rank out Private.

Tucker, Clinton M. - Rank in Private. Rank out Private.

Underwood, George - Rank in Private. Rank out Private.

Wildman, J.D. - Rank in Private. Rank out Private.

Wileman, James D. - Rank in Private. Rank out Private.

Wileman, William - Rank in Private. Rank out Private.

Wilkerson, J.H.P. - Rank in Private. Rank out Private.

Wilkinson, James K.P. - Rank in Private. Rank out Private.

Williams, H.M. - Rank in Private. Rank out Private.

Williams, J.B. - Rank in Private. Rank out Private.

Williams, James H. - Rank in Private. Rank out Corporal.

Williams, Jerome B. - Rank in Private. Rank out Private.

Winton, G.G. - Rank in Private. Rank out Private.

Winton, George - Rank in Private. Rank out Private.

Winton, James - Rank in Private. Rank out Private.

Withrow, John F. - Rank in Private. Rank out Private.

Withrow, Samuel - Rank in Private. Rank out Private.

Womack, Francis M. - Rank in Sergeant. Rank out Private.

Womack, William H.H. - Rank in Private. Rank out Private.

Original roster of "The Duck River Riflemen"

'Duck River Rifles'

24th Co. G Roster

Captain, James M. Billington, (resigned April 1862).

1st Lieut. J. Lon Secrest. (killed at Perryville, Oct. 8,1862).

2nd Lieut. Wm. M. Shires, (resigned April 1862. Living near Old Lasea).

2nd Lieut. Joel L. Hardison, (killed at Murfreesboro, Dec. 31, 1862).

2nd Lieut. (Brevet) B. Frank Rowlett,(discharged 1862).

1st Sergt. David M. Hardison, (living near Old Berlin).

2nd Sergt. Rob't W. Tindall, (living at Leftwich).

3rd Sergt. John E. Hardeman, (living in Texas).

4th Sergt. Jasper W. Dillehay.(dead)

5th Sergt. Sam W. Daimwood (living near Columbia).

1st Corp. James A. Dougherty, (living near Chapel Hill).

3rd Corp. Wm. A. Collins (living near Franklin).

Privates

Sam Booker Aldridge (living near Caney Springs in 1904)

John F. Barham (died at Fulton, KY)

John L. Biggers (died in Texas)

Jacob Bennett (living in Arkansas in 1904)

Robert Brown (living near Kedron in 1904)

David S. Black (living near Columbia in 1904)

Sidney Black (died in Maury County)

Robert Brown (living near Kedron in 1904)

Calvin Modrell Cheek (mortally wounded at Resaca, May 15, 1864)

James Clark (wouded at Shiloh. living in Marshall Co. in 1904)

Joseph Clark (died in Maury County)

Robert D. Clark (living in Hickman Co. in 1904)

Thomas Clark (died in Maury Co.)

William A. Collins (wounded at Shiloh)

George C. Daimwood (wounded at Shiloh, living near Columbia in 1904)

T. Anderson Daniel (wounded at Shiloh, living near Bethesda in 1904)

John Davis (on detatched service as Division Teamster, living near Smyrna in 1904)

Joseph Dean (lost in retreat from Bowling Green KY 1862)

Andrew Jackson Derryberry (killed at Shiloh at the first fire, shot through the heart)

John H. Derryberry (died on way home to Maury Co. in 1864 of dysentery)

Joseph L. Derryberry (living near Caney Springs in 1904)

Thomas N. Doughtery (living near Chapel Hill in 1904)

William L. Doughtery (wounded at Shiloh, living in West Tennessee in 1904)

Major E. Dowell Jr. (killed at the first fire, shot through the breast)

Major E. Dowell Sr. discharged for disability, buried in Williams Cemetery)

Edom Edwards (discharged for wounds at Shiloh, died on Bear Creek)

William Edwards (discharged for disability, living at Chapel Hill in 1904)

Sid Evans (wounded at Shiloh, captured and died in prison two months later)

William Erwin (moved to Obion Co.)

James Evins (killed at Shiloh at the first fire, shot through the brain)

Joseph Dean Evins (lost in retreat from Bowling Green KY 1862)

E. Fitzgerald (killed at Shiloh at the first fire, shot in the head)

James Fuller(killed at Shiloh)

William Graham (living in Lamar Co. Texas in 1904)

David M. Hardison (wounded at Shiloh)

George W. Hardison (wounded at Franklin, died at Hillsboro, TN)

James Hardison (died from measles at Camp Trousdale Oct. 1861)

Martin V. Hardison (wounded three times, once at Shiloh, living near Hardison's Mill in 1904.

Dr. Sam T. Hardison (inclined to Calvary 1865, banker in Lewisburg in 1904)

William Duncan Hardison (captured twice, living near Rock Springs in 1904, buried in Charles Hardison Cemetery)

William Joshua Hardison (contracted measles, sent home to die, buried in Joshua Hardison Cemetery)

Holland Harmon (dischared for disability Jan. 1862)

Tom Harmon (wounded at Shiloh, living at Dabbletown in 1904)

Edmond Harris (discharged in 1862, died at Hardison's Mill)

Merrill Hinson (died from wounds at Shiloh)

Thomas Hosford (killed at Shiloh)

William Hosford (died in Hickman Co., Gen Cheatham remarked "he was the best soldier in the Army")

David A. Jackson Jr. (wounded at Shiloh, killed at Pulaski Dec. 1864)

David A. Jackson Sr. (discharged 1862, died in 25th district)

John Johnson (discharged for wounds at Shiloh, shot through both hips)

Davy Crockett Jones (living in the Tugas Bend in 1904)

Robert Jones (discharged for disability, living near New Lasea in 1904)

Samuel Jones (died from measles at Camp Trousdale, Oct 1861)

Thomas H. Jones (a boy discharged 1862, living near Sowell's Mill in 1904)

Willis A. Jones (killed at Murfreesboro, placed on the Confederate Roll of Honor at Richmond)

Pole King (wounded at Shiloh, living near Chapel Hill in 1904)

William T. Lee (wounded at Murfreesboro, dead)

William J. Lovett (wounded at Shiloh)

A. B. (Wood) Mackay (discharged for disability, died at Beechland in 1903)

Simon L. Mcfadden (wounded at Shiloh, went to Lamar Co. Texas)

John Martin (discharged for disability)

Porter Mayfield (died in Marshall Co.)

Austin Moore (died at Flat Creek about 1890)

Charles G. Nicholson (killed at Franklin)

John M. Nicholson (died in Maury Co.)

Thomas Addison Orr (killed at Shiloh at the first fire, shot through the breast)

George W. Pinkleton (wounded at Shiloh, lost at Missionary Ridge)

Newton Reed (killed at Shiloh at the first fire, shot in the head)

Sergt. George W. Rummage (wounded at Shiloh, killed at Atlanta)

Sam Secrest (died from measles at Camp Trousdale, Oct. 9, 1861)

W.H. Secrest (living near South Berlin in 1904)

Thomas Ansberry Sharp (wounded at Shiloh, died in Maury Co. 1890)

William Anderson Sharp (living near Old Lasea in 1904, died in Maury Co. 1922)

Christian N. Shires (lving in Obion Co. in 1904)

Jacob Shires (captured at Missionary Ridge, living near Match in 1904)

Peter Shires (went to Washington Territory)

William M. Shires captured at Missionary Ridge, living near Rally Hill in 1904, buried at Shires Memorial Cemetery)

Hazard Cappon Tindall (wounded at Missionary Ridge, died Feb 20, 1864)

William Henry Harrison Tindell (buried at Jackson Cemetery #2)

George W. Underwood (discharged Oct 1861, living near Match in 1904)

Jeff Weatherly (killed at Shiloh at the first fire, shot in the breast)

Hiram M. Williams (lost at Shiloh & never heard of again)

Franklin J. Wright (wounded at Shiloh, went to Texas)

Hanson M. Wright (died at Madison GA Hospital July 1864)

Roster made at close of war by 2nd Sergt. R. W. Tindall C.S.A. 1865 and published in Columbia Tennessee's "Daily Herald" By Judge Frank H. Smith in 1904.

REF: http://duckriverrifles.50megs.com/about.html

Company H

Anderson, S.W - Rank in Private. Rank out Private.

Anderson, D.C. - Rank in Private. Rank out Private.

Anderson, J.G. - Rank in First Lieutenant. Rank out First Lieutenant.

Anderson, J.N. - Rank in Sergeant. Rank out Lieutenant.

Anderson, R.M. - Rank in Private. Rank out Private.

Anderson, W.S. - Rank in Private. Rank out Private.

Anderson, William S. - Rank in Private. Rank out Private.

Anglen, N.J. - Rank in Private. Rank out Private.

Anglin, F.M. - Rank in Private. Rank out Private.

Anglin, J.N. - Rank in Private. Rank out Private.

Anglin, N.J. - Rank in Private. Rank out Private.

Anglin, Newton - Rank in Private. Rank out Private.

Anglin, W. - Rank in Private. Rank out Private.

Angling, N.J. - Rank in Private. Rank out Private.

Armistead, David H. - Rank in Private. Rank out Private.

Armistead, Robert B. - Rank in Sergeant. Rank out Second Lieutenant.

Arnold, W.D. - Rank in Private. Rank out Private.

Arnold, William - Rank in Private. Rank out Private.

Babb, W.F.P. - Rank in Private. Rank out Private.

Baird, A.G. - Rank in Private. Rank out Private.

Baird, W.C. - Rank in Private. Rank out Private.

Baker, W.D. - Rank in Corporal. Rank out Corporal.

Ballard, F.M. - Rank in Private. Rank out Second Lieutenant.

Bates, R.H. - Rank in Private. Rank out Private.

Bates, Z.B. - Rank in Private. Rank out Private.

Beale, C.W. - Rank in Captain. Rank out Captain.

Beard, W.B. - Rank in Private. Rank out Private.

Beard, W.C. - Rank in Private. Rank out Private.

Beasley, E.R. - Rank in Private. Rank out Private.

Beasley, Isaac J. - Rank in Private. Rank out Private.

Beasley, William R. - Rank in Private. Rank out Private.

Beesly, Isaac J. - Rank in Private. Rank out Private.

Beesly, William H. - Rank in Private. Rank out Private.

Berry, William G. - Rank in Sergeant. Rank out Sergeant.

Bradley, M. M. - Rank in Private. Rank out Corporal.

Bratton, R.F. - Rank in Sergeant. Rank out Private.

Brickle, J.A. - Rank in Private. Rank out Corporal.

Brown, Lewis C. - Rank in Private. Rank out Private.

Campbell, H. C. - Rank in First Sergeant. Rank out Captain.

Cardwell, Joseph L. - Rank in Second Lieutenant. Rank out Second Lieutenant.

Cardwell, Silas H. - Rank in Corporal. Rank out Corporal.

Cardwell, William L. - Rank in Private. Rank out Private.

Carnwell, R.S. - Rank in Second Lieutenant. Rank out Second Lieutenant.

Carter, Isaac - Rank in Private. Rank out Private.

Carter, William H. - Rank in Private. Rank out Private.

Clark, J.H. - Rank in Private. Rank out First Sergeant.

Cleavland, Alex P. - Rank in Sergeant. Rank out Sergeant.

Climer, J.D. - Rank in Private. Rank out Private.

Climor, J.D. - Rank in Private. Rank out Private.

Clymer, J.D. - Rank in Private. Rank out Private.

Cook, James C. - Rank in Private. Rank out Private.

Cooper, G.W. - Rank in Private. Rank out Private.

Coopper, G.W. - Rank in Private. Rank out Private.

Cornwell, Benjamin S. - Rank in Second Lieutenant. Rank out Second Lieutenant.

Cox, James M. - Rank in Private. Rank out Private.

Craghead, Joesph - Rank in Private. Rank out Private.

Craghead, Marlin - Rank in Private. Rank out Private.

Craighead, Marlin - Rank in Private. Rank out Private.

Cunningham, Thomas - Rank in Private. Rank out Private.

Davis, Rufus - Rank in Private. Rank out Private.

Dawson, L.H. - Rank in Private. Rank out Private.

Dawson, R.K. - Rank in Second Lieutenant. Rank out Second Lieutenant.

Deal, W.M. - Rank in Private. Rank out Private.

Dean, R.A. - Rank in Private. Rank out Private.

Dean, Robert A. - Rank in Private. Rank out Private.

Deel, W. M. - Rank in Private. Rank out Private.

Deen, R.A. - Rank in Private. Rank out Private.

Dellehay, John H. - Rank in Private. Rank out Private.

Dewire, Patrick - Rank in Private. Rank out Private.

Dickens, James F. - Rank in Private. Rank out Private.

Dillahay, James A. - Rank in Private. Rank out Corporal.

Dillahay, James P. - Rank in Private. Rank out Private.

Dillahay, James T. - Rank in Corporal. Rank out Corporal.

Dillahay, John H. - Rank in Private. Rank out Private.

Dillahay, Robert J. - Rank in Private. Rank out Private.

Dillehay, James A. - Rank in Private. Rank out Corporal.

Dillehay, James P. - Rank in Private. Rank out Private.

Dillehay, James T. - Rank in Corporal. Rank out Corporal.

Dillehay, John H. - Rank in Private. Rank out Private.

Dillehay, Robert J. - Rank in Private. Rank out Private.

Dillihay, J. A. - Rank in Private. Rank out Corporal.

Dixon, John G. - Rank in Private. Rank out Private.

Doyse, Patrick - Rank in Private. Rank out Private.

Dunlap, James - Rank in Private. Rank out Private.

Dyer, Dixon - Rank in Private. Rank out Private.

Ferguson, Charles L. - Rank in Musician. Rank out Musician.

Fly, J.M. - Rank in Private. Rank out Private.

Ford, James C. - Rank in Private. Rank out Private.

Furgerson, Archibald W. - Rank in Private. Rank out Private.

Furgerson, C.L. - Rank in Musician. Rank out Musician.

Furgerson, Charles - Rank in Musician. Rank out Musician.

Furman, R. - Rank in Private. Rank out Private.

Giles, W. C. J. - Rank in Private. Rank out Private.

Goad, Jefferson - Rank in Private. Rank out Private.

Goad, Joshua - Rank in Private. Rank out Private.

Goard, Jefferson - Rank in Private. Rank out Private.

Goard, Joshua - Rank in Private. Rank out Private.

Good, Jefferson - Rank in Private. Rank out Private.

Goud, Jefferson - Rank in Private. Rank out Private.

Greer, J.H. - Rank in Private. Rank out Second Lieutenant.

Gregory, William Jesse - Rank in Private. Rank out Private.

Groves, G.W. - Rank in Private. Rank out Private.

Groves, Henry - Rank in Private. Rank out Private.

Halibuston, L.S. - Rank in Private. Rank out Private.

Halliburton, L.L. - Rank in Private. Rank out Private.

Halliburton, Leroy S. - Rank in Private. Rank out Private.

Hance, Erastus S. - Rank in First Lieutenant. Rank out Captain.

Harris, J.H. - Rank in Private. Rank out Private.

Hart, Henry W. - Rank in Captain. Rank out Captain.

Haynie, Thomas M. - Rank in Sergeant. Rank out Sergeant.

Herron, William F. - Rank in Private. Rank out Private.

Hogg, Shelby J. - Rank in Private. Rank out Private.

Hollamon, William Z. - Rank in Private. Rank out Private.

Hollerman, William S. - Rank in Private. Rank out Private.

Hunter, W.H. - Rank in Corporal. Rank out Corporal.

Kemp, Henry - Rank in Private. Rank out .

Kemp, Jinks H. - Rank in Private. Rank out Private.

Kemp, John M. - Rank in Private. Rank out Private.

Kemp, William L. - Rank in Private. Rank out Private.

King, Wellington - Rank in Private. Rank out Private.

Kirby, Wade H. - Rank in Private. Rank out Sergeant.

Law, Henry D. - Rank in Private. Rank out Private.

Law, Hugh L. - Rank in Private. Rank out Private.

Long, Charles S. - Rank in Private. Rank out Private.

MClellan, David L. - Rank in First Sergeant. Rank out Ordnance Sergeant.

Mass, T.F. - Rank in Private. Rank out Private.

Massey, George W. - Rank in Private. Rank out Private.

Mathers, E. - Rank in Private. Rank out Private.

Mathews, Benjamin - Rank in Private. Rank out Private.

Mathews, Enoch - Rank in Private. Rank out Private.

Mathews, James D. - Rank in Private. Rank out Private.

McCall, Hugh L. - Rank in Private. Rank out Private.

McCard, W.C. - Rank in Sergeant. Rank out Private.

McClellan, W.C. - Rank in Private. Rank out .

McClelland, David L. - Rank in First Sergeant. Rank out Ordnance Sergeant.

McCord, J.H. - Rank in Private. Rank out Private.

McCord, Jerome H. - Rank in Private. Rank out Private.

McCord, W.C. - Rank in Sergeant. Rank out Private.

McCord, W.H. - Rank in Private. Rank out Private.

McCowen, I.H. - Rank in Private. Rank out Private.

McCoy, Robert - Rank in Private. Rank out Private.

Monday, Bailey P. - Rank in Private. Rank out Private.

Monday, Thomas - Rank in Private. Rank out Private.

Mondy, B.P. - Rank in Private. Rank out Private.

Mondy, Thomas - Rank in Private. Rank out Private.

Montgomery, Felix G. - Rank in Private. Rank out Private.

Moore, R.T. - Rank in Private. Rank out Private.

Morris, Daniel E. - Rank in Private. Rank out Private.

Moss, G. - Rank in Private. Rank out Private.

Moss, J.F. - Rank in Private. Rank out Private.

Moss, N.F. - Rank in Private. Rank out Private.

Moss, T.F. - Rank in Private. Rank out Private.

Moss, Thomas Fletcher - Rank in Private. Rank out Private.

Munday, Bailey P. - Rank in Private. Rank out Private.

Munday, Thomas - Rank in Private. Rank out Private.

Mundy, Bailey P. - Rank in Private. Rank out Private.

Mundy, Thomas - Rank in Private. Rank out Private.

Neely, W.A. - Rank in Private. Rank out Private.

Odum, Josiah - Rank in Private. Rank out .

Overby, Alexander - Rank in Private. Rank out Private.

Overby, Wilson - Rank in Private. Rank out Private.

Pamell, Andrew - Rank in Private. Rank out Private.

Parker, S.P. - Rank in Private. Rank out Sergeant.

Parker, Samuel P. - Rank in Private. Rank out Sergeant.

Parker, Samuel P. - Rank in Private. Rank out Sergeant.

Parker, W.A. - Rank in Private. Rank out Private.

Pate, William H.H. - Rank in Private. Rank out Private.

Paual, Andrew - Rank in Private. Rank out Private.

Payne, Hampton W. - Rank in Private. Rank out Private.

Payne, John - Rank in Private. Rank out Private.

Pendergrass, B.H. - Rank in Private. Rank out Private.

Pinkerton, James - Rank in Private. Rank out Private.

Pistole, Thomas J. - Rank in Private. Rank out Private.

Porter, John - Rank in Private. Rank out Private.

Poual, Andrew - Rank in Private. Rank out Private.

Powell, Andrew - Rank in Private. Rank out Private.

Powell, Jesse - Rank in Private. Rank out Private.

Prichard, G.H. - Rank in Private. Rank out Private.

Primm, H.G. - Rank in Private. Rank out Private.

Pritchett, G.H. - Rank in Private. Rank out Private.

Ragsdale, J.P. - Rank in Private. Rank out Private.

Ragsdale, W.N. - Rank in Private. Rank out Private.

Ray, Albert N. - Rank in Private. Rank out Private.

Reaves, L.E. - Rank in Corporal. Rank out Private.

Reaves, Leonidas E. - Rank in Corporal. Rank out Private.

Reaves, S.J. - Rank in Private. Rank out Private.

Reece, Abraham - Rank in Private. Rank out Private.

Reece, James W. - Rank in Private. Rank out Private.

Reece, Wade H. - Rank in Private. Rank out Private.

Reece, William H. - Rank in Private. Rank out Private.

Reed, Braddock - Rank in Private. Rank out Private.

Reese, Abraham - Rank in Private. Rank out Private.

Reese, Wade - Rank in Private. Rank out Private.

Reid, Braddock - Rank in Private. Rank out Private.

Richardson, Riley S. - Rank in Private. Rank out Private.

Richerson, Riley S. - Rank in Private. Rank out Private.

Richmond, J.W. - Rank in Private. Rank out Private.

Ried, Braddock - Rank in Private. Rank out Private.

Riley, Isaac N. - Rank in Private. Rank out Second Lieutenant.

Riley, James N. - Rank in Private. Rank out Second Lieutenant.

Robbins, William T. - Rank in Corporal. Rank out Private.

Roberts, J.A. - Rank in Private. Rank out Private.

Roberts, William T. - Rank in Corporal. Rank out Private.

Royster, Charles E. - Rank in Private. Rank out Private.

Russell, H.T. - Rank in Private. Rank out .

Russell, James T. - Rank in Private. Rank out Private.

Sanders, William V. - Rank in Musician. Rank out Musician.

Scruggs, T. S. J. - Rank in Private. Rank out Private.

Shaw, J.M. - Rank in Private. Rank out Corporal.

Sholders, William L. - Rank in Private. Rank out Private.

Shoulders, David T. - Rank in Private. Rank out Private.

Shoulders, William S. - Rank in Private. Rank out Private.

Shoulter, William L. - Rank in Private. Rank out Private.

Sims, Zachariah - Rank in Private. Rank out Private.

Slayden, A.J. - Rank in Private. Rank out Private.

Slayden, Andrew J. - Rank in Private. Rank out Private.

Sloan, S.N. - Rank in Private. Rank out Corporal.

Sloan, Sidney M. - Rank in Private. Rank out Corporal.

Slone, Sidney M. - Rank in Private. Rank out Corporal.

Smith, Harrison - Rank in Corporal. Rank out Corporal.

Smith, John N. - Rank in Private. Rank out Second Lieutenant.

Smith, Walter - Rank in Private. Rank out Sergeant.

Smith, William H. - Rank in Private. Rank out Private.

Stephens, Albert H. - Rank in Private. Rank out Private.

Stephens, Charles - Rank in Private. Rank out Private.

Sterns, A.H. - Rank in Private. Rank out Private.

Stevens, Albert - Rank in Private. Rank out Private.

Stevens, Charles - Rank in Private. Rank out Private.

Stevens, J.H. - Rank in Private. Rank out Private.

Stevens, J.K. - Rank in Private. Rank out Private.

Taylor, John D. - Rank in Private. Rank out Private.

Taylor, Joseph B. - Rank in Private. Rank out Private.

Taylor, Joseph D. - Rank in Private. Rank out Private.

Taylor, Peter H. - Rank in Private. Rank out Private.

Termon, B.B. - Rank in Private. Rank out Private.

Termon, Kerney - Rank in Private. Rank out Private.

Termon, Thomas - Rank in Private. Rank out Private.

Thomas, John F. - Rank in Private. Rank out Private.

Thomas, William A. - Rank in Private. Rank out Private.

Truett, J.M. - Rank in Private. Rank out Private.

Truitt, J.M. - Rank in Private. Rank out Private.

Turman, Kerney - Rank in Private. Rank out Private.

Turman, Thomas - Rank in Private. Rank out Private.

Tyler, J. W. - Rank in Corporal. Rank out Private.

Tyler, James W. - Rank in Corporal. Rank out Private.

Underhill, D. H. - Rank in Private. Rank out Private.

Underhill, Daniel - Rank in Private. Rank out Private.

Wakefield, William C. - Rank in Private. Rank out Private.

Wakefield, William Clay - Rank in Private. Rank out Private.

Wallace, Robert - Rank in Private. Rank out .

Warf, B.S. - Rank in Private. Rank out Private.

Warf, E.D. - Rank in Private. Rank out Private.

Warren, W.C. - Rank in Private. Rank out Private.

Watson, G.W. - Rank in Private. Rank out Private.

Williams, Allen W. - Rank in Private. Rank out Color Sergeant.

Williams, Bailey P. - Rank in Private. Rank out Private.

Williams, Daly T. - Rank in Private. Rank out Private.

Williams, James H. - Rank in Private. Rank out Private.

Winkleer, Henderson W. - Rank in Private. Rank out Private.

Winkler, Henderson - Rank in Private. Rank out Private.

Worf, B.S. - Rank in Private. Rank out Private.

Young, G.W. - Rank in Second Lieutenant. Rank out Second Lieutenant.

Company I

Anderson, S.W - Rank in Private. Rank out Private.

Adcock, Allen - Rank in Private. Rank out Private.

Adcox, Alen - Rank in Private. Rank out Private.

Alexander, Thomas - Rank in Private. Rank out Private.

Anderson, D.C. - Rank in Private. Rank out Private.

Anderson, J.T. - Rank in Private. Rank out Private.

Anglen, N.J. - Rank in Private. Rank out Private.

Anglin, J.N. - Rank in Private. Rank out Private.

Anglin, N.J. - Rank in Private. Rank out Private.

Anglin, Newton - Rank in Private. Rank out Private.

Anglin, W. - Rank in Private. Rank out Private.

Angling, N.J. - Rank in Private. Rank out Private.

Armstrong, Nathaniel W. - Rank in Private. Rank out Private.

Arnold, Benjamin F. - Rank in Private. Rank out Private.

Arnold, W.D. - Rank in Private. Rank out Private.

Askins, Alonzo - Rank in Private. Rank out Private.

Baird, W.J. - Rank in Private. Rank out Private.

Baker, Elijah - Rank in Private. Rank out Private.

Baker, Milow - Rank in Private. Rank out Private.

Barber, Wiley A. - Rank in Private. Rank out Private.

Bates, Adolphus - Rank in Private. Rank out Private.

Bates, B.B. - Rank in Private. Rank out Private.

Bates, Dennis - Rank in Private. Rank out Private.

Bates, Moses - Rank in Private. Rank out Private.

Baysdale, M. - Rank in Private. Rank out Private.

Beatty, A.H. - Rank in Private. Rank out Private.

Beatty, Thomas S. - Rank in Second Lieutenant. Rank out Second Lieutenant.

Bedford, John - Rank in Private. Rank out Private.

Bradford, John - Rank in Private. Rank out Private.

Bratton, J.A. - Rank in Private. Rank out Private.

Bratton, James A. - Rank in Private. Rank out Private.

Bratton, M.J.A. - Rank in Private. Rank out Private.

Brown, C.L. - Rank in Private. Rank out Private.

Brown, S.C. - Rank in Private. Rank out Private.

Brudford, John - Rank in Private. Rank out Private.

Buchanan, Elias - Rank in Private. Rank out Private.

Campbell, F. M. - Rank in Private. Rank out Private.

Campbell, John F. M. - Rank in Private. Rank out Private.

Campbell, William D. - Rank in Private. Rank out Corporal.

Campbell, William J. - Rank in Private. Rank out Private.

Cash, William - Rank in Private. Rank out Private.

Cavender, G.B. - Rank in Private. Rank out Private.

Chapell, Francis C. - Rank in Corporal. Rank out Private.

Climer, J.D. - Rank in Private. Rank out Private.

Climor, J.D. - Rank in Private. Rank out Private.

Cook, John T. - Rank in Private. Rank out Private.

Cook, W.J. - Rank in Private. Rank out Private.

Cook, William J. - Rank in Private. Rank out Private.

Cooper, David M. - Rank in Private. Rank out Private.

Cooper, G.W. - Rank in Private. Rank out Private.

Coopper, G.W. - Rank in Private. Rank out Private.

Cotham, William S. - Rank in Private. Rank out Private.

Cottone, Wm. - Rank in Private. Rank out Private.

Cox, G.W. - Rank in Private. Rank out Private.

Cox, John - Rank in Private. Rank out Private.

Cross, Harvy N. - Rank in Private. Rank out Private.

Cunningham, Thomas - Rank in Private. Rank out Private.

Curl, Thomas B. - Rank in Private. Rank out Private.

Curl, William Y. - Rank in Corporal. Rank out Private.

Daugherty, James A. - Rank in Corporal. Rank out Corporal.

Deal, W.M. - Rank in Private. Rank out Private.

Dean, R.A. - Rank in Private. Rank out Private.

Dean, Robert A. - Rank in Private. Rank out Private.

Deel, W. M. - Rank in Private. Rank out Private.

Deen, R.A. - Rank in Private. Rank out Private.

Depriest, Andrew J. - Rank in Private. Rank out Private.

Depriest, William F. - Rank in Private. Rank out Private.

Dewire, Patrick - Rank in Private. Rank out Private.

Doyse, Patrick - Rank in Private. Rank out Private.

Duke, James M. - Rank in Private. Rank out Private.

Dunbar, Samuel M. - Rank in First Sergeant. Rank out Private.

Duncan, T.H. - Rank in Private. Rank out Private.

Duncan, Thomas H. - Rank in Private. Rank out Private.

Duncan, Thomas J. - Rank in Private. Rank out Private.

Dunkin, T.H. - Rank in Private. Rank out Private.

Early, E.W. - Rank in Captain. Rank out Captain.

Easley, Andrew D. - Rank in Private. Rank out Private.

Easley, Edward W - Rank in Captain. Rank out Captain.

Easley, Thomas S. - Rank in Private. Rank out Second Lieutenant.

Edmonds, J.T. - Rank in Private. Rank out Drummer.

Edmonds, Joseph H. - Rank in Private. Rank out Drummer.

Edmonds, Joseph S. - Rank in Private. Rank out Drummer.

Emison, Frank A. - Rank in Private. Rank out Private.

Emler, Frank - Rank in Private. Rank out Private.

Emler, Henderson - Rank in Private. Rank out Private.

Emmerson, F.A. - Rank in Private. Rank out Private.

Esells, A.D. - Rank in Private. Rank out Private.

Fentress, James - Rank in Private. Rank out Private.

Fielder, C.W. - Rank in Private. Rank out Private.

Fielder, N.C. - Rank in Private. Rank out Private.

Fielder, Newton C. - Rank in Private. Rank out Private.

Furgerson, Frank - Rank in Private. Rank out Private.

Garner, William C. - Rank in Private. Rank out Private.

Garrett, Austin S. - Rank in Private. Rank out Private.

Garrett, Eli H. - Rank in Private. Rank out Private.

Garrett, T.J. - Rank in Private. Rank out Private.

Garrette, I.T. - Rank in Private. Rank out Private.

Geins, J.R. - Rank in Private. Rank out Private.

Gentry, Samuel - Rank in Private. Rank out Private.

Giles, W. C. J. - Rank in Private. Rank out Private.

Goens, J.R. - Rank in Private. Rank out Private.

Goins, J.R. - Rank in Private. Rank out Private.

Goins, Jordan R. - Rank in Private. Rank out Private.

Graves, Thomas J. - Rank in Private. Rank out Private.

Gray, John V. - Rank in Private. Rank out Private.

Green, Robert F. - Rank in Sergeant. Rank out Sergeant.

Greer, J.H. - Rank in Private. Rank out Second Lieutenant.

Griffin, Lewis J. - Rank in Private. Rank out Corporal.

Griffin, Newton P. - Rank in Private. Rank out Private.

Griffin, Willis C. - Rank in Private. Rank out Private.

Groves, G.W. - Rank in Private. Rank out Private.

Gunter, Perry - Rank in Private. Rank out Private.

Halbrooks, Robert C. - Rank in Private. Rank out Private.

Hale, W.F. - Rank in Private. Rank out Private.

Hammock, James M. - Rank in Private. Rank out Private.

Harrington, J.D. - Rank in Private. Rank out Private.

Harrington, James D. - Rank in Private. Rank out Private.

Harrington, W.W. - Rank in Private. Rank out First Sergeant.

Harrington, Wilson - Rank in Private. Rank out First Sergeant.

Harris, Benjamin F. - Rank in Private. Rank out Private.

Harris, J.H. - Rank in Private. Rank out Private.

Hassell, F.M. - Rank in Private. Rank out Private.

Hendricks, S.G. - Rank in Private. Rank out Sergeant.

Hendricks, Smith G. - Rank in Private. Rank out Sergeant.

Hendrix, S.G. - Rank in Private. Rank out Sergeant.

Henry, Franklin B. - Rank in Private. Rank out First Lieutenant.

Hensiley, J.D. - Rank in Private. Rank out Private.

Herrington, James B. - Rank in Private. Rank out Private.

Holmes, J.A. - Rank in Private. Rank out Captain.

Holmes, William - Rank in Private. Rank out Second Lieutenant.

Holms, J.A. - Rank in Private. Rank out Captain.

Holms, Thomas - Rank in Private. Rank out Second Lieutenant.

Hooper, James - Rank in Private. Rank out Private.

Hooten, J.B. - Rank in Private. Rank out Private.

Hooton, J.B. - Rank in Private. Rank out Private.

Hoper, James - Rank in Private. Rank out Private.

Huchenson, Elijah - Rank in Private. Rank out Private.

Hutcherson, Elijah - Rank in Private. Rank out Private.

Hutcherson, Francis M. - Rank in Private. Rank out Private.

Hutcherson, James - Rank in Private. Rank out Private.

Hutcherson, James C. - Rank in Private. Rank out Private.

Hutchinson, James C. - Rank in Private. Rank out Private.

Hutchison, F.M. - Rank in Private. Rank out Private.

Inman, K. - Rank in Private. Rank out Private.

Jenkins, James - Rank in Private. Rank out Private.

Jenkins, William - Rank in Private. Rank out Private.

Jinkens, James - Rank in Private. Rank out Private.

Jinkens, William - Rank in Private. Rank out Private.

Killough, J.G. - Rank in Private. Rank out Private.

Kunkle, John A. - Rank in Private. Rank out Private.

Lancaster, William J. - Rank in Private. Rank out Private.

Lane, Elias - Rank in Private. Rank out Private.

Lawson, J. C. - Rank in Private. Rank out Private.

Lawson, Shadrick S. - Rank in Private. Rank out Private.

Lovelass, William - Rank in Private. Rank out Private.

Loveless, William - Rank in Private. Rank out Private.

Maberry, Henry - Rank in Sergeant. Rank out Private.

Maberry, John S. - Rank in Private. Rank out Private.

Maberry, P.S. - Rank in Second Lieutenant. Rank out Second Lieutenant.

Malugin, G.W. - Rank in Private. Rank out Sergeant.

Malugin, Robert B. - Rank in Private. Rank out Private.

Mass, T.F. - Rank in Private. Rank out Private.

Mayberry, Henry - Rank in Sergeant. Rank out Private.

Mayberry, P.S. - Rank in Second Lieutenant. Rank out Second Lieutenant.

McCaleb, F.P. - Rank in Private. Rank out Private.

McCaleb, Franklin P. - Rank in Private. Rank out Private.

McCard, W.C. - Rank in Sergeant. Rank out Private.

McClanahan, J.L. - Rank in Private. Rank out Private.

McClanahan, John L. - Rank in Private. Rank out Private.

McClanahan, Robert - Rank in Private. Rank out Private.

McClaren, Adolphus - Rank in Private. Rank out Private.

McClaren, Robert - Rank in Private. Rank out Private.

McClarin, Robert - Rank in Private. Rank out Private.

McCord, J.H. - Rank in Private. Rank out Private.

McCord, Jerome H. - Rank in Private. Rank out Private.

McCord, W.C. - Rank in Sergeant. Rank out Private.

McCowen, I.H. - Rank in Private. Rank out Private.

McLanahan, J.L. - Rank in Private. Rank out Private.

McLarin, Adolphus - Rank in Private. Rank out Private.

McLuren, Adolphes - Rank in Private. Rank out Private.

Melt, Robert - Rank in Private. Rank out Private.

Mett, Robert - Rank in Private. Rank out Private.

Milam, Burris M. - Rank in Private. Rank out Private.

Milam, George W. - Rank in Private. Rank out Private.

Milam, W.M. - Rank in Private. Rank out Private.

Milom, Charles - Rank in Private. Rank out Private.

Miloms, C.M. - Rank in Private. Rank out Private.

Morrison, Joel P. - Rank in Private. Rank out Private.

Moss, G. - Rank in Private. Rank out Private.

Moss, J.F. - Rank in Private. Rank out Private.

Moss, N.F. - Rank in Private. Rank out Private.

Moss, T.F. - Rank in Private. Rank out Private.

Moss, Thomas Fletcher - Rank in Private. Rank out Private.

Mumley, John A. - Rank in Private. Rank out Private.

Nunelly, J.D.L. - Rank in First Lieutenant. Rank out First Lieutenant.

Nunley, J.A. - Rank in Private. Rank out Private.

Nunnelee, J.A. - Rank in Private. Rank out Private.

Nunnelee, James D.L. - Rank in First Lieutenant. Rank out First Lieutenant.

Nunneley, John A. - Rank in Private. Rank out Private.

Nunnelley, John A. - Rank in Private. Rank out Private.

Nutt, R.C. - Rank in Private. Rank out Private.

Nutt, Robert - Rank in Private. Rank out Private.

Oliver, W.E. - Rank in Private. Rank out Private.

Overby, Alexander - Rank in Private. Rank out Private.

Pace, Pleasant G. - Rank in Private. Rank out Private.

Pace, Samuel - Rank in Private. Rank out Private.

Pace, Wilson - Rank in Private. Rank out Private.

Parker, Andrew J. - Rank in Second Sergeant. Rank out Second Sergeant.

Parker, James P. - Rank in Private. Rank out Private.

Parker, Moses E. - Rank in Private. Rank out Private.

Parker, S.P. - Rank in Private. Rank out Sergeant.

Parker, Samuel P. - Rank in Private. Rank out Sergeant.

Parker, Samuel P. - Rank in Private. Rank out Sergeant.

Peeler, Josiah G. - Rank in Private. Rank out Second Lieutenant.

Peeler, W.T. - Rank in Private. Rank out Private.

Perry, Benjamin - Rank in Private. Rank out Private.

Pickard, Jesse A. - Rank in Private. Rank out Private.

Pickard, John L. - Rank in Private. Rank out Private.

Pinkerton, Dave C. - Rank in Private. Rank out Private.

Pinkerton, William - Rank in Private. Rank out Private.

Pinkerton, Jr., William - Rank in Private. Rank out Private.

Poplin, M.P. - Rank in Private. Rank out Private.

Poptin, M.P. - Rank in Private. Rank out Private.

Primm, H.G. - Rank in Private. Rank out Private.

Ragsdale, W.N. - Rank in Private. Rank out Private.

Reaves, David - Rank in Private. Rank out Private.

Reaves, J.J. - Rank in Private. Rank out Private.

Reaves, L.E. - Rank in Corporal. Rank out Private.

Reaves, Leonidas E. - Rank in Corporal. Rank out Private.

Reaves, S.J. - Rank in Private. Rank out Private.

Reece, James M. - Rank in Private. Rank out Private.

Reese, James M. - Rank in Private. Rank out Private.

Rivers, Daniel D. - Rank in Corporal. Rank out Corporal.

Rivers, Joel - Rank in Private. Rank out Private.

Rivers, Martin M. - Rank in Private. Rank out Private.

Roberts, F.A. - Rank in Private. Rank out Private.

Robinson, Newton J. - Rank in Private. Rank out Private.

Sanders, Wiley M. - Rank in Drummer. Rank out Private.

Sisco, Fielders H. - Rank in Private. Rank out Private.

Sisco, John - Rank in Private. Rank out Private.

Sisco, John E. - Rank in Private. Rank out Private.

Smith, W.G. - Rank in Private. Rank out Private.

Stephen, J.P. - Rank in Private. Rank out Private.

Stephens, Albert H. - Rank in Private. Rank out Private.

Stephens, Charles - Rank in Private. Rank out Private.

Stephens, J.K. - Rank in Private. Rank out Private.

Stephens, John - Rank in Private. Rank out Private.

Sterns, A.H. - Rank in Private. Rank out Private.

Stevens, Albert - Rank in Private. Rank out Private.

Stevens, Charles - Rank in Private. Rank out Private.

Stevens, J.K. - Rank in Private. Rank out Private.

Stevens, J.P. - Rank in Private. Rank out Private.

Stevens, John - Rank in Private. Rank out Private.

Steward, Wiley - Rank in Private. Rank out Private.

Stewart, Wiley - Rank in Private. Rank out Private.

Stoops, William H. - Rank in Private. Rank out Private.

Stuard, Wiley - Rank in Private. Rank out Private.

Tatum, Sublet A. - Rank in Private. Rank out Private.

Termon, Kerney - Rank in Private. Rank out Private.

Thomptin, William B. - Rank in Private. Rank out Private.

Thornton, William B. - Rank in Private. Rank out Private.

Thurman, J.A. - Rank in Private. Rank out Corporal.

Thurman, James A. - Rank in Private. Rank out Corporal.

Thurman, Jay A. - Rank in Private. Rank out Corporal.

Tibbs, William A. - Rank in Private. Rank out Private.

Tolly, M.W. - Rank in Private. Rank out Private.

Tucker, James H. - Rank in Private. Rank out Private.

Turman, Kerney - Rank in Private. Rank out Private.

Turner, Andrew J. - Rank in Private. Rank out Private.

Turner, Elias - Rank in Private. Rank out Private.

Turner, Willis - Rank in Corporal. Rank out Private.

Turnlaw, J. A. - Rank in Private. Rank out Private.

Twilley, Elias P. - Rank in Private. Rank out Private.

Tyler, J. W. - Rank in Corporal. Rank out Private.

Tyler, James W. - Rank in Corporal. Rank out Private.

Underhill, D. H. - Rank in Private. Rank out Private.

Underhill, Daniel - Rank in Private. Rank out Private.

Wafford, W.P. - Rank in Private. Rank out Private.

Walker, T.J. - Rank in Private. Rank out Private.

Warf, W.T. - Rank in Private. Rank out Private.

Warford, W.P. - Rank in Private. Rank out Private.

Warford, W.P. - Rank in Private. Rank out Private.

Warren, E.T. - Rank in Private. Rank out .

Warren, Elijah - Rank in Private. Rank out Private.

Warren, Elijah W. - Rank in Private. Rank out Private.

Warren, John T. - Rank in Private. Rank out Private.

Warren, R.W. - Rank in Private. Rank out Private.

Warren, Ralph - Rank in Private. Rank out Private.

Warren, Robert J. - Rank in Private. Rank out Private.

Warren, T.J. - Rank in Private. Rank out Private.

White, Andrew J. - Rank in Fifer. Rank out Regimental Fifer.

Williams, J.J. - Rank in Captain. Rank out Lieutenant Colonel.

Wofford, William P. - Rank in Private. Rank out Private.

Worf, B.S. - Rank in Private. Rank out Private.

Worf, W.T. - Rank in Private. Rank out Private.

Wright, Frederick B. - Rank in Private. Rank out Private.

Wright, George - Rank in Private. Rank out Private.

Wright, Robert - Rank in Private. Rank out Private.

Young, Nathaniel - Rank in Private. Rank out First Lieutenant.

Company K

Adams, Felix V. - Rank in Private. Rank out Corporal.

Alison, F.T. - Rank in Private. Rank out Private.

Alison, L.T. - Rank in Private. Rank out Private.

Allison, L.D. - Rank in Private. Rank out Private.

Allison, L.T. - Rank in Private. Rank out Private.

Anderson, A.J. - Rank in Private. Rank out Corporal.

Anderson, Andrew - Rank in Private. Rank out Corporal.

Anderson, Elijah - Rank in Private. Rank out Private.

Anderson, Marion - Rank in Private. Rank out Private.

Anderson, William J. - Rank in Private. Rank out Private.

Angell, George W. - Rank in Private. Rank out Private.

Angle, G.W. - Rank in Private. Rank out Private.

Arnold, W.M. - Rank in Private. Rank out Private.

Barton, Daniel J. - Rank in Private. Rank out Private.

Barton, James C. - Rank in Private. Rank out Private.

Bashaw, William B. - Rank in Private. Rank out Private.

Baysdale, M. - Rank in Private. Rank out Private.

Bennett, James D. - Rank in Third Lieutenant. Rank out Second Lieutenant.

Berton, James C. - Rank in Private. Rank out Private.

Bowers, Giles C. - Rank in Private. Rank out Private.

Brown, David O. - Rank in Private. Rank out Private.

Brown, John - Rank in Private. Rank out Private.

Brown, Thomas - Rank in Private. Rank out Private.

Burger, Joshua M. - Rank in Private. Rank out Private.

Calaham, Achilles H. - Rank in Corporal. Rank out Sergeant.

Callahan, Achilles H - Rank in Corporal. Rank out Sergeant.

Calloham, A. H. - Rank in Corporal. Rank out Sergeant.

Campey, James B. - Rank in Private. Rank out Private.

Campsey, James B. - Rank in Private. Rank out Private.

Clay, William H. - Rank in Private. Rank out Private.

Coulson, David G. - Rank in Private. Rank out Private.

Crick, John - Rank in Private. Rank out Private.

Crick, McDonald - Rank in Private. Rank out Private.

Daniel, Joseph W. - Rank in Private. Rank out Private.

Davenport, Benjamin - Rank in Private. Rank out Private.

Dayton, J.W. - Rank in Private. Rank out Private.

Denny, W.B. - Rank in Private. Rank out Private.

Denton, James M. - Rank in Private. Rank out Private.

Denton, James W. - Rank in Private. Rank out Private.

Denton, T.W. - Rank in Private. Rank out Private.

Dice, Silas - Rank in Private. Rank out Private.

Eaton, James H. - Rank in Private. Rank out Private.

Edwards, I.W. - Rank in Sergeant. Rank out Private.

Edwards, S. Walker - Rank in Sergeant. Rank out Private.

Eubanks, George W. - Rank in Private. Rank out Private.

Fletcher, Greenville - Rank in Private. Rank out Private.

Fletcher, James P. - Rank in Private. Rank out Private.

Foard, James C. - Rank in Private. Rank out Private.

Frazier, A.J. - Rank in Private. Rank out Private.

Frazier, Harmon A. - Rank in Sergeant. Rank out Private.

Frazier, Isaac T. - Rank in Private. Rank out Corporal.

Furguson, Marshall - Rank in Private. Rank out Private.

Gett, George W. - Rank in Private. Rank out Private.

Gill, Albert B. - Rank in Private. Rank out Private.

Gill, Alfred B. - Rank in Private. Rank out Private.

Glenn, Caleb M. - Rank in Private. Rank out Private.

Goodner, T.C. - Rank in Captain. Rank out Captain.

Harlan, Thomas J. - Rank in Private. Rank out First Lieutenant.

Harland, Thomas J. - Rank in Private. Rank out Lieutenant.

Harland, Thos - Rank in Private. Rank out First Lieutenant.

Harlin, T.J. - Rank in Private. Rank out First Lieutenant.

Harmon, James K. - Rank in Corporal. Rank out Corporal.

Harper, James M. - Rank in Private. Rank out Corporal.

Hickerson, Joseph - Rank in Private. Rank out Private.

Hodge, Martin C. - Rank in Private. Rank out Private.

Hoggatt, John W. - Rank in Private. Rank out Private.

Hoggett, John W. - Rank in Private. Rank out Private.

Ingram, James A. - Rank in Private. Rank out Corporal.

Jarrell, Charles - Rank in Private. Rank out Private.

Jarrell, James C. - Rank in Private. Rank out Private.

Jenkins, Daniel E. - Rank in Private. Rank out Private.

Jerald, Charles - Rank in Private. Rank out Private.

Jerald, James C. - Rank in Private. Rank out Private.

Jett, Edward - Rank in Private. Rank out Private.

Jett, George W. - Rank in Private. Rank out Private.

Jett, Thomas B. - Rank in Private. Rank out Private.

Johnson, Harvey - Rank in Private. Rank out Private.

Jones, George - Rank in Sergeant. Rank out Sergeant.

Jones, Nathan M. - Rank in Private. Rank out Private.

Jones, Nathan N. - Rank in Private. Rank out Private.

Kallahan, A.H. - Rank in Corporal. Rank out Sergeant.

Koger, Peter H. - Rank in Private. Rank out Private.

Lusk, Edmond - Rank in Private. Rank out Private.

Martin, Joseph E. - Rank in Private. Rank out Private.

Martin, W.P. - Rank in Private. Rank out Private.

Martin, William T. - Rank in Private. Rank out Private.

McBrown, Henry C. - Rank in Second Lieutenant. Rank out Second Lieutenant.

McCall, David D. - Rank in Private. Rank out Private.

McCall, Henry B. - Rank in Private. Rank out Second Lieutenant.

McCammey, William B. - Rank in Private. Rank out Private.

McCammry, William B. - Rank in Private. Rank out Private.

McCanny, William B. - Rank in Private. Rank out Private.

McCarny, William B. - Rank in Private. Rank out Private.

McConnald, J.A. - Rank in Sergeant. Rank out Private.

McCrea, Nathan T. - Rank in Private. Rank out Private.

McCutchan, Robert A. - Rank in Private. Rank out Private.

McCutcheon, R.A. - Rank in Private. Rank out Private.

McCutchun, R.A. - Rank in Private. Rank out Private.

McDonald, Joseph A. - Rank in Sergeant. Rank out Private.

McDonald, Roderick C. - Rank in Private. Rank out Private.

McGuire, Robert - Rank in Private. Rank out Second Lieutenant.

McGuire, William J. - Rank in Private. Rank out Private.

McGuire, William Jackson - Rank in Private. Rank out Private.

McKanny, W.B. - Rank in Private. Rank out Private.

McKinney, W.B. - Rank in Private. Rank out Private.

Melven, Nathan F. - Rank in Private. Rank out Private.

Melvin, Nathan N. - Rank in Private. Rank out Private.

Melvin, Nathan T. - Rank in Private. Rank out Private.

Melvin, Nathan T. - Rank in Private. Rank out Private.

Moore, John S. - Rank in Private. Rank out Private.

Morrow, Bethel A. - Rank in Corporal. Rank out Private.

Morrow, David - Rank in Private. Rank out Private.

North, William P. - Rank in Private. Rank out Sergeant.

Nunley, John - Rank in Private. Rank out Private.

Nunnelly, John - Rank in Private. Rank out Private.

Nunnely, John - Rank in Private. Rank out Private.

Ofield, Allen - Rank in Private. Rank out Private.

Oldfield, Allen - Rank in Private. Rank out Private.

Owen, John Green - Rank in Private. Rank out Private.

Pemberton, Daniel W. - Rank in Private. Rank out Private.

Pemberton, J.C. - Rank in Private. Rank out Private.

Petty, Thomas C. - Rank in Private. Rank out Private.

Phillips, Newsom - Rank in Private. Rank out Private.

Ponder, Benjamin - Rank in Private. Rank out Private.

Powers, Anderson - Rank in First Sergeant. Rank out First Sergeant.

Powers, Andrew J. - Rank in Private. Rank out Private.

Puckett, Samuel M. - Rank in Private. Rank out Private.

Ragsdale, Francis H. - Rank in Second Lieutenant. Rank out Captain.

Scissom, William W. - Rank in Private. Rank out Private.

Seay, William A. - Rank in First Lieutenant. Rank out First Lieutenant.

Sissom, William W. - Rank in Private. Rank out Private.

Smith, Egbert P. - Rank in Private. Rank out Private.

Stephens, A.K. - Rank in Private. Rank out Private.

Stevens, A.K. - Rank in Private. Rank out Private.

Stevens, Lilburn H. - Rank in Private. Rank out Corporal.

Swann, Churchwell - Rank in Private. Rank out Private.

Swann, Thomas F. - Rank in Private. Rank out Private.

Taylor, Hardin H. - Rank in Private. Rank out Private.

Taylor, John M. - Rank in Private. Rank out First Sergeant.

Taylor, William J. - Rank in Private. Rank out Private.

Teal, Robert - Rank in Private. Rank out Private.

Teel, Robert - Rank in Private. Rank out Private.

Tucker, James D. - Rank in Private. Rank out Private.

Tucker, Telem H. - Rank in Private. Rank out Private.

Turman, B.B. - Rank in Private. Rank out Private.

Waite, George B. - Rank in Private. Rank out Private.

Waite, George W. - Rank in Private. Rank out Private.

Walker, H.N. - Rank in Private. Rank out Private.

West, Daniel T. - Rank in Private. Rank out Private.

White, William T. - Rank in Private. Rank out Private.

Williams, A.N. - Rank in Private. Rank out Chief Musician.

Williams, Benjamin B. - Rank in Private. Rank out Private.

Williams, James M. - Rank in Private. Rank out Musician.

Williams, Joshua A. - Rank in Private. Rank out Private.

Williams, N.B. - Rank in Musician. Rank out Musician.

Williams, Z.T. - Rank in Musician. Rank out Musician.

Wilson, Edward - Rank in Private. Rank out Sergeant.

Wiser, J.W. - Rank in Private. Rank out Private.

Wiser, John W. - Rank in Private. Rank out Private.

Wooten, Leroy C. - Rank in Private. Rank out Private.

Wright, G.W. - Rank in Private. Rank out Private.

Wright, G.W. - Rank in Private. Rank out Private.

Wright, Joseph N. - Rank in Corporal. Rank out Corporal.

Company L

Bennett, Lycurgus L. - Rank in First Sergeant. Rank out Ordnance Sergeant.

Dyar, Joseph S. - Rank in Private. Rank out Private.

Dyer, Joseph S. - Rank in Private. Rank out Private.

Finney, John L. - Rank in Private. Rank out Private.

Finney, John T. - Rank in Private. Rank out Private.

Finny, John T. - Rank in Private. Rank out Private.

Gibson, Decalb C. - Rank in Private. Rank out Private.

Gipson, Decalb C. - Rank in Private. Rank out Private.

Herrin, John - Rank in Private. Rank out Private.

Hindman, Alex - Rank in Private. Rank out Private.

Hipp, David D. - Rank in Third Lieutenant. Rank out Second Lieutenant.

Johnson, A.S. - Rank in Private. Rank out Private.

Johnson, Aaron L. - Rank in Private. Rank out Private.

Johnson, Calvin - Rank in Private. Rank out Private.

Johnson, W. Calvin - Rank in Private. Rank out Private.

Jones, Thomas F. - Rank in Private. Rank out Private.

Linton, Marcus E. - Rank in Private. Rank out Private.

Linton, W.C. - Rank in Private. Rank out Private.

Long, A. Samuel - Rank in Private. Rank out Private.

Long, J.P.K. - Rank in Private. Rank out Private.

Long, James K.P. - Rank in Private. Rank out Private.

Long, James P. - Rank in Private. Rank out Private.

Long, Samuel A. - Rank in Private. Rank out Private.

Lonton, Marcus - Rank in Private. Rank out Private.

Lusk, George W. - Rank in Corporal. Rank out Corporal.

Lynch, William - Rank in Private. Rank out Private.

Nevels, John S. - Rank in Private. Rank out Corporal.

Nevill, John L. - Rank in Private. Rank out Corporal.

Newman, Isham B. - Rank in Private. Rank out Private.

Newsom, Andrew J. - Rank in Private. Rank out Private.

Oliver, John H. - Rank in Second Lieutenant. Rank out Captain.

Partin, F.M. - Rank in Private. Rank out Private.

Parton, Francis M. - Rank in Private. Rank out Private.

Pearson, Farrar - Rank in Private. Rank out Private.

Perry, William P. - Rank in Private. Rank out Private.

Persons, Farrar - Rank in Private. Rank out Private.

Pool, James - Rank in Private. Rank out Private.

Purdie, Pleasant P. - Rank in Private. Rank out Private.

Purdy, P.P. - Rank in Private. Rank out Private.

Quinn, Hugh - Rank in Private. Rank out Private.

Rice, William A. - Rank in Private. Rank out First Lieutenant/Adjutant.

Roddy, Albert D. - Rank in Private. Rank out Private.

Roddy, Benjamin F. - Rank in Private. Rank out Private.

Roddy, Joseph G. - Rank in Private. Rank out Second Lieutenant.

Rose, Martin V. - Rank in Private. Rank out Private.

Rutherford, A.Sidney - Rank in Private. Rank out Private.

Smith, John - Rank in Private. Rank out Private.

Wildman, J.D. - Rank in Private. Rank out Private.

Wileman, James D. - Rank in Private. Rank out Private.

Wileman, William - Rank in Private. Rank out Private.

Wilson, Francis M. - Rank in Private. Rank out Corporal.

Wilson, Marquis D. L. - Rank in Private. Rank out Private.

Winton, G.G. - Rank in Private. Rank out Private.

Winton, George - Rank in Private. Rank out Private.

Withrow, John F. - Rank in Private. Rank out Private.

Withrow, Samuel - Rank in Private. Rank out Private.

Womack, Francis M. - Rank in Sergeant. Rank out Private.

Company Unknown

Anderson, S.W - Rank in Private. Rank out Private.

Aldridge (Aldrige), S.B. - Rank in Private. Rank out Private.

Allison, Joseph A. - Rank in Private. Rank out Private.

Anderson, A.S. - Rank in Private. Rank out Private.

Anderson, Alex P. - Rank in Private. Rank out Private.

Anderson, D.C. - Rank in Private. Rank out Private.

Anderson, George N. - Rank in Private. Rank out Sergeant.

Anderson, George W. - Rank in Private. Rank out Sergeant.

Anderson, J.G. - Rank in First Lieutenant. Rank out First Lieutenant.

Anderson, J.N. - Rank in Sergeant. Rank out Lieutenant.

Anderson, James - Rank in Private. Rank out Private.

Anderson, R.M. - Rank in Private. Rank out Private.

Anderson, T.W. - Rank in Private. Rank out Sergeant.

Anderson, William S. - Rank in Private. Rank out Private.

Anglin, F.M. - Rank in Private. Rank out Private.

Armistead, David H. - Rank in Private. Rank out Private.

Armistead, Robert B. - Rank in Sergeant. Rank out Second Lieutenant.

Arnold, John B. - Rank in Corporal. Rank out First Lieutenant.

Arnold, W.D. - Rank in Private. Rank out Private.

Arnold, W.M. - Rank in Private. Rank out Private.

Arnold, William - Rank in Private. Rank out Private.

Auldredg, S.B. - Rank in Private. Rank out Private.

Bain, F.M. - Rank in Private. Rank out Private.

Baird, A.G. - Rank in Private. Rank out Private.

Baird, W.C. - Rank in Private. Rank out Private.

Baker, W.D. - Rank in Corporal. Rank out Corporal.

Ballard, F.M. - Rank in Private. Rank out Second Lieutenant.

Bane, F.M. - Rank in Private. Rank out Private.

Bates, R.H. - Rank in Private. Rank out Private.

Bates, Z.B. - Rank in Private. Rank out Private.

Beale, C.W. - Rank in Captain. Rank out Captain.

Beard, W.B. - Rank in Private. Rank out Private.

Beard, W.C. - Rank in Private. Rank out Private.

Beasley, E.R. - Rank in Private. Rank out Private.

Beasley, Isaac J. - Rank in Private. Rank out Private.

Beasley, William R. - Rank in Private. Rank out Private.

Beesly, Isaac J. - Rank in Private. Rank out Private.

Beesly, William H. - Rank in Private. Rank out Private.

Beggers, John L. - Rank in Private. Rank out Private.

Bennett, James D. - Rank in Third Lieutenant. Rank out Second Lieutenant.

Borroughs, G.G. - Rank in Private. Rank out Private.

Bradley, M. M. - Rank in Private. Rank out Corporal.

Bratton, R.F. - Rank in Sergeant. Rank out Private.

Brickle, J.A. - Rank in Private. Rank out Corporal.

Brixey, Samuel H. - Rank in Private. Rank out Private.

Burrows, George G. - Rank in Private. Rank out Private.

Campbell, H. C. - Rank in First Sergeant. Rank out Captain.

Cardwell, William L. - Rank in Private. Rank out Private.

Carter, Isaac - Rank in Private. Rank out Private.

Carter, William H. - Rank in Private. Rank out Private.

Charles, John O. - Rank in Private. Rank out Private.

Cheek, C.M. - Rank in Private. Rank out Private.

Clark, J.H. - Rank in Private. Rank out First Sergeant.

Clark, Joseph - Rank in Private. Rank out Private.

Clark, R.D. - Rank in Private. Rank out Private.

Clark, Robert D. - Rank in Private. Rank out Private.

Clark, Thomas W. - Rank in Private. Rank out Private.

Cleavland, Alex P. - Rank in Sergeant. Rank out Sergeant.

Clymer, J.D. - Rank in Private. Rank out Private.

Cook, James C. - Rank in Private. Rank out Private.

Cornwell, Benjamin S. - Rank in Second Lieutenant. Rank out Second Lieutenant.

Cox, James M. - Rank in Private. Rank out Private.

Crownover, C.B. - Rank in Private. Rank out Private.

Crownover, Charles P. - Rank in Private. Rank out Private.

Davis, Rufus - Rank in Private. Rank out Private.

Dawrighty, J.A. - Rank in Corporal. Rank out Corporal.

Dawson, L.H. - Rank in Private. Rank out Private.

Dawson, R.K. - Rank in Second Lieutenant. Rank out Second Lieutenant.

Dean, J.W. - Rank in Private. Rank out Private.

Deen, J.W. - Rank in Private. Rank out Private.

Dellehay, John H. - Rank in Private. Rank out Private.

Derryberry, A.J. - Rank in Private. Rank out Private.

Derryberry, J.H. - Rank in Private. Rank out Private.

Dickens, James F. - Rank in Private. Rank out Private.

Dillahay, James A. - Rank in Private. Rank out Corporal.

Dillahay, James P. - Rank in Private. Rank out Private.

Dillahay, James T. - Rank in Corporal. Rank out Corporal.

Dillahay, John H. - Rank in Private. Rank out Private.

Dillahay, Robert J. - Rank in Private. Rank out Private.

Dillehay, James A. - Rank in Private. Rank out Corporal.

Dillehay, James P. - Rank in Private. Rank out Private.

Dillehay, James T. - Rank in Corporal. Rank out Corporal.

Dillehay, John H. - Rank in Private. Rank out Private.

Dillehay, Robert J. - Rank in Private. Rank out Private.

Dillihay, J. A. - Rank in Private. Rank out Corporal.

Dixon, John G. - Rank in Private. Rank out Private.

Dotson, William C. - Rank in Private. Rank out Private.

Dougherty, James H. - Rank in Corporal. Rank out Corporal.

Dowell Jr., M.C. - Rank in Private. Rank out Private.

Dunlap, James - Rank in Private. Rank out Private.

Dyer, Dixon - Rank in Private. Rank out Private.

Farris, William G. - Rank in Private. Rank out Private.

Ferguson, Charles L. - Rank in Musician. Rank out Musician.

Fly, J.M. - Rank in Private. Rank out Private.

Foard, James C. - Rank in Private. Rank out Private.

Ford, James C. - Rank in Private. Rank out Private.

Fuller, J.H. - Rank in Private. Rank out Private.

Fuller, J.W. - Rank in Private. Rank out Private.

Furgerson, Archibald W. - Rank in Private. Rank out Private.

Furgerson, C.L. - Rank in Musician. Rank out Musician.

Furgerson, Charles - Rank in Musician. Rank out Musician.

Furman, R. - Rank in Private. Rank out Private.

Gregory, William Jesse - Rank in Private. Rank out Private.

Groves, Henry - Rank in Private. Rank out Private.

Gwinn, James - Rank in Private. Rank out Private.

Hance, Erastus S. - Rank in First Lieutenant. Rank out Captain.

Read, N.B. - Rank in Private. Rank out Private.

Rice, Steaphen C. - Rank in Private. Rank out Private.

Richardson, Riley S. - Rank in Private. Rank out Private.

Ried, Braddock - Rank in Private. Rank out Private.

Riley, Isaac N. - Rank in Private. Rank out Second Lieutenant.

Riley, James N. - Rank in Private. Rank out Second Lieutenant.

Riley, John H. - Rank in Private. Rank out Private.

Robbins, William T. - Rank in Corporal. Rank out Private.

Roberts, Isaac T. - Rank in First Lieutenant. Rank out Captain.

Roulett, B.F. - Rank in Second Lieutenant. Rank out Second Lieutenant.

Rowlett, B.F. - Rank in Second Lieutenant. Rank out Second Lieutenant.

Russell, H.T. - Rank in Private. Rank out .

Russell, William S. - Rank in Private. Rank out Private.

Rutherford, Elliott - Rank in Private. Rank out Private.

Sanders, William V. - Rank in Musician. Rank out Musician.

Sansom, Green F. - Rank in Private. Rank out Sergeant.

Scruggs, T. S. J. - Rank in Private. Rank out Private.

Scully, Thomas - Rank in Private. Rank out Private.

Secres, W.S. - Rank in Private. Rank out Private.

Secrest, Dock - Rank in Private. Rank out Private.

Secrest, I.S. - Rank in First Lieutenant. Rank out First Lieutenant.

Secrest, S.W. - Rank in Private. Rank out Private.

Sharp, Thomas A. - Rank in Private. Rank out Private.

Sharp, William A. - Rank in Private. Rank out Private.

Shaw, J.M. - Rank in Private. Rank out Corporal.

Shires, W.H. - Rank in First Sergeant. Rank out First Lieutenant.

Sholders, William L. - Rank in Private. Rank out Private.

Sims, Zachariah - Rank in Private. Rank out Private.

Slayden, A.J. - Rank in Private. Rank out Private.

Slayden, Andrew J. - Rank in Private. Rank out Private.

Sloan, S.N. - Rank in Private. Rank out Corporal.

Slone, Sidney M. - Rank in Private. Rank out Corporal.

Smith, Harrison - Rank in Corporal. Rank out Corporal.

Smith, John N. - Rank in Private. Rank out Second Lieutenant.

Smith, Walter - Rank in Private. Rank out Sergeant.

Smith, William H. - Rank in Private. Rank out Private.

Stephens, Anther N. - Rank in Private. Rank out Private.

Stevens, J.K. - Rank in Private. Rank out Private.

Thomas, John F. - Rank in Private. Rank out Private.

Thomas, Joseph W. - Rank in Private. Rank out Second Lieutenant.

Thomas, William A. - Rank in Private. Rank out Private.

Thomas, William J. - Rank in Private. Rank out Private.

Thompson, B.J. - Rank in Private. Rank out Private.

Thompson, Benjamin B. - Rank in Sergeant. Rank out Private.

Tyler, J. W. - Rank in Corporal. Rank out Private.

Tyler, James W. - Rank in Corporal. Rank out Private.

Warren, W.C. - Rank in Private. Rank out Private.

Wilkerson, J.H.P. - Rank in Private. Rank out Private.

Wilkinson, James K.P. - Rank in Private. Rank out Private.

Williams, Bailey P. - Rank in Private. Rank out Private.

Williams, Daly T. - Rank in Private. Rank out Private.

Williams, H.M. - Rank in Private. Rank out Private.

Williams, J.B. - Rank in Private. Rank out Private.

Williams, James H. - Rank in Private. Rank out Corporal.

Williams, Jerome B. - Rank in Private. Rank out Private.

Womack, William H.H. - Rank in Private. Rank out Private.

Worf, B.S. - Rank in Private. Rank out Private.

Bibliography

Tennessee 24th Infantry Regiment

Confederate Military History, Extended Edition. Vol. 10: Tennessee. 806 p. E484C65.1987v10. (Contains numerous, scattered references to Tennessee units). This book is included on our Civil War in Tennessee CD-ROM and is also available on CD-ROM as a part of The Confederate Military History

Crute, Joseph H., Jr. **Units of the Confederate States Army.** Midlothian, VA: Derwent Books, 1987. Ref. Concise summary of the regiment's service.

Ferguson, Edwin L. **Sumner County, Tennessee In the Civil War**

Lindsley, John B., ed. **The Military Annals of Tennessee: Confederate.** Nashville, TN: Lindsley, 1886. E579.4L75. (Brief unit history).

Sifakis, Stewart. **Compendium of the Confederate Armies: Tennessee.** NY: Facts on File, 1992. E579S53.1992. (Unit organizational history).

Tennessee. CW Centennial Comm. **Tennesseans in the Civil War: A Military History of Union and Confederate Units...** Nashville, TN: By the Comm, 1964. E579.5A53v1. (Brief unit history)

On Line Sites:

http:www.tngenweb.org/sumner/sumnfg7c.htm

http://www.tngenweb.org/dekalb/goodners.htm#Co.%20F

http://www.tngenweb.org/dekalb/goodners.htm#Co.%20F

http://duckriverrifles.50megs.com/custom2.html

Index

Anderson, S.W ~ Co. I H
Abraham, B.Ellis ~ Co. C
Adams, Felix V. ~ Co. K
Adams, P.L. ~ Co. F
Adams, S.D. ~ Co. C
Adams, William L. ~ Co. C
Adcock, Allen ~ Co. I
Adcox, Alen ~ Co. I
Albright, J.W. ~ Co. E
Aldridge, A.J. ~ Co. D
Aldridge, S.B. ~ Co. 1 G
Aldrige, S.B. ~ Co. 1 G
Alexander, Thomas ~ Co. I
Alison, F.T. ~ Co. K
Alison, L.T. ~ Co. K
Alldridge, A.J. ~ Co. D
Allen, D.L. ~ Co. F
Allen, David L. ~ Co. F
Allen, H.H. ~ Co. D
Allison, Alfred J. ~ Co. A
Allison, Andrew J. ~ Co. A
Allison, Joseph ~ Co. F
Allison, Joseph A. ~ Co. 2 G
Allison, L.D. ~ Co. K
Allison, L.T. ~ Co. K
Allison, R.D. ~ Co. F
Allison, Robert ~ Co. F
Allman, John ~ Co. F
Allmon, J.A. ~ Co. F
Anderson, A.J. ~ Co. K
Anderson, A.S. ~ Co. 2 G
Anderson, Alex P. ~ Co. 2 G
Anderson, Andrew ~ Co. K
Anderson, C.H. ~ Co. E
Anderson, D.C. ~ Co. H I
Anderson, Elijah ~ Co. K
Anderson, George N. ~ Co. 2 G
Anderson, George W. ~ Co. 2 G
Anderson, J.G. ~ Co. 1 H
Anderson, J.N. ~ Co. 1 H

Anderson, J.T. ~ Co. I
Anderson, James ~ Co. 2 G
Anderson, Marion ~ Co. K
Anderson, R.M. ~ Co. 1 H
Anderson, T.W. ~ Co. 2 G
Anderson, W.S. ~ Co. 1 H
Anderson, William J. ~ Co. K
Anderson, William S. ~ Co. 1 H
Angell, George W. ~ Co. K
Angle, G.W. ~ Co. K
Anglen, N.J. ~ Co. 1HI
Anglin, F.M. ~ Co. 1 H
Anglin, J.N. ~ Co. 1HI
Anglin, N.J. ~ Co. 1HI
Anglin, Newton ~ Co. 1HI
Anglin, W. ~ Co. 1HI
Angling, N.J. ~ Co. 1HI
Arbuckle, C.T.L. ~ Co. A
Armistead, David H. ~ Co. 2 H
Armistead, Robert B. ~ Co. 2 H
Armstrong, Nathaniel W. ~ Co. I
Arnold, Benjamin F. ~ Co. I
Arnold, Henry ~ Co. A
Arnold, John B. ~ Co. 2 G
Arnold, W.D. ~ Co. 1 H
Arnold, W.D. ~ Co. I
Arnold, W.M. ~ Co. 1 K
Arnold, William ~ Co. 1 H
Aronheart, W.A. ~ Co. D
Askew, J.T. ~ Co. F
Askins, Alonzo ~ Co. I
Auldredg, S.B. ~ Co. 1 G
Austin, H.M. ~ Co. E
Austin, Henry M. ~ Co. E
Auston, H.M. ~ Co. E
Babb, W.F.P. ~ Co. H
Bain, Ed. C. ~ Co. B
Bain, F.M. ~ Co. 1 G
Baird, A.G. ~ Co. 1 H
Baird, W.C. ~ Co. 1 H

Baird, W.J. ~ Co. I
Baker, Elijah ~ Co. I
Baker, L.B. ~ Co. F
Baker, L.R. ~ Co. F
Baker, Luther B. ~ Co. F
Baker, Milow ~ Co. I
Baker, W.D. ~ Co. 1 H
Ballard, F.M. ~ Co. 1 H
Bane, F.M. ~ Co. 1 G
Barbee, E.A. ~ Co. F
Barbee, Ealumonson A. ~ Co. F
Barbee, Eanderson ~ Co. F
Barber, Wiley A. ~ Co. I
Barham, John F. ~ Co. 1G
Barham, John H. ~ Co. D
Barnes, John H. ~ Co. B
Barnon, Henry C. ~ Co. C
Barns, John A. ~ Co. B
Barrett, James A. ~ Co. F
Barrow, H.C. ~ Co. C
Barrow, Henry C. ~ Co. C
Barrows, H.C. ~ Co. C
Barton, Daniel J. ~ Co. K
Barton, James C. ~ Co. K
Basdal, Jesse ~ Co. B
Basdal, John H. ~ Co. B
Basdal, William D. ~ Co. B
Bashaw, William B. ~ Co. K
Baskerville, John A. ~ Co. E
Baskerville, Richard K. ~ Co. E
Bass, Daniel S. ~ Co. B
Bates, Adolphus ~ Co. I
Bates, B.B. ~ Co. I
Bates, Dennis ~ Co. I
Bates, Moses ~ Co. I
Bates, R.H. ~ Co. 1 H
Bates, Z.B. ~ Co. 1 H
Batey, James K. ~ Co. F
Bauland, J.P. ~ Co. A
Baw, James ~ Co. F
Baysdale, M. ~ Co. 1KI

Bazdale, J.M. ~ Co. B
Bazdale, Jesse J. ~ Co. B
Bazdale, W.D. ~ Co. B
Bazell, George W. ~ Co. B
Bazell, William D. ~ Co. B
Bazen, William D. ~ Co. B
Bazzell, G.M. ~ Co. B
Bazzell, James M. ~ Co. B
Bazzell, Jesse J. ~ Co. B
Bazzell, John H. ~ Co. B
Beadle, R.O. ~ Co. F
Beadle, Richard O. ~ Co. F
Beale, C.W. ~ Co. 1 H
Beard, A.P. ~ Co. B
Beard, W.B. ~ Co. 1 H
Beard, W.C. ~ Co. 1 H
Beasley, E.R. ~ Co. 1 H
Beasley, Isaac J. ~ Co. 2 H
Beasley, James R. ~ Co. B
Beasley, James R. ~ Co. B
Beasley, Jesse ~ Co. M
Beasley, William R. ~ Co. 2 H
Beasly, James R. ~ Co. B
Beatty, A.H. ~ Co. I
Beatty, James K. ~ Co. F
Beatty, Thomas S. ~ Co. I
Bedford, John ~ Co. I
Beech, R.T. ~ Co. B
Beech, Richard ~ Co. B
Beech, William ~ Co. B
Beeck, R.T. ~ Co. B
Beedle, R.O. ~ Co. F
Beesly, Isaac J. ~ Co. 2 H
Beesly, William H. ~ Co. 2 H
Beggers, John L. ~ Co. 1 G
Belt, S.K. ~ Co. C
Belt, W.H. ~ Co. C
Bennett, Jacob ~ Co. B
Bennett, James D. ~ Co. 2 K
Bennett, Lycurgus L. ~ Co. L
Bennett, Thomas A. ~ Co. B

Bennett, W.M. ~ Co. 2G
Bennett, W.P. ~ Co. F
Benton, James C. ~ Co. A
Berge, J.P. ~ Co. B
Berge, William A. ~ Co. B
Berry, William G. ~ Co. 2H
Berton, James C. ~ Co. K
Bertrand, R.B. ~ Co. E
Betts, E.W. ~ Co. F
Betty, James K. ~ Co. F
Betty, James R. ~ Co. F
Bezell, William D. ~ Co. B
Biggar, John R. ~ Co. D
Bigger, John R. ~ Co. D
Bigger, L.C. ~ Co. D
Bigger, William L. ~ Co. D
Biggers, J.L. ~ Co. 1GB
Biggers, John L. ~ Co. 1GB
Billington, James M. ~ Co. G
Black, D.S. ~ Co. 1GB
Black, David ~ Co. 1GB
Black, H. M. ~ Co. C
Black, S. S. ~ Co. 1GB
Black, William F. ~ Co. B
Blackman, Joseph ~ Co. E
Bond, James H. ~ Co. D
Bond, James O. ~ Co. D
Borroughs, G.G. ~ Co. 1 G
Bosdol, James M. ~ Co. B
Bowers, B. ~ Co.
Bowers, G.L. ~ Co. F
Bowers, George M. ~ Co. F
Bowers, Giles C. ~ Co. K
Boyce, A. ~ Co. A
Bozzell, J.H. ~ Co. B
Bradford, A.J. ~ Co. F
Bradford, John ~ Co. I
Bradley, M. M. ~ Co. 1 H
Bradley, Thomas F. ~ Co. F
Branham, J. R. ~ Co. E
Braswell, John ~ Co. F

Braswell, M.D. ~ Co. F
Braswell, Mathew D. ~ Co. F
Braswell, Sampson ~ Co. F
Bratton, H.L.W. ~ Co. C
Bratton, J.A. ~ Co. I
Bratton, James A. ~ Co. I
Bratton, M.J.A. ~ Co. I
Bratton, R.F. ~ Co. 1 H
Bratton, R.W. ~ Co. C
Bratton, Robert Wilson ~ Co. C
Brickle, J.A. ~ Co. 1 H
Bridges, Joseph N. ~ Co. -
Briggs, Samuel ~ Co. F
Britton, Abraham ~ Co. F
Brixey, Samuel H. ~ Co. 2 G
Bromley, James P. ~ Co. E
Brown, C.L. ~ Co. I
Brown, David O. ~ Co. K
Brown, E. G. ~ Co. A
Brown, J.C. ~ Co. C
Brown, J.G. ~ Co. C
Brown, John ~ Co. K
Brown, Lewis C. ~ Co. 2H
Brown, Robert ~ Co. 1GB
Brown, S.C. ~ Co. I
Brown, Thomas ~ Co. K
Brown, Thomas B. ~ Co. F
Brown, Thomas F. ~ Co. F
Brown, W.J. ~ Co. A
Brudford, John ~ Co. I
Brumley, J.P. ~ Co. E
Brumley, T.S. ~ Co. E
Brumley, W.J. ~ Co. E
Buchanan, Elias ~ Co. I
Burge, J.P. ~ Co. B
Burge, William ~ Co. B
Burger, Joshua M. ~ Co. K
Burk, N.C. ~ Co. B
Burk, T.A. ~ Co. B
Burk, Thomas H. ~ Co. B
Burns, C.B. ~ Co. E

Burrow, J.A. ~ Co. C
Burrow, J.W. ~ Co. C
Burrows, George G. ~ Co. 2 G
Burtrand, R.B. ~ Co. E
Butts, Elijah W. ~ Co. F
Buzzell, J.H. ~ Co. B
Byrnes, C.B. ~ Co. E
Cacy, Fleming ~ Co. B
Calaham, Achilles H. ~ Co. K
Caldwell, Thomas H. ~ Co. B
Callahan, Achilles H ~ Co. K
Calloham, A. H. ~ Co. K
Cambell, H. C. ~ Co.
Cambell, James ~ Co. E
Campbell, F. M. ~ Co. I
Campbell, H. C. ~ Co. 1 H
Campbell, James ~ Co. E
Campbell, John F. M. ~ Co. I
Campbell, William D. ~ Co. I
Campbell, William J. ~ Co. I
Campey, James B. ~ Co. K
Campsey, James B. ~ Co. K
Cappee, Henry M. ~ Co. F
Cappee, Robert ~ Co. F
Cardwell, Joseph L. ~ Co. H
Cardwell, Silas H. ~ Co. 2H
Cardwell, William L. ~ Co. 2 H
Carlton, D.O. ~ Co. A
Carlton, J.M. ~ Co. A
Carlton, J.N. ~ Co. A
Carlton, W.J. ~ Co. A
Carn, Franklin W. ~ Co. C
Carnes, W.D.G. ~ Co. F
Carnwell, R.S. ~ Co. 2H
Carr, C.S. ~ Co. C
Carr, D.A. ~ Co. C
Carr, F.W. ~ Co. C
Carr, Franklin W. ~ Co. C
Carr, James A. ~ Co. C
Carr, M.A. ~ Co. C
Carr, Matthew R. ~ Co. C

Carr, N.H. ~ Co. C
Carr, W.K. ~ Co. C
Carsen, J.M. ~ Co. A
Carsen, R.G. ~ Co. A
Carson, J.M. ~ Co. A
Carson, James M. ~ Co. A
Carson, R.G. ~ Co. A
Carson, R.J. ~ Co. A
Carson, W.H.H. ~ Co. A
Carson, William H.H. ~ Co. A
Carter, Isaac ~ Co. 2 H
Carter, J.W. ~ Co. E
Carter, John E. ~ Co. C
Carter, R.L. ~ Co. C
Carter, Richard L. ~ Co. C
Carter, W.B. ~ Co. F
Carter, William H. ~ Co. 2 H
Cash, William ~ Co. I
Casleman, J.J. ~ Co. A
Castleman, J.J. ~ Co. A
Cathey, John A. ~ Co. D
Cauley, John ~ Co. C
Cavender, G.B. ~ Co. I
Cayce, Flemming S. ~ Co. B
Cerbett, J. ~ Co. D
Chadwell, Everett ~ Co. B
Chadwell, John ~ Co. B
Chadwin, John ~ Co. B
Chamberlain, W.F. ~ Co. C
Chamberlain, William L. ~ Co. C
Chamberland, William ~ Co. C
Chamberlin, W.F. ~ Co. C
Chambers, T.J. ~ Co. B
Chamlin, W.F. ~ Co. C
Chandler, T.M. ~ Co. F
Chandler, Thomas ~ Co. F
Chapell, Francis C. ~ Co. I
Chapman, Isaac ~ Co. -
Charles, John O. ~ Co. 2 G
Chartwell, John ~ Co. B
Chatwell, John ~ Co. B

Cheek, C.M. ~ Co. 1 G
Cherry, Isaac J. ~ Co. D
Chrisman, John ~ Co. D
Chrissman, John A. ~ Co. D
Chrisswell, Laban ~ Co. D
Chrisswell, Samuel D. ~ Co. D
Christopher, Alfred N. ~ Co. D
Christwell, S.D. ~ Co. D
Cissoms, J.M. ~ Co. E
Claiborne, J.W. ~ Co. C
Claiborne, W.D. ~ Co. C
Claiborne, W.H.H. ~ Co. C
Claiborne, William H. ~ Co. C
Clara, J.H.T. ~ Co. E
Clark, J.A. ~ Co. F
Clark, J.H. ~ Co. 1 H
Clark, James S. ~ Co. B
Clark, Joseph ~ Co. 1 G
Clark, R.D. ~ Co. 1 G
Clark, Robert D. ~ Co. 1 G
Clark, Thomas W. ~ Co. 1 G
Clay, William H. ~ Co. K
Cleavland, Alex P. ~ Co. 2 H
Cleveland, F.G. ~ Co. A
Clieveland, F.G. ~ Co. A
Climer, J.D. ~ Co. 1HI
Climor, J.D. ~ Co. 1HI
Cloar, J.H.T. ~ Co. E
Clymer, J.D. ~ Co. 1 H
Coal, J.M. ~ Co. E
Cochran, R.A. ~ Co. F
Cochrhan, R.A. ~ Co. F
Cockrhan, R.A. ~ Co. F
Coffee, H.M. ~ Co. F
Coffee, Henry M. ~ Co. F
Coffee, R.D. ~ Co. F
Coffee, Robert ~ Co. F
Cole, A.W. ~ Co. A
Cole, J.M. ~ Co. E
Collens, M.J. ~ Co. A
Collens, W.J. ~ Co. A

Collines, W.A. ~ Co. 1G
Collins, M. J. ~ Co. A
Collins, William A. ~ Co. 1GB
Conger, Josiah ~ Co. F
Congo, Josiah ~ Co. F
Cook, H. C. ~ Co. D
Cook, J. K. ~ Co. A
Cook, J. P. ~ Co. A
Cook, James C. ~ Co. 2 H
Cook, John T. ~ Co. I
Cook, W.J. ~ Co. I
Cook, William J. ~ Co. I
Cooper, David M. ~ Co. I
Cooper, G.W. ~ Co. 1HI
Cooper, Isaac ~ Co. F
Coopper, G.W. ~ Co. 1HI
Copeland, J.B. ~ Co. B
Copeland, John ~ Co. B
Corbett, James ~ Co. D
Corbett, John ~ Co. D
Corbitte, James ~ Co. D
Corbitte, John R. ~ Co. D
Corley, Nathan ~ Co. F
Corly, Nathan ~ Co. F
Cornwell, Benjamin S. ~ Co. 2 H
Cornwell, John S. ~ Co. 4
Cosey, W.L. ~ Co. A
Cotham, William S. ~ Co. I
Cottone, Wm. ~ Co. I
Coulson, David G. ~ Co. K
Coursey, J.B. ~ Co. A
Coursey, Joseph ~ Co. A
Coursey, T.H. ~ Co. A
Coursey, W.L. ~ Co. A
Coursey, William ~ Co. A
Cousey, W.L. ~ Co. A
Covington, Larkin M. ~ Co. D
Covington, M. ~ Co. D
Covington, M.J. ~ Co. F
Covington, R.M. ~ Co. D
Covington, Robert W. ~ Co. D

Covington, W.F. ~ Co. D
Covington, William ~ Co. D
Cowan, George W. ~ Co. B
Cowan, Jo. W. ~ Co. B
Cowen, J.W. ~ Co. B
Cox, G.W. ~ Co. I
Cox, Henry ~ Co. E
Cox, James M. ~ Co. 2 H
Cox, John ~ Co. I
Cozort, Benjamin ~ Co. D
Craddock, J.C.J. ~ Co. F
Craddock, N.L. ~ Co. F
Craftin, Jeseph ~ Co. D
Crafton, Joseph ~ Co. D
Craghead, Joesph ~ Co. 2H
Craghead, Marlin ~ Co. 2H
Craighead, Marlin ~ Co. 2H
Crawford, James ~ Co. C
Crawford, Joseph ~ Co. C
Crawford, T.J. ~ Co. C
Creasey, Frank ~ Co. C
Creasey, Franklin ~ Co. C
Creasey, J.M. ~ Co. C
Creasey, John ~ Co. C
Creek, Samuel ~ Co. D
Creesey, J.M. ~ Co. C
Creesey, John ~ Co. C
Crenshaw, N.D. ~ Co. E
Cresswell, Thomas A. ~ Co. D
Crest, I.L.C. ~ Co. G
Crick, John ~ Co. K
Crick, Joseph W. ~ Co. D
Crick, McDonald ~ Co. K
Crick, Samuel R. ~ Co. D
Crisswell, Thomas A. ~ Co. D
Criswell, Laban ~ Co. D
Criswell, Thomas A. ~ Co. D
Crockett, George B. ~ Co. B
Cromer, Joseph H. ~ Co. D
Cromwell, J.S. ~ Co. M
Cross, Harvy N. ~ Co. I

Crouder, Alex. ~ Co. F
Crowder, A.P. ~ Co. F
Crownover, C.B. ~ Co. 2 G
Crownover, Charles P. ~ Co. 2 G
Culberson, S.H. ~ Co. B
Culbertson, Sam H. ~ Co. B
Cullom, J.W. ~ Co.
Cunningham, Robert W. ~ Co. B
Cunningham, Thomas ~ Co. 1HI
Curl, Thomas B. ~ Co. I
Curl, William Y. ~ Co. I
Curren, Everette P. ~ Co. B
Currin, E.P. ~ Co. B
Curtis, William C. ~ Co. F
Cutler, John J. ~ Co. F
Cutter, John J. ~ Co. F
Daimwood, G.G. ~ Co. 1GB
Daimwood, S.W. ~ Co. B
Dainwood, G.G. ~ Co. 1GB
Dainwood, S.W. ~ Co. B
Dais, Robert ~ Co. C
Dalbins, J.A. ~ Co. E
Dalbins, W.H. ~ Co. E
Dallas, W.M. ~ Co. C
Daniel, Joseph W. ~ Co. K
Daniel, Thomas A. ~ Co. 1GB
Danwood, George G. ~ Co. 1GB
Darity, J.A. ~ Co. 1GB
Darity, T.N. ~ Co. B
Darity, W.L. ~ Co. 1GB
Darmwood, G.G. ~ Co. 1GB
Daugherty, James A. ~ Co. 1IB
Daughrity, James A. ~ Co. 1GB
Daughrity, T.N. ~ Co. B
Daughrity, W.C. ~ Co. 1GB
Daughrity, W.L. ~ Co. 1GB
Daughrity, W.L. ~ Co. 1GB
Davenport, Benjamin ~ Co. K
Davis, George F. ~ Co. B
Davis, John ~ Co. 1GB
Davis, John C. ~ Co. 1GB

The TN 24th Infantry Regiment

Davis, R.G. ~ Co. F
Davis, R.James ~ Co. F
Davis, Robert ~ Co. C
Davis, Robert J. ~ Co. F
Davis, Rufus ~ Co. 2 H
Davis, S.T. ~ Co. A
Davis, W.C. ~ Co. F
Davis, W.E. ~ Co. A
Dawrighty, J.A. ~ Co. 1 G
Dawson, L.H. ~ Co. 1 H
Dawson, R.K. ~ Co. 1 H
Day, E. ~ Co. E
Dayton, J.W. ~ Co. K
Deal, W.M. ~ Co. 1HI
Dean, J.W. ~ Co. 1 G
Dean, R.A. ~ Co. 1HI
Dean, Robert A. ~ Co. 1HI
Dearing, A.J. ~ Co. C
Deel, W. M. ~ Co. 1HI
Deen, J.W. ~ Co. 1 G
Deen, R.A. ~ Co. 1HI
Deerin, A.J. ~ Co. C
Dellehay, J.W. ~ Co. 1GB
Dellehay, John H. ~ Co. 2 H
Deney, W.B. ~ Co. F
Denney, W.B. ~ Co. F
Dennie, W.B. ~ Co. F
Denny, B.R. ~ Co. A
Denny, W.B. ~ Co. K
Denton, James M. ~ Co. K
Denton, James W. ~ Co. K
Denton, T.W. ~ Co. K
Depriest, Andrew J. ~ Co. I
Depriest, William F. ~ Co. I
Dering, A.J. ~ Co. C
Derrin, Adam J. ~ Co. C
Derryberry, A.J. ~ Co. 1 G
Derryberry, J.H. ~ Co. 1 G
Derryberry, John H. ~ Co. 1GB
Dewire, Patrick ~ Co. 1HI
Dias, Robert ~ Co. C

Dice, Silas ~ Co. K
Dickens, J.A. ~ Co. A
Dickens, J.H. ~ Co. E
Dickens, James F. ~ Co. 2 H
Dickens, W.T. ~ Co. A
Dickerson, M. T. ~ Co. E
Dies, Robert ~ Co. C
Dillahay, James A. ~ Co. 2 H
Dillahay, James P. ~ Co. 2 H
Dillahay, James T. ~ Co. 2 H
Dillahay, John H. ~ Co. 2 H
Dillahay, Robert J. ~ Co. 2 H
Dillehay, J. N. ~ Co. 1GB
Dillehay, James A. ~ Co. 2 H
Dillehay, James P. ~ Co. 2 H
Dillehay, James T. ~ Co. 2 H
Dillehay, Jasper N. ~ Co. 1GB
Dillehay, John H. ~ Co. 2 H
Dillehay, Robert J. ~ Co. 2 H
Dillehay, T. N. ~ Co. 1GB
Dilleyhay, J. N. ~ Co. 1GB
Dilleyhay, J. W. ~ Co. 1GB
Dillihay, J. A. ~ Co. 2 H
Dinkins, J. H. ~ Co. E
Dixon, J. A. ~ Co. C
Dixon, John G. ~ Co. 2 H
Dobbins, F. D. ~ Co. E
Dobbins, F. L. ~ Co. E
Dobbins, Foster ~ Co. E
Dobbins, J. A. ~ Co. E
Dobbins, W. H. ~ Co. E
Dobbins, William ~ Co. E
Dobbs, H. S. ~ Co. E
Donwood, George G. ~ Co. 1GB
Dorris, W.A. ~ Co. E
Dorwood, George G. ~ Co. 1CB
Doss, M.F. ~ Co. F
Dotson, William C. ~ Co. 2 G
Dougherty, James H. ~ Co. 1 G
Dowdy, H.L. ~ Co. D
Dowdy, L.H. ~ Co. D

Dowdy, Robert J. ~ Co. D
Dowell, A.P. ~ Co. F
Dowell, H.P. ~ Co. F
Dowell Jr., M.C. ~ Co. 1 G
Dowell Sr., M.C. ~ Co. 1GB
Dowley, R.J. ~ Co. D
Dowly, L.H. ~ Co. D
Doyse, Patrick ~ Co. 1HI
Duke, James M. ~ Co. I
Duke, Micajah ~ Co. C
Duke, W.J. ~ Co. C
Dunbar, Samuel M. ~ Co. I
Duncan, T.H. ~ Co. I
Duncan, Thomas H. ~ Co. I
Duncan, Thomas J. ~ Co. I
Duncan, W.A. ~ Co. C
Dunkin, T.H. ~ Co. I
Dunlap, James ~ Co. 1 H
Dunn, C.W. ~ Co. A
Dunn, E.F. ~ Co. A
Dunn, W.D. ~ Co. A
Durrin, A.J. ~ Co. C
Dutton, Wiley ~ Co. E
Dyar, Joseph S. ~ Co. L
Dyer, Dixon ~ Co. 2 H
Dyer, Joseph S. ~ Co. L
Early, E.W. ~ Co. I
Earnheart, William A ~ Co. D
Easley, Andrew D. ~ Co. I
Easley, Edward W ~ Co. I
Easley, Thomas S. ~ Co. I
Eassonheart, W.A. ~ Co. D
Eaton, James H. ~ Co. K
Edminson, R.C. ~ Co. D
Edmonds, J.T. ~ Co. D2I
Edmonds, Joseph H. ~ Co. D2I
Edmonds, Joseph S. ~ Co. D2I
Edmondson, R.C. ~ Co. D
Edmons, J.S. ~ Co. D
Edmons, Joseph T. ~ Co. D
Edmonson, R.C. ~ Co. D

Edwards, Edom ~ Co. 1GB
Edwards, I.W. ~ Co. K
Edwards, S. Walker ~ Co. K
Edwards, William ~ Co. 1GB
Ellis, Abe ~ Co. C
Ellis, P.P. ~ Co. C
Ellison, Joseph ~ Co. G
Elmer, Henry ~ Co. D
Elmore, Henry ~ Co. D
Elmore, P.H. ~ Co. D
Elmore, W.H. ~ Co. D
Emison, Frank A. ~ Co. I
Emler, Frank ~ Co. I
Emler, Henderson ~ Co. I
Emmerson, F.A. ~ Co. I
Esells, A.D. ~ Co. I
Estes, J.D. ~ Co. F
Estis, J.D. ~ Co. F
Etheridge, G.W. ~ Co. E
Eubanks, George W. ~ Co. K
Evans, James ~ Co. 1G
Evans, Sidney ~ Co. 1G
Evins, J. ~ Co. 1G
Evins, S. ~ Co. 1G
Fain, T.J. ~ Co. A
Fain, W.G. ~ Co. A
Fain, William W. ~ Co. A
Fain Jr., R.W. ~ Co. A
Faris, J.W. ~ Co. A
Faris, Richard W. ~ Co. A
Faris, William J.S. ~ Co. A
Farrar, William A. ~ Co. D
Farris, John W. ~ Co. A
Farris, R.W. ~ Co. A
Farris, W.J.S. ~ Co. A
Farris, William G. ~ Co. 2 G
Featherston, Calvin ~ Co. A
Fentress, James ~ Co. I
Fergerson, C.D. ~ Co. B
Fergerson, J.C. ~ Co. A
Fergerson, Nimrod ~ Co. B

Ferguson, A. ~ Co. B
Ferguson, C.D. ~ Co. B
Ferguson, Charles L. ~ Co. 2 H
Ferguson, James A. ~ Co. B
Ferguson, Nimrod ~ Co. B
Ferguson, Thomas ~ Co. B
Ferguson, Wilson T. ~ Co. C
Fergusson, W.T. ~ Co. C
Ferrell, C. ~ Co. F
Fetherston, Calvin ~ Co. A
Fielder, C.W. ~ Co. I
Fielder, N.C. ~ Co. I
Fielder, Newton C. ~ Co. I
Fielding, William C. ~ Co. F
Fields, Henry ~ Co. B
Fingerton, George W. ~ Co. 1GB
Finney, John L. ~ Co. 2GL
Finney, John T. ~ Co. 2GL
Finney, Patton A. ~ Co. 2G
Finney, Patton P. ~ Co. 2G
Finney, Preston P. ~ Co. 2G
Finney, William J. ~ Co. 2G
Finny, John T. ~ Co. 2GL
Fisher, W.F. ~ Co. C
Fisher, W.H. ~ Co. C
Fisher, William Franklin ~ Co. C
Fite, L.H. ~ Co. F
Fitzgerals, J.A. ~ Co. 1G
Fletcher, Greenville ~ Co. K
Fletcher, James P. ~ Co. K
Floyd, Drury A. ~ Co. D
Floyd, J.A. ~ Co. D
Floyd, Joshua ~ Co. D
Floyd, Monroe ~ Co. D
Floyd, R.M. ~ Co. D
Floyd, W.J. ~ Co. D
Fly, J.M. ~ Co. 1 H
Foard, D.M. ~ Co. C
Foard, E.G. ~ Co. C
Foard, James C. ~ Co. 2 K
Ford, D.M. ~ Co. C

Ford, Daniel M. ~ Co. C
Ford, E.G. ~ Co. C
Ford, James C. ~ Co. 2 H
Fouch, John C. ~ Co. F
Fouquier, James ~ Co. C
Fowler, Lawrence ~ Co. F
Fox, Willis H. ~ Co. B
Frazier, A.J. ~ Co. K
Frazier, Harmon A. ~ Co. K
Frazier, Isaac T. ~ Co. K
Freeman, Richard ~ Co. C
Frey, James B. ~ Co. D
Fry, James B. ~ Co. D
Fugull, James ~ Co. C
Fuller, J.H. ~ Co. 1 G
Fuller, J.W. ~ Co. 1 G
Fuqua, James ~ Co. C
Furgerson, Archibald W. ~ Co. 2 H
Furgerson, C.L. ~ Co. 2 H
Furgerson, Charles ~ Co. 2 H
Furgerson, Frank ~ Co. I
Furgerson, J.C. ~ Co. A
Furgerson, W.F. ~ Co. C
Furguson, H. ~ Co. B
Furguson, Marshall ~ Co. K
Furguson, Thomas ~ Co. B
Furgusson, W.T. ~ Co. C
Furman, R. ~ Co. 1 H
Furrel, C. ~ Co. F
Galtny, J.F. ~ Co. F
Gammon, Moses ~ Co. C
Gammons, Moses ~ Co. C
Garner, William C. ~ Co. I
Garrett, Austin S. ~ Co. I
Garrett, Eli H. ~ Co. I
Garrett, J.M. ~ Co. C
Garrett, James W. ~ Co. D
Garrett, T.J. ~ Co. I
Garrett, T.W. ~ Co. A
Garrett, W.H. ~ Co. A
Garrette, I.T. ~ Co. I

Gaulden, J.C. ~ Co. C
Gaulding, James C. ~ Co. C
Geins, J.R. ~ Co. I
Gentry, Samuel ~ Co. I
Gentry, W.H. ~ Co. A
Gett, George W. ~ Co. K
Gibson, Decalb C. ~ Co. L
Gifford, Brice ~ Co. C
Gilaspie, J. S. ~ Co. D
Giles, W. C. J. ~ Co. 1HI
Gill, Albert B. ~ Co. K
Gill, Alfred B. ~ Co. K
Gillespie, J. S. ~ Co. D
Gillespie, James J. ~ Co. D
Gilliam, G. J. ~ Co. 2G
Gilliam, William ~ Co. 2G
Gillispee, J. S. ~ Co. D
Gipson, Decalb C. ~ Co. L
Glen, Joseph S. ~ Co. F
Glen, Josiah S. ~ Co. F
Glenn, Caleb M. ~ Co. K
Goad, Jefferson ~ Co. 2H
Goad, Joshua ~ Co. 2H
Goard, Jefferson ~ Co. 2H
Goard, Joshua ~ Co. 2H
Goens, J.R. ~ Co. I
Goins, J.R. ~ Co. I
Goins, Jordan R. ~ Co. I
Gold, J.P. ~ Co. F
Gold, James E. ~ Co. F
Gold, John E. ~ Co. F
Good, Jefferson ~ Co. 2H
Goodner, T.C. ~ Co. K
Gordon, G.W. ~ Co. F
Goud, Jefferson ~ Co. H
Gould, J.E. ~ Co. F
Gould, J.P. ~ Co. F
Goulding, James C. ~ Co. C
Gowen, Washington ~ Co. B
Graham, W.B. ~ Co. 1GB
Graham, William ~ Co. D

Grandham, Lewis ~ Co. E
Grantham, Lewis ~ Co. E
Granthan, Lewis ~ Co. E
Graves, B.H. ~ Co. E
Graves, B.M. ~ Co. E
Graves, Bannister M. ~ Co. E
Graves, Thomas J. ~ Co. I
Gray, Daniel J. ~ Co. D
Gray, John V. ~ Co. I
Green, Jo John ~ Co. B/F
Green, Robert F. ~ Co. I
Greer, J.H. ~ Co. 1HI
Gregory, A. ~ Co. E
Gregory, Abraham ~ Co. A
Gregory, J.L. ~ Co. E
Gregory, John A. ~ Co. F
Gregory, William ~ Co. E
Gregory, William A. ~ Co. E
Gregory, William Jesse ~ Co. 2 H
Grey, D.J. ~ Co. D
Griffin, Lewis J. ~ Co. I
Griffin, Newton P. ~ Co. I
Griffin, Willis C. ~ Co. I
Grigg, J.R. ~ Co. C
Grigg, John ~ Co. E
Griggs, J.R. ~ Co. C
Grigors, Willim A. ~ Co. E
Grigory, Abraham ~ Co. A
Grigory, John A. ~ Co. F
Grigory, William ~ Co. E
Grinadge, J.R. ~ Co. A
Gross, V.B. ~ Co. C
Groves, G.W. ~ Co. H1I
Groves, Henry ~ Co. 1 H
Gualtney, J.F. ~ Co. F
Guinn, James ~ Co. 2F
Guinn, Jesse ~ Co. E
Guinn, Literel ~ Co. B
Gunter, Perry ~ Co. I
Guthrie, W.P. ~ Co. E
Gwaltney, J.F. ~ Co. F

Gwin, Jesse ~ Co. E
Gwinn, James ~ Co. 2 G
Hagan, H.D.P. ~ Co. B
Haincs, John A. ~ Co. D
Hains, W.D. ~ Co. C
Halbrooks, Robert C. ~ Co. I
Hale, G.W. ~ Co. F
Hale, J.R. ~ Co. F
Hale, W.F. ~ Co. I
Haley, William ~ Co. C
Halibuston, L.S. ~ Co. H
Hall, B.F. ~ Co. F
Hall, Benjamin ~ Co. F
Hall, G.W. ~ Co. F
Hall, J.P. ~ Co. F
Hall, P.A. ~ Co. F
Halliburton, L.L. ~ Co. H
Halliburton, Leroy S. ~ Co. H
Halstead, J.O. ~ Co. A
Halstead, J.P. ~ Co. A
Halsted, J.O. ~ Co. A
Haly, William ~ Co. C
Hamer, George ~ Co. B
Hammock, James M. ~ Co. I
Hampton, J.H. ~ Co. B
Hampton, Jerry ~ Co. B
Hampton, P. ~ Co. D
Hampton, Smith ~ Co. D
Hampton, T. ~ Co. D
Hance, Erastus S. ~ Co. 2 H
Hanes, F.P. ~ Co. C
Hanes, John A. ~ Co. D
Hanes, W.D. ~ Co. C
Hanman, Thomas ~ Co. B
Hanson, H.C. ~ Co. D
Hardaman, J.E. ~ Co. B
Hardeman, John E. ~ Co. B
Hardison, David M. ~ Co. B
Hardison, G.W. ~ Co. B
Hardison, George ~ Co. B
Hardison, Joel S. ~ Co. B

Hardison, Martin V. ~ Co. G/B
Hardison, S.T. ~ Co. B
Hardison, W.J. ~ Co. G
Hardison, William D. ~ Co. B
Haris, W.N. ~ Co. A
Harlan, Thomas J. ~ Co. K
Harland, Thomas J. ~ Co. K
Harland, Thos ~ Co. K
Harlin, T.J. ~ Co. K
Harman, H.D. ~ Co. G/B
Harman, Thomas ~ Co. B
Harmen, Thomas ~ Co. B
Harmon, H.D. ~ Co. G,B
Harmon, James K. ~ Co. K
Harmon, Thomas ~ Co. B
Harmond, Thomas ~ Co. B
Harp, William H. ~ Co. F
Harper, James M. ~ Co. K
Harper, W.F. ~ Co. B
Harrell, R.F. ~ Co. E
Harrington, J.D. ~ Co. I
Harrington, James D. ~ Co. I
Harrington, W.W. ~ Co. I
Harrington, Wilson ~ Co. I
Harris, Benjamin F. ~ Co. I
Harris, Edward ~ Co. B
Harris, J.H. ~ Co. H,I
Harris, J.W. ~ Co. A
Harris, Richard A. ~ Co. D
Harris, W.N. ~ Co. A
Harrison, W.H. ~ Co. E
Harrison, William H. ~ Co. B
Harroll, R.T. ~ Co. E
Harshaw, Benjamin ~ Co. E
Hart, Henry W. ~ Co. M,H
Hart, Seaborn J. ~ Co. M
Hartley, Washington ~ Co. D
Hartley, William ~ Co. D
Hartly, W. ~ Co. D
Haskings, Samuel B. ~ Co. A
Hasley, Wash ~ Co. D

Hassell, F.M. ~ Co. I
Hasten, A.J. ~ Co. C
Hastin, A.J. ~ Co. C
Hastings, A.J. ~ Co. C
Hawe, G.W. ~ Co. F
Hayes, William H. ~ Co. F
Haynes, A.J. ~ Co. D
Haynes, F.P. ~ Co. C
Haynes, J.H. ~ Co. A
Haynes, John A. ~ Co. D
Haynes, T.H. ~ Co. A
Haynes, W.D. ~ Co. C
Haynie, Thomas M. ~ Co. H
Hays, William H. ~ Co. F
Heartley, W. ~ Co. D
Heath, David ~ Co. A
Heath, J.W. ~ Co. A
Heflin, Jonathan ~ Co. F
Heftin, Jonathan ~ Co. F
Hellmentoller, Arch D. ~ Co. F
Helmantallow, A.D. ~ Co. F
Helmintaller, A.D. ~ Co. F
Helmontaller, A.D. ~ Co. F
Hemphill, George R. ~ Co. D
Hendricks, Francis J. ~ Co. D
Hendricks, Isaac H. ~ Co. D
Hendricks, S.G. ~ Co. I
Hendricks, Smith G. ~ Co. I
Hendrix, F.J. ~ Co. D
Hendrix, Isaac H. ~ Co. D
Hendrix, John G. ~ Co. D
Hendrix, S.G. ~ Co. I
Hendrix, W.F. ~ Co. D
Hendrix, Jr., E.W. ~ Co. A
Hendrucks, J. ~ Co. D
Henry, Franklin B. ~ Co. I
Henry, Jo E. ~ Co. E
Henry, Owen ~ Co. E
Hensiley, J.D. ~ Co. I
Herbert, R.H ~ Co. B
Herbert, Richard N. ~ Co. B

Herrin, John ~ Co. L
Herrington, James B. ~ Co. I
Herron, William F. ~ Co. H
Hibbett, A.J. ~ Co. E
Hibbett, J.L. ~ Co. F&S
Hickerson, Joseph ~ Co. K
Hicks, John M. ~ Co. D
Hill, Albert ~ Co. B
Hill, Andrew D. ~ Co. B
Hill, F.M. ~ Co. B
Hill, J.B. ~ Co. E
Hill, James A. ~ Co. B
Hill, James W.M. ~ Co. B
Hill, R.G. ~ Co. E
Hill, W.H. ~ Co. E
Hime, William J. ~ Co. G
Hindman, Alex ~ Co. L
Hinson, H.C. ~ Co. D
Hinson, John ~ Co. D
Hinson, M.C. ~ Co. D
Hinson, Merril ~ Co. G,B
Hipp, David D. ~ Co. L
Hodge, Martin C. ~ Co. K
Hogan, H.D.P. ~ Co. B
Hoges, William H. ~ Co. F
Hogg, Shelby J. ~ Co. M,H
Hoggatt, John W. ~ Co. K
Hoggett, John W. ~ Co. K
Holden, George W. ~ Co. A
Holden, J.H. ~ Co. A
Holden, J.M. ~ Co. A
Holder, J.A. ~ Co. A
Holder, James A. ~ Co. A
Holdon, George W. ~ Co. A
Holdon, J.R. ~ Co. D
Hollamon, William Z. ~ Co. H
Holland, F.A. ~ Co. B
Holland, Frank A. ~ Co. B
Holland, J.R. ~ Co. C
Holland, T.J. ~ Co. E
Holland, W.C. ~ Co. D

Hollen, J.R. ~ Co. C
Hollerman, William S. ~ Co. H
Holmes, J.A. ~ Co. I
Holmes, William ~ Co. I
Holms, J.A. ~ Co. I
Holms, Thomas ~ Co. I
Holt, J.S. ~ Co. E
Holt, James ~ Co. E
Holton, John R. ~ Co. D
Hooper, James ~ Co. I
Hooten, J.B. ~ Co. I
Hooton, J.B. ~ Co. I
Hoper, James ~ Co. I
Horseford, William ~ Co. G,B
Horsford, T. ~ Co. G
Horsford, William ~ Co. G,B
Hosford, Henry ~ Co. B
Hosford, Thomas ~ Co. G
Hosford, William ~ Co. G,B
Hoskins, Samuel B. ~ Co. A
House, M.P. ~ Co. E
Howard, John J.P. ~ Co. G
Howe, William W. ~ Co. G
Howell, F. ~ Co. B
Howell, Harrison ~ Co. B
Howell, Lafayette ~ Co. B
Howell, Martin ~ Co. C
Hubbard, J.M. ~ Co. F
Hubbard, Richard H. ~ Co. B
Hubboard, J.M. ~ Co. F
Hubbord, J.M. ~ Co. F
Huchenson, Elijah ~ Co. I
Hudson, D.D. ~ Co. F
Hudson, John C. ~ Co. A
Hudson, John D. ~ Co. F
Hudson, John T. ~ Co. F
Hughes, Joseph ~ Co. C
Hughes, William ~ Co. B
Hughs, Joseph ~ Co. C
Hughs, Josephus H. ~ Co. C
Hughs, William ~ Co. B

Hunt, J.S. ~ Co. E
Hunt, J.W. ~ Co. E
Hunt, James ~ Co. E
Hunter, D.L. ~ Co. E
Hunter, F.M. ~ Co. E
Hunter, W.H. ~ Co. H
Hurcleman, John E. ~ Co. B
Hurdeman, John E. ~ Co. B
Hurdiman, J.E. ~ Co. B
Hurley, Washington ~ Co. D
Huse, William ~ Co. B
Hutcherson, Elijah ~ Co. I
Hutcherson, Francis M. ~ Co. I
Hutcherson, J.A. ~ Co. C
Hutcherson, James ~ Co. I
Hutcherson, James C. ~ Co. I
Hutcherson, John S. ~ Co. A
Hutcheson, J.A. ~ Co. C
Hutchinson, J.S. ~ Co. A
Hutchinson, James C. ~ Co. I
Hutchinson, John A. ~ Co. C
Hutchison, F.M. ~ Co. I
Hutchison, J.A. ~ Co. C
Hutton, W.M. ~ Co. F&S
Ingram, James A. ~ Co. K
Inman, K. ~ Co. I
Irvin, W.H. ~ Co. B
Irwin, W.H. ~ Co. B
Ivines, J. ~ Co. G
Ivines, S. ~ Co. G
Jackson, D.C. ~ Co. A
Jackson, David ~ Co. G,B
Jackson, David A. ~ Co. G,B
Jackson, F.M. ~ Co. A
Jackson, J.C. ~ Co. A
Jackson, John L. ~ Co. A
Jackson, M.R. ~ Co. A
Jackson, W.H.H. ~ Co. A
Jackson, William ~ Co. A
Jackson, Sr., W.H. ~ Co. A
Jacques, W. Isaac ~ Co. F

James, W.C. ~ Co. A
Jamison, Thomas R. ~ Co. B
Jaquees, J.W. ~ Co. F
Jaquess, Isaac W. ~ Co. F
Jarden, William ~ Co. E
Jarrell, Charles ~ Co. K
Jarrell, James C. ~ Co. K
Jenkins, Daniel E. ~ Co. K
Jenkins, James ~ Co. I
Jenkins, Jesse J. ~ Co. G
Jenkins, William ~ Co. I
Jenkins, William H. ~ Co. G
Jerald, Charles ~ Co. K
Jerald, James C. ~ Co. K
Jett, Edward ~ Co. K
Jett, George W. ~ Co. K
Jett, Thomas B. ~ Co. K
Jimerson, Thomas ~ Co. B
Jinkens, James ~ Co. I
Jinkens, William ~ Co. I
Johnson, A.S. ~ Co. L
Johnson, Aaron L. ~ Co. L
Johnson, B.D. ~ Co. B
Johnson, Calvin ~ Co. L
Johnson, Harvey ~ Co. K
Johnson, J.R. ~ Co. A
Johnson, James M. ~ Co. C
Johnson, James R. ~ Co. A
Johnson, James W. ~ Co. C
Johnson, John A. ~ Co. G,B
Johnson, Joshua ~ Co. D
Johnson, R.A.W. ~ Co. B
Johnson, Samuel C. ~ Co. D
Johnson, T.L. ~ Co. F
Johnson, Thomas P. ~ Co. E
Johnson, W. Calvin ~ Co. L
Johnson, W.F. ~ Co. D
Johnson, W.H. ~ Co. C
Johnson, W.T. ~ Co. D
Johnston, E.M. ~ Co. F
Johnston, J.M. ~ Co. C

Johnston, J.W. ~ Co. C
Johnston, W.H. ~ Co. C
Jones, B.A. ~ Co. A
Jones, C.J. ~ Co. C
Jones, Cornelius ~ Co. A
Jones, D.A. ~ Co. A
Jones, D.S. ~ Co. G,B
Jones, David A. ~ Co. A
Jones, E.D. ~ Co. A
Jones, Edward D. ~ Co. A
Jones, George ~ Co. K
Jones, J.C. ~ Co. A
Jones, J.E. ~ Co. C
Jones, J.M. ~ Co. C
Jones, J.W. ~ Co. E
Jones, J.W. ~ Co. C
Jones, John J. ~ Co. A
Jones, John M. ~ Co. G
Jones, Nathan M. ~ Co. K
Jones, Nathan N. ~ Co. K
Jones, R.H. ~ Co. A
Jones, Robert ~ Co. G,B
Jones, Samuel ~ Co. G
Jones, Spencer ~ Co. B
Jones, Stephen ~ Co. B
Jones, T.D. ~ Co. C
Jones, T.H. ~ Co. G,B
Jones, Thomas E. ~ Co. F&S
Jones, Thomas F. ~ Co. L
Jones, W.A. ~ Co. C
Jones, W.A. ~ Co. B
Jones, W.P. ~ Co. B
Jones, W.P. ~ Co. F
Jones, W.T. ~ Co. F
Jones, Wiley ~ Co. B
Jones, Willis ~ Co. G,B
Jordan, John A. ~ Co. D
Jordan, W.A. ~ Co. D
Jordan, William ~ Co. E
Jordan, William A. ~ Co. D
Kallahan, A.H. ~ Co. K

Karr, D.A. ~ Co. C
Karr, W.R. ~ Co. C
Keany, James M. ~ Co. C
Kearley, James H. ~ Co. C
Kearley, James N. ~ Co. C
Kearly, James M. ~ Co. C
Kelley, Enoch B. ~ Co. D
Kelly, Enoch Beal ~ Co. D
Kelly, S.B. ~ Co. D
Kemp, Henry ~ Co. H
Kemp, Jinks H. ~ Co. M,H
Kemp, John M. ~ Co. M,H
Kemp, William L. ~ Co. M,H
Kerley, D.W. ~ Co. E
Kerley, J.H. ~ Co. C
Kerley, R.H. ~ Co. C
Kerley, Robert ~ Co. C
Key, C.P. ~ Co. E
Key, W.T. ~ Co. E
Kidian, Henry ~ Co. A
Killough, J.G. ~ Co. I
Kimens, J.E. ~ Co. A
Kimmins, J.E. ~ Co. A
King, Andrew L. ~ Co. B
King, J.A. ~ Co. F
King, J.J. ~ Co. A
King, James ~ Co. A
King, N.K. ~ Co. G
King, R.W. ~ Co. A
King, Sampsom J. ~ Co. F
King, W.R. ~ Co. F
King, Wellington ~ Co. H
Kirby, R.H. ~ Co. C
Kirby, Wade H. ~ Co. H
Kirk, John H. ~ Co. F&S
Kirley, R.H. ~ Co. C
Kirly, D.W. ~ Co. E
Knight, Robert ~ Co. F
Knight, W.J. ~ Co. F
Koger, Peter H. ~ Co. K
Kunkle, John A. ~ Co. I

Kurley, R.H. ~ Co. C
Ladd, John C. ~ Co. B
Laflin, William H.H. ~ Co. D
Laine, W.J. ~ Co. B
Lamb, N.H. ~ Co. A
Lamb, Nicholas H. ~ Co. D
Lamb, W.H. ~ Co. D
Lamb, Wilis ~ Co. D
Lamb, William M. ~ Co. A
Lancaster, William J. ~ Co. I
Lane, Elias ~ Co. I
Lane, William J. ~ Co. B
Langford, Silas J. ~ Co. M
Laptin, William H.H. ~ Co. D
Law, Addison H. ~ Co. M
Law, Henry D. ~ Co. M,H
Law, Hugh L. ~ Co. M,H
Lawrence, A.H. ~ Co. F
Lawrence, Augustus H. ~ Co. F
Lawrence, J.L. ~ Co. F
Lawrence, John ~ Co. M
Lawrence, Pleasant W. ~ Co. M
Lawrence, William ~ Co. B
Lawson, J. C. ~ Co. I
Lawson, Shadrick S. ~ Co. I
Layne, W. J. ~ Co. B
Leath, Thomas ~ Co. C
Lee, Andrew J. ~ Co. G
Lee, Henry J. ~ Co. G
Lee, James M. ~ Co. F
Lee, W.T. ~ Co. B
Leverett, Robert ~ Co. A
Levingston, Robert ~ Co. E
Lewis, B.W. ~ Co. A
Lewis, J.W. ~ Co. A
Lillard, M.C. ~ Co. D
Lincoln, W.H. ~ Co. F
Linton, Marcus E. ~ Co. L
Linton, W.C. ~ Co. L
Linville, J.N. ~ Co. C
Livingston, J.F. ~ Co. E

Livingston, R.N. ~ Co. E
Livingston, Robert ~ Co. E
Llyon, F.E.P. ~ Co. F
Loftin, William H.H. ~ Co. D
Lofton, N.H.H. ~ Co. D
Long, A. Samuel ~ Co. L,G
Long, Charles S. ~ Co. M,H
Long, J.P.K. ~ Co. L,G
Long, James K.P. ~ Co. L,G
Long, James P. ~ Co. L,G
Long, Samuel A. ~ Co. L
Lonton, Marcus ~ Co. L
Lovein, William ~ Co. C
Loveings, William ~ Co. C
Lovelass, William ~ Co. I
Loveless, William ~ Co. I
Lovett, J.N. ~ Co. B
Lovett, N.J. ~ Co. B
Lovit, N.J. ~ Co. B
Lucas, Henry V. ~ Co.
Luckey, J.C. ~ Co. F
Luckey, John F. ~ Co. F
Luckey, S.C. ~ Co. F
Luckey, Samuel ~ Co. F
Luckey, W.H. ~ Co. F
Luckey, William ~ Co. F
Lucus, Henry N. ~ Co.
Lusk, Edmond ~ Co. K
Lusk, George W. ~ Co. L
Lynch, W.S. ~ Co. F
Lynch, W.T. ~ Co. F
Lynch, William ~ Co. L,G
MClellan, David L. ~ Co. H
Maberry, Henry ~ Co. I
Maberry, John S. ~ Co. I
Maberry, P.S. ~ Co. I
Mackey, A.B. ~ Co. G,B
Maddox, F.F. ~ Co. A
Maddox, T.F. ~ Co. A
Malugin, G.W. ~ Co. I
Malugin, Robert B. ~ Co. I

Mangram, Jesse ~ Co. A
Mangrum, J.W. ~ Co. A
Mangrum, Jesse ~ Co. A
Mangrun, Jesse ~ Co. A
Manire, A.W. ~ Co. A
Manire, D.C. ~ Co. A
Manire, Lemuel ~ Co. A
Manire, Leonard ~ Co. A
Marcrum, J.W. ~ Co. C
Markes, Baily ~ Co. F
Markram, J.W. ~ Co. C
Markrum, J.W. ~ Co. C
Marks, Bailey ~ Co. F
Marshall, J.M. ~ Co. C
Marshall, W.J. ~ Co. D
Marshall, William S. ~ Co. D
Martin, B.F. ~ Co. B
Martin, C.C. ~ Co. F
Martin, J.F. ~ Co. E
Martin, J.T. ~ Co. B
Martin, John C. ~ Co. G
Martin, Joseph E. ~ Co. K
Martin, W.P. ~ Co. K
Martin, William T. ~ Co. K
Mash, Albert D. ~ Co. G
Mass, T.F. ~ Co. H,I
Massey, George W. ~ Co. H
Mathers, E. ~ Co. H
Mathews, Benjamin ~ Co. H
Mathews, Enoch ~ Co. H
Mathews, James D. ~ Co. H
Maupen, G.W. ~ Co. D
Maupin, James A. ~ Co. B
Maupin, James M. ~ Co. B
Maxwell, J.A. ~ Co. A
May, William W. ~ Co. G
Mayberry, Henry ~ Co. I
Mayberry, P.S. ~ Co. I
Mayfield, A.P. ~ Co. G,B
Maynard, Gibson ~ Co. M
McBrown, Henry C. ~ Co. K

McCaleb, F.P. ~ Co. I
McCaleb, Franklin P. ~ Co. I
McCall, David D. ~ Co. K
McCall, Henry B. ~ Co. K
McCall, Hugh L. ~ Co. H
McCammey, William B. ~ Co. K
McCammry, William B. ~ Co. K
McCanny, William B. ~ Co. K
McCard, W.C. ~ Co. H,I
McCarny, William B. ~ Co. K
McClanahan, J.L. ~ Co. I
McClanahan, John L. ~ Co. I
McClanahan, Robert ~ Co. I
McClaren, Adolphus ~ Co. I
McClaren, Robert ~ Co. I
McClarin, Robert ~ Co. I
McClellan, W.C. ~ Co. H
McClelland, David L. ~ Co. H
McConnald, J.A. ~ Co. K
McCord, J.H. ~ Co. H,I
McCord, Jerome H. ~ Co. H,I
McCord, W.C. ~ Co. H,I
McCord, W.H. ~ Co. H
McCowen, I.H. ~ Co. H,I
McCoy, Robert ~ Co. H
McCrea, Nathan T. ~ Co. K
McCucheon, J.F. ~ Co. F&S
McCutchan, John T. ~ Co. F&S
McCutchan, Robert A. ~ Co. K
McCutchen, J.F. ~ Co. F&S
McCutcheon, J.F. ~ Co. F&S
McCutcheon, R.A. ~ Co. K
McCutchun, R.A. ~ Co. K
McDonald, Joseph A. ~ Co. K
McDonald, Roderick C. ~ Co. K
McDowell, William ~ Co. A
McFadden, S.L. ~ Co. G,B
McFaddin, S.L. ~ Co. G,B
McGee, Robert ~ Co. E
McGowan, T.M. ~ Co. A
McGowen, T.M. ~ Co. A

McGowin, M. ~ Co. A
McGuire, Robert ~ Co. K
McGuire, William J. ~ Co. K
McGuire, William Jackson ~ Co. K
McKanny, W.B. ~ Co. K
McKinney, W.B. ~ Co. K
McLanahan, A.H. ~ Co. F
McLanahan, J.L. ~ Co. I
McLarin, Adolphus ~ Co. I
McLaron, A.J. ~ Co. D
McLuren, Adolphes ~ Co. I
McMahan, And. A. ~ Co. B
McMahon, Andrew A. ~ Co. B
McMahon, Henry A. ~ Co. B
McMayhan, A.A. ~ Co. B
McMayhan, L.L. ~ Co. B
McMayhan, Lem L. ~ Co. B
McMillen, A.J. ~ Co. G
McMillin, A.J. ~ Co. G
McMurray, J.F. ~ Co. B
McMurray, S.J. ~ Co. B
McMurry, Samuel J. ~ Co. B
McNeely, R.D. ~ Co. E
McWhirter, J.S. ~ Co. E
McWhirter, James ~ Co. E
Mclaron, A.J. ~ Co. D
Meader, John ~ Co. C
Meaders, W.C. ~ Co. C
Meador, D.F. ~ Co. C
Meador, Ira ~ Co. C
Meador, J.I. ~ Co. E
Meador, J.W. ~ Co. C
Meador, John ~ Co. C
Meador, P.G. ~ Co. C
Meador, W.J. ~ Co. E
Meadors, I.J. ~ Co. C
Meadors, J.D. ~ Co. C
Meadows, W.C. ~ Co. G
Medders, William C. ~ Co. G
Megee, Robert ~ Co. E
Melt, Robert ~ Co. I

Melven, Nathan F. ~ Co. K
Melvin, Nathan N. ~ Co. K
Melvin, Nathan T. ~ Co. K
Melvin, Nathan T. ~ Co. K
Mett, Robert ~ Co. I
Milam, Burris M. ~ Co. I
Milam, George W. ~ Co. I
Milam, W.M. ~ Co. I
Milom, Charles ~ Co. I
Miloms, C.M. ~ Co. I
Modlin, William M. ~ Co. B
Moncrief, C.T. ~ Co. E
Moncrief, T.J. ~ Co. E
Moncrief, Thomas J. ~ Co. E
Monday, Bailey P. ~ Co. H
Monday, Thomas ~ Co. H
Mondy, B.P. ~ Co. H
Mondy, Thomas ~ Co. H
Moneyhan, J. ~ Co. F
Moneyhan, J. ~ Co. F
Mongle, D.G. ~ Co. C
Montgomery, Felix G. ~ Co. H
Mooneyham, J.A. ~ Co. F
Mooneyham, Joel ~ Co. F
Moonigham, J.A. ~ Co. F
Moonigham, Joel. ~ Co. F
Mooningham, James A. ~ Co. F
Mooningham, Joel ~ Co. F
Moor, Austin ~ Co. G,B
Moore, A. ~ Co. G,B
Moore, John S. ~ Co. K
Moore, R.T. ~ Co. H
Moore, Thomas ~ Co. D
Moot, William H. ~ Co.
Moppin, George W. ~ Co. D
More, Austen ~ Co. G,B
Moreton, James C. ~ Co. G
Morgan, James W. ~ Co. D
Morgan, Thomas D. ~ Co. D
Morgin, J.W. ~ Co. D
Moris, J.H. ~ Co. E

Morris, Daniel E. ~ Co. H
Morris, J.W. ~ Co. E
Morris, James H. ~ Co. E
Morris, John W. ~ Co. E
Morris, Joseph H. ~ Co. E
Morrison, Joel P. ~ Co. I
Morrison, W.E. ~ Co. C
Morrow, Bethel A. ~ Co. K
Morrow, David ~ Co. K
Morton, Green W. ~ Co. B
Morton, James C. ~ Co. G
Mosear, A.M. ~ Co. F
Moseley, Henry ~ Co. A
Mosely, Henry ~ Co. A
Mosely, William C. ~ Co. D
Mosher, Amzi ~ Co. F
Mosiar, A. M. ~ Co. F
Mosier, A.M. ~ Co. F
Mosier, Amzi ~ Co. F
Mosley, Henry ~ Co. A
Mosley, William C. ~ Co. D
Moss, G. ~ Co. H,I
Moss, J.F. ~ Co. H,I
Moss, N.F. ~ Co. H,I
Moss, T.F. ~ Co. H,I
Moss, Thomas Fletcher ~ Co. H,I
Mott, W.H. ~ Co. F
Mumley, John A. ~ Co. I
Munday, Bailey P. ~ Co. H
Munday, Thomas ~ Co. H
Mundy, Bailey P. ~ Co. H
Mundy, Thomas ~ Co. H
Mungal, D.G. ~ Co. C
Mungle, D.G. ~ Co. C
Murfrey, E.M. ~ Co. A
Murphey, Clay F. ~ Co. M
Murphrey, E.M. ~ Co. D
Myrick, Russell ~ Co. E
Nance, Benjamin F. ~ Co. A
Nance, John W. ~ Co. A
Neal, W.H. ~ Co. E

Neal, Wilson S. ~ Co. F
Neathery, J.J. ~ Co. G
Neel, W.H. ~ Co. E
Neeley, Miles E. ~ Co. B
Neely, W.A. ~ Co. H
Nethery, J. J. ~ Co. G
Nevels, John S. ~ Co. L,G
Nevill, John L. ~ Co. L,G
Newman, Isham B. ~ Co. L,G
Newsom, Andrew J. ~ Co. L,G
Nichols, C.W. ~ Co. C
Nicholson, C.G. ~ Co. G,B
Nicholson, John M. ~ Co. G,B
Nolen, J.F. ~ Co. F
Nolen, Joseph ~ Co. F
North, William P. ~ Co. K
Norval, C.B. ~ Co. A
Norval, D.G. ~ Co. A
Norvell, D.G. ~ Co. A
Norvell, Daniel G. ~ Co. A
Norville, D.G. ~ Co. A
Norville, D.Z. ~ Co. A
Nunelly, J.D.L. ~ Co. I
Nunley, J.A. ~ Co. I
Nunley, John ~ Co. K
Nunnelee, J.A. ~ Co. I
Nunnelee, James D.L. ~ Co. I
Nunneley, John A. ~ Co. I
Nunnelley, John A. ~ Co. I
Nunnelly, John ~ Co. K
Nunnely, John ~ Co. K
Nutt, R.C. ~ Co. I
Nutt, Robert ~ Co. I
O'Briant, W.C. ~ Co. D
O'Bryane, W.C. ~ Co. D
Odum, Josiah ~ Co. H
Ofield, Allen ~ Co. K
Oglesbey, J.K.P. ~ Co. C
Ogley, John H. ~ Co. C
Oldfield, Allen ~ Co. K
Oliver, John H. ~ Co. GFL

Oliver, W.E. ~ Co. I
Olldridge, A.J. ~ Co. D
Orr, T.A. ~ Co. G
Overby, Alexander ~ Co. H,I
Overby, Wilson ~ Co. H
Overton, J.W. ~ Co. E
Owen, James H. ~ Co. A
Owen, John Green ~ Co. K
Owen, L.B.R. ~ Co. B
Owens, Jasper ~ Co. F
Pace, Pleasant G. ~ Co. I
Pace, Samuel ~ Co. I
Pace, Wilson ~ Co. I
Palmore, Rob F. ~ Co. B
Pamell, Andrew ~ Co. H
Parker, Andrew J. ~ Co. I
Parker, James P. ~ Co. I
Parker, Moses E. ~ Co. I
Parker, S.P. ~ Co. H,I
Parker, Samuel P. ~ Co. H,I
Parker, Samuel P. ~ Co. H,I
Parker, W.A. ~ Co. H
Parrett, Lewis ~ Co. F
Parsley, G.H. ~ Co. D
Parsley, J.W. ~ Co. A
Parsley, Newton J. ~ Co. D
Partin, F.M. ~ Co. G,L
Parton, Francis M. ~ Co. G,L
Pate, William H.H. ~ Co. H
Patterson, W.W. ~ Co. F
Paty, William Smith ~ Co. F
Paual, Andrew ~ Co. H
Payne, Hampton W. ~ Co. H
Payne, John ~ Co. H,M
Pearson, Farrar ~ Co. G,L
Peebles, Thomas H. ~ Co. B
Peeler, Josiah G. ~ Co. I
Peeler, W.T. ~ Co. I
Pemberton, Daniel W. ~ Co. K
Pemberton, J.C. ~ Co. K
Pendergrass, B.H. ~ Co. H

Penn, Joshua H. ~ Co. G
Perry, Benjamin ~ Co. I
Perry, S.M. ~ Co. E
Perry, William P. ~ Co. G,L
Persons, Farrar ~ Co. G,L
Petry, Amos ~ Co. F
Pettriss, Amos ~ Co. F
Petty, Thomas C. ~ Co. K
Phelps, J.H. ~ Co. E
Phillips, Newsom ~ Co. K
Pickard, Jesse A. ~ Co. I
Pickard, John L. ~ Co. I
Pingleton, G.W. ~ Co. G,B
Pingleton, George W. ~ Co. G,B
Pinkerton, Dave C. ~ Co. I
Pinkerton, James ~ Co. H
Pinkerton, William ~ Co. I
Pinkerton, Jr., William ~ Co. I
Pinn, Joshua H. ~ Co. G
Pistole, Thomas J. ~ Co. H,M
Ponder, Benjamin ~ Co. K
Pool, James ~ Co. G,L
Pope, Ezell ~ Co. A
Pope, F.M. ~ Co. A
Pope, Francis M. ~ Co. A
Pope, John K. ~ Co. A
Poplin, M.P. ~ Co. I
Poptin, M.P. ~ Co. I
Porter, John ~ Co. H
Potts, J.S. ~ Co. B
Potts, W.M. ~ Co. B
Potts, William S. ~ Co. B
Poual, Andrew ~ Co. H
Powell, Andrew ~ Co. H
Powell, Jesse ~ Co. H,M
Powell, John H. ~ Co. F
Powell, Samuel A. ~ Co. F
Powers, Anderson ~ Co. K
Powers, Andrew J. ~ Co. K
Prentice, W.B. ~ Co. F
Prentis, W.B. ~ Co. F

Prentis, W.D. ~ Co. F
Preston, W.C. ~ Co. F
Preston, William C. ~ Co. F
Pretcher, James C. ~ Co. F
Price, Ewel C. ~ Co. G
Prichard, G.H. ~ Co. H
Prichard, J.C. ~ Co. F
Prichard, James C. ~ Co. F
Primm, H.G. ~ Co. H,I
Pritchard, James C. ~ Co. F
Pritchett, G.H. ~ Co. H
Prowell, J.H. ~ Co. F
Prowell, John H. ~ Co. F
Puckett, Samuel M. ~ Co. K
Pulley, Sly G. ~ Co. B
Pully, S.J. ~ Co. B
Pumroy, J.W. ~ Co. B
Pumroy, James P. ~ Co. B
Purdie, Pleasant P. ~ Co. L
Purdie, Thomas J. ~ Co. G
Purdy, P.P. ~ Co. L
Purdy, Thomas J. ~ Co. G
Purdy, Thomas R. ~ Co. G
Pyram, W.H. ~ Co. D
Pyrin, W.H. ~ Co. D
Pyron, W.H. ~ Co. D
Quinn, Hugh ~ Co. G,L
Quinn, T.B. ~ Co. C
Ragan, J.B. ~ Co. F
Ragsdale, Francis H. ~ Co. K
Ragsdale, J.P. ~ Co. H
Ragsdale, W.N. ~ Co. H,I
Rainey, Joseph ~ Co. F
Raney, Joseph ~ Co. F
Ransom, Richard ~ Co. A
Ray, Albert N. ~ Co. H,M
Ray, John ~ Co. B
Ray, N.J. ~ Co. A
Read, Eldridge H. ~ Co. G
Read, H.E. ~ Co. C
Read, N.B. ~ Co. 1 G

Read, T.R. ~ Co. C
Reagan, J.B. ~ Co. F
Reany, Joseph ~ Co. F
Reaves, David ~ Co. I
Reaves, J.J. ~ Co. I
Reaves, L.E. ~ Co. H,I
Reaves, Leonidas E. ~ Co. H,I
Reaves, S.J. ~ Co. H,I
Redchick, James P. ~ Co. E
Reddick, J.P. ~ Co. E
Reddick, James P. ~ Co. E
Reece, Abraham ~ Co. H
Reece, E.P. ~ Co. F
Reece, J.S. ~ Co. F
Reece, James M. ~ Co. I
Reece, James W. ~ Co. H,M
Reece, Wade H. ~ Co. H,M
Reece, William H. ~ Co. H,M
Reed, Braddock ~ Co. 2HM
Reed, E.H. ~ Co. G
Reed, N.B. ~ Co. G
Reese, Abraham ~ Co. H
Reese, James M. ~ Co. I
Reese, Wade ~ Co. M,H
Reeves, R.C. ~ Co. E
Reid, Braddock ~ Co. H,M
Reid, H.E. ~ Co. C
Reid, T.R. ~ Co. C
Renney, Joseph ~ Co. F
Rennie, Joseph ~ Co. F
Retelick, James P. ~ Co. E
Rice, Septimus C. ~ Co. G
Rice, Steaphen C. ~ Co. 2 G
Rice, T.P. ~ Co. E
Rice, William A. ~ Co. G,L
Rice, William B. ~ Co. E
Richardson, Jesse ~ Co. E
Richardson, Riley S. ~ Co. 2 H
Richerson, Riley S. ~ Co. H,M
Richmond, J.W. ~ Co. H
Ried, Braddock ~ Co. 2 H

Riley, Isaac N. ~ Co. 2 H
Riley, James N. ~ Co. 2 H
Riley, John A. ~ Co. D
Riley, John H. ~ Co. 2 G
Rivers, Daniel D. ~ Co. I
Rivers, J.A. ~ Co. B
Rivers, J.B. ~ Co. B
Rivers, Joel ~ Co. I
Rivers, Martin M. ~ Co. I
Rives, R.C. ~ Co. E
Robberts, C.W. ~ Co. E
Robbins, William T. ~ Co. 2 H
Roberson, A.J. ~ Co. C
Roberson, J.H. ~ Co. C
Roberts, B.F. ~ Co. B
Roberts, C.W. ~ Co. E
Roberts, Cyrus W. ~ Co. E
Roberts, F.A. ~ Co. I
Roberts, Isaac T. ~ Co. 2 G
Roberts, J.A. ~ Co. H
Roberts, John H. ~ Co. B
Roberts, William T. ~ Co. B
Roberts, William T. ~ Co. 2HM
Robertson, N.J. ~ Co. D
Robertson, W.D. ~ Co. A
Robinson, A.J. ~ Co. C
Robinson, J.H. ~ Co. C
Robinson, Newton J. ~ Co. DI
Roddy, Albert D. ~ Co. L
Roddy, Benjamin F. ~ Co. 2GL
Roddy, Joseph G. ~ Co. 2GL
Roland, James K. ~ Co. A
Rolland, James K. ~ Co. A
Rollands, Amon ~ Co. F
Rollands, L.A. ~ Co. F
Rollins, Amon ~ Co. F
Rollins, L.A. ~ Co. F
Rollins, Leonidas A. ~ Co. F
Rose, J.W. ~ Co. C
Rose, John W. ~ Co. C
Rose, Martin V. ~ Co. L

Roulett, B.F. ~ Co. 1 G
Rowland, J.K.P. ~ Co. A
Rowland, James K. ~ Co. A
Rowlett, B.F. ~ Co. 1 G
Royster, Charles E. ~ Co. 2HM
Rucker, John E. ~ Co. B
Rumage, George ~ Co. 1GB
Rummage, George ~ Co. 1GB
Russell, H.T. ~ Co. 2 H
Russell, James T. ~ Co. 2HM
Russell, John A.J. ~ Co. -
Russell, W.J. ~ Co. D
Russell, William ~ Co. A
Russell, William S. ~ Co. D M
Rutherford, A.Sidney ~ Co. 2GL
Rutherford, Elliott ~ Co. 2 G
Rutherford, T.F. ~ Co. F
Rutledge, W.C. ~ Co. A
Ryan, W.M.P. ~ Co. D
Ryan, William P. ~ Co. D
Ryley, John A. ~ Co. D
Rylie, John A. ~ Co. D
Sage, Oliver ~ Co. B
Sanders, S.H. ~ Co. C
Sanders, Wiley M. ~ Co. I
Sanders, William V. ~ Co. 2 H
Sanford, J.R. ~ Co. E
Sansom, Green F. ~ Co. 2 G
Savage, William ~ Co. A
Scales, Pleasant D. ~ Co. D
Scissom, William W. ~ Co. K
Scott, Charles ~ Co. F
Scott, William ~ Co. B
Scruggs, T. S. J. ~ Co. 1 H
Scully, Charles ~ Co. G
Scully, Thomas ~ Co. 2 G
Seay, William A. ~ Co. K
Secres, W.S. ~ Co. 1 G
Secrest, Dock ~ Co. 1 G
Secrest, I.S. ~ Co. 1 G
Secrest, S.W. ~ Co. 1 G

Secrest, W.H. ~ Co. 1GB
Sephen, A.J. ~ Co. F
Seward, B.R. ~ Co. B
Shannon, Samuel C. ~ Co. B
Sharber, M.R. ~ Co. D
Sharbro, M.R. ~ Co. D
Sharp, Thomas A. ~ Co. 1 G
Sharp, William A. ~ Co. 1 G
Shaver, J.T. ~ Co. F
Shaver, John ~ Co. F
Shaver, John T. ~ Co. F
Shavers, John ~ Co. F
Shaw, J.M. ~ Co. 1 H
Shiers, William ~ Co. 1GB
Shires, C.N. ~ Co. 1GB
Shires, Ira ~ Co. 1GB
Shires, Jacob B. ~ Co. 1GB
Shires, Peter ~ Co. 1GB
Shires, W.H. ~ Co. 1 G
Shires, W.M. ~ Co. 1GB
Shires, William ~ Co. 1GB
Shires, William H. ~ Co. 1GB
Shivers, Ira ~ Co. 1GB
Sholders, William L. ~ Co. 2 H
Short, J. D. ~ Co. C
Shoulders, David T. ~ Co. 2H
Shoulders, John B. ~ Co. M
Shoulders, William S. ~ Co. 2H
Shoulter, William L. ~ Co. 2H
Simmons, J.A. ~ Co. E
Simpson, Lewis E. ~ Co. F
Simpson, Luke ~ Co. F
Simpson, S.E. ~ Co. F
Sims, Zachariah ~ Co. 1 H
Sisco, Fielders H. ~ Co. I
Sisco, John ~ Co. I
Sisco, John E. ~ Co. I
Sissom, J.M. ~ Co. E
Sissom, James ~ Co. E
Sissom, William W. ~ Co. K
Sisson, James ~ Co. E

Sisson, Joseph ~ Co. E
Slayden, A.J. ~ Co. 1 H
Slayden, Andrew J. ~ Co. 1 H
Sloan, S.N. ~ Co. 2 H
Sloan, Sidney M. ~ Co. H
Slone, Sidney M. ~ Co. 2 H
Smith, Egbert P. ~ Co. K
Smith, Harrison ~ Co. 2 H
Smith, J.C. ~ Co. C
Smith, John ~ Co. F
Smith, John ~ Co. L
Smith, John A. ~ Co. D
Smith, John N. ~ Co. 1 H
Smith, Samuel ~ Co. E
Smith, T.B. ~ Co. A
Smith, T.P. ~ Co. A
Smith, T.P. ~ Co. D
Smith, Thomas J. ~ Co. D
Smith, Thomas P. ~ Co. A
Smith, W.F. ~ Co. D
Smith, W.G. ~ Co. I
Smith, W.L. ~ Co. A
Smith, Walter ~ Co. 1 H
Smith, William ~ Co. E
Smith, William H. ~ Co. 2 H
Smitherland, J. ~ Co. A
Smotherman, Barton ~ Co. A
Smotherman, C.C. ~ Co. A
Smotherman, Calvin C. ~ Co. A
Smotherman, D.D. ~ Co. A
Smotherman, J.T. ~ Co. A
Smotherman, J.W. ~ Co. A
Smotherman, John W. ~ Co. A
Smotherman, Joseph ~ Co. A
Smotherman, William ~ Co. A
Smuthermon, Barton ~ Co. A
Smuthermon, C.C. ~ Co. A
Smuthermon, D.D. ~ Co. A
Smuthermon, J.W. ~ Co. A
Smuthermon, Joseph ~ Co. A
Smuthermon, William ~ Co. A

Snell, John S. ~ Co. D
Solomon, J ~ Co. C
Spence, Francis ~ Co. A
Spence, Francis M. ~ Co. A
Spence, Francis N. ~ Co. A
Spencer, F.V. ~ Co. A
Spradlin, A.L. ~ Co. E
Spradlin, J.B. ~ Co. E
Spradm, A.L. ~ Co. E
Stegall, John G. ~ Co. A
Stegall, W.J. ~ Co. A
Stem, J.E. ~ Co. A
Stephen, J.P. ~ Co. I
Stephens, A.J. ~ Co. F
Stephens, A.K. ~ Co. K
Stephens, Albert H. ~ Co. 1HI
Stephens, Anther N. ~ Co. 2 G
Stephens, Charles ~ Co. 1HI
Stephens, J.K. ~ Co. I
Stephens, J.P. ~ Co. B
Stephens, J.S. ~ Co. E
Stephens, James ~ Co. E
Stephens, John ~ Co. I
Stephens, Milton ~ Co. B
Stepns, Andrew ~ Co. F
Sterns, A.H. ~ Co. 1HI
Stevens, A.J. ~ Co. F
Stevens, A.K. ~ Co. K
Stevens, Albert ~ Co. 1HI
Stevens, Charles ~ Co. 1HI
Stevens, J.H. ~ Co. 1H
Stevens, J.K. ~ Co. 1 H
Stevens, J.K. ~ Co. I
Stevens, J.P. ~ Co. I
Stevens, John ~ Co. I
Stevens, John P. ~ Co. B
Stevens, Lilburn H. ~ Co. K
Stevens, Milton ~ Co. B
Steward, Alexander ~ Co. F
Steward, Wiley ~ Co. I
Stewart, Alexander ~ Co. F

Stewart, Alexander L. ~ Co. F
Stewart, Andrew ~ Co. F
Stewart, J.J. ~ Co. G
Stewart, J.W. ~ Co. F
Stewart, Wiley ~ Co. I
Stigall, J.G. ~ Co. A
Stigall, W.G. ~ Co. A
Stigall, W.J. ~ Co. A
Stignor, J.M. ~ Co. B
Stinson, A.J. ~ Co. C
Stinson, A.W. ~ Co. C
Stinson, John ~ Co. B
Stinson, W.B. ~ Co. B
Stokes (Stoaks), Absalom ~ Co. F
Stone, James R. ~ Co. A
Stooks, Absalom ~ Co. F
Stoops, William H. ~ Co. I
Stryedlin, A.L. ~ Co. E
Stuard, Wiley ~ Co. I
Stuart, Alexander ~ Co. F
Stuart, Andrew ~ Co. F
Stuart, J.A. ~ Co. F
Stuart, J.W. ~ Co. F
Stugall, J.G. ~ Co. A
Stugall, W.G. ~ Co. A
Stull, J.E. ~ Co. A
Sullivan, James ~ Co. C
Sullivan, Joseph M. ~ Co. C
Sullivan, Josephus ~ Co. C
Sutton, H.J. ~ Co. 2G
Swann, Churchwell ~ Co. K
Swann, Thomas F. ~ Co. K
Tanner, Robert ~ Co. A
Tatum, Sublet A. ~ Co. I
Taylor, C.P. ~ Co. A
Taylor, Charles P. ~ Co. A
Taylor, Edward E. ~ Co. D
Taylor, Hardin H. ~ Co. K
Taylor, J.A. ~ Co. A
Taylor, James A. ~ Co. 2G
Taylor, John D. ~ Co. 2H

Taylor, John M. ~ Co. K
Taylor, Joseph B. ~ Co. 2H
Taylor, Joseph D. ~ Co. 2H
Taylor, Peter H. ~ Co. 2H
Taylor, R.A. ~ Co. D
Taylor, R.H. ~ Co. D
Taylor, William A. ~ Co. 2G
Taylor, William J. ~ Co. K
Teal, Robert ~ Co. K
Teel, Robert ~ Co. K
Templeton, E.G. ~ Co. E
Templeton, E.J. ~ Co. E
Templeton, L. ~ Co. E
Termon, B.B. ~ Co. 1H
Termon, Kerney ~ Co. 1HI
Termon, Thomas ~ Co. 1H
Thacker, E. Newton ~ Co. 2G
Thomas, Alexander C. ~ Co. 2G
Thomas, Freeman H. ~ Co. 2G
Thomas, J.H. ~ Co. C
Thomas, John F. ~ Co. 2 H
Thomas, Joseph W. ~ Co. 2 G
Thomas, W.H. ~ Co. F
Thomas, William A. ~ Co. 2 H
Thomas, William H. ~ Co. F
Thomas, William J. ~ Co. 2 G
Thompson, B.J. ~ Co. 2 G
Thompson, Benjamin B. ~ Co. 2 G
Thompson, James W. ~ Co. B
Thompson, Robert H. ~ Co. B
Thomptin, William B. ~ Co. I
Thornton, William B. ~ Co. I
Thurman, J.A. ~ Co. I
Thurman, James A. ~ Co. I
Thurman, Jay A. ~ Co. I
Tibbs, William A. ~ Co. I
Tigner, John M. ~ Co. B
Tignor, John M. ~ Co. B
Timberlake, J.F. ~ Co.
Timberlake, W.M. ~ Co. F
Tindall, H.C. ~ Co. 1GB

Tindall, R.W. ~ Co. 1GB
Tindell, H.C. ~ Co. 1GB
Tindell, Robert W. ~ Co. 1GB
Tindill, R.W. ~ Co. 1GB
Tisdale, F.M. ~ Co. B
Toliver, Henry ~ Co. A
Tolliver, Henry ~ Co. A
Tolly, M.W. ~ Co. I
Townsend, A.J. ~ Co. 2G
Townsend, Andre' J. ~ Co. 2G
Townsend, F.M. ~ Co. 2G
Tracy, D.R. ~ Co. F
Truett, J.M. ~ Co. 1H
Truitt, J.M. ~ Co. 1H
Tucker, Clinton M. ~ Co. 2G
Tucker, James D. ~ Co. K
Tucker, James H. ~ Co. I
Tucker, Telem H. ~ Co. K
Turman, B.B. ~ Co. 1K
Turman, Kerney ~ Co. 1HI
Turman, Thomas ~ Co. 1H
Turner, Andrew J. ~ Co. I
Turner, Ed P. ~ Co. F&S
Turner, Elias ~ Co. I
Turner, F.P. ~ Co. C
Turner, Robert ~ Co. A
Turner, S. H. ~ Co. D
Turner, Stephen ~ Co. D
Turner, Willis ~ Co. I
Turnlaw, J. A. ~ Co. I
Twilley, Elias P. ~ Co. I
Tyler, J. W. ~ Co. H I
Tyler, James W. ~ Co. H I
Uhls, J. M. ~ Co. C
Uhls, Jacob M. ~ Co. C
Underhill, D. H. ~ Co. 1HI
Underhill, Daniel ~ Co. 1HI
Underwood, Atariah ~ Co. A
Underwood, George ~ Co. 1G
Underwood, J. E. ~ Co. A
Underwood, John ~ Co. A

Underwood, W. A. ~ Co. A
Underwood, William ~ Co. A
Vantreas, G. W. ~ Co. F
Vantrease, Nicholas D. ~ Co. F
Vantrees, Nicholas ~ Co. F
Vantrees, Wash. ~ Co. F
Vaughn, Jerry H. ~ Co. B
Vernon, James A. ~ Co. B
Vernon, James Alex ~ Co. B
Vernon, Richard T. ~ Co. B
Vernon, W. T. ~ Co. A
Vickrey, Burnett ~ Co. A
Vicory, Burnet ~ Co. A
Vincent, Moses ~ Co. A
Vincent, W.A. ~ Co. A
Vinson, W. ~ Co. A
Wafford, W.P. ~ Co. I
Waite, George B. ~ Co. K
Waite, George W. ~ Co. K
Wakefield, William C. ~ Co. M2H
Wakefield, William Clay ~ Co. M2H
Walker, H.N. ~ Co. K
Walker, Henry J. ~ Co. B
Walker, T.J. ~ Co. I
Walker, William H. ~ Co. M
Wallace, Robert ~ Co. 2H
Walters, Thomas L. ~ Co. B
Ward, B.B. ~ Co. A
Warf, B.S. ~ Co. 1H
Warf, E.D. ~ Co. 1H
Warf, W.T. ~ Co. I
Warford, W.P. ~ Co. I
Warford, W.P. ~ Co. I
Warren, A. ~ Co. F
Warren, E.T. ~ Co. I
Warren, Elijah ~ Co. I
Warren, Elijah W. ~ Co. I
Warren, Jesse ~ Co. B
Warren, Jesse A. ~ Co. B
Warren, John ~ Co. B
Warren, John B. ~ Co. B

Warren, John B. ~ Co. B
Warren, John M. ~ Co. B
Warren, John T. ~ Co. I
Warren, R.M. ~ Co. B
Warren, R.W. ~ Co. I
Warren, Ralph ~ Co. I
Warren, Randle ~ Co. B
Warren, Robert J. ~ Co. I
Warren, T.J. ~ Co. I
Warren, Thomas J. ~ Co. B
Warren, W.C. ~ Co. 1 H
Warren, William ~ Co. B
Washburn, J.L. ~ Co. F
Washburn, Lewis ~ Co. F
Watson, G.W. ~ Co. H
Webb, Frank ~ Co. E
Wellborn, W. T. ~ Co.
Welsin, James ~ Co. B
West, A. J. ~ Co. E
West, Daniel T. ~ Co. K
Whitby, Richard B. ~ Co. B
White, Andrew J. ~ Co. I
White, Caleb ~ Co. C
White, David ~ Co. D
White, Joseph S. ~ Co. D
White, T.J. ~ Co. E
White, Thomas ~ Co. D
White, W.H. ~ Co. C
White, W.H. ~ Co. D
White, William A. ~ Co. D
White, William J. ~ Co. D
White, William T. ~ Co. K
Whiteas, R.L. ~ Co. A
Whites, Robert L. ~ Co. A
Whitfield, Smith ~ Co. B
Whitice, R.L. ~ Co. A
Whitley, J.W. ~ Co. F
Whitley, John ~ Co. B
Whitley, John W. ~ Co.
Whitly, John ~ Co. B
Whitly, John W. ~ Co. ...

Whitmore, Richard S. ~ Co. F
Whittemore, R.S. ~ Co. F
Whittemore, Richard ~ Co. F
Whittemore, Richard ~ Co. F
Whitts, Robert L. ~ Co. A
Wildman, J.D. ~ Co. L2G
Wileman, James D. ~ Co. L2G
Wileman, William ~ Co. L2G
Wilkerson, J.H.P. ~ Co. 2 G
Wilkinson, James K.P. ~ Co. 2 G
Willborn, W.T. ~ Co.
Williams, A.N. ~ Co. K
Williams, Allen W. ~ Co. M2H
Williams, Bailey P. ~ Co. 2 H
Williams, Benjamin B. ~ Co. K
Williams, Daly T. ~ Co. 2 H
Williams, Daniel G. ~ Co. E
Williams, Francis M. ~ Co. B
Williams, George W. ~ Co. B
Williams, H.A. ~ Co. B
Williams, H.M. ~ Co. 1 G
Williams, Harrison ~ Co. B
Williams, J.B. ~ Co. 2 G
Williams, J.J. ~ Co. I
Williams, James H. ~ Co. 2 G
Williams, James H. ~ Co. M2H
Williams, James M. ~ Co. K
Williams, Jerome B. ~ Co. 2 G
Williams, Joshua A. ~ Co. K
Williams, N.B. ~ Co. K
Williams, W.E. ~ Co. F
Williams, William E.L. ~ Co. F
Williams, Z.T. ~ Co. K
Williamson, John Arch ~ Co. D
Wilson, Edward ~ Co. K
Wilson, Francis M. ~ Co. L
Wilson, Henry R. ~ Co. D
Wilson, J.D. ~ Co. B
Wilson, J.M. ~ Co. E
Wilson, James B. ~ Co. D
Wilson, Jason ~ Co. B

Wilson, John A. ~ Co. D
Wilson, John Miller ~ Co. E
Wilson, Joseph D. ~ Co. B
Wilson, Lafaycttc ~ Co. D
Wilson, M.L. ~ Co. D
Wilson, Marquis D. L. ~ Co. 1L
Wilson, William A. ~ Co. D
Wilson, Z.M. ~ Co. D
Wilson, Zacheus M. ~ Co. D
Windrow, I.N. ~ Co. D
Winfree, B.C. ~ Co. F
Winfree, Bennett C. ~ Co. F
Winfree, J.A. ~ Co. F
Winfree, J.T. ~ Co. F
Winfree, James T. ~ Co. F
Winfrey, Bemont ~ Co. F
Winfrey, J.A. ~ Co. F
Winfrey, J.T. ~ Co. F
Winfrey, John A. ~ Co. F
Winfrie, John A. ~ Co. F
Winfry, J.T. ~ Co. F
Winfry, John H. ~ Co. F
Wing, S.K. ~ Co. F
Winkleer, Henderson W. ~ Co. M2H
Winkler, Henderson ~ Co. M2H
Winn, L.A. ~ Co. A
Winton, G.G. ~ Co. L2G
Winton, George ~ Co. L2G
Winton, James ~ Co. G
Wiser, J.W. ~ Co. K
Wiser, John W. ~ Co. K
Withrow, John F. ~ Co. L2G

Withrow, Samuel ~ Co. L2G
Wix, Marshall ~ Co. C
Wix, Robert ~ Co. E
Wofford, William P. ~ Co. I
Womack, Francis M. ~ Co. L2G
Womack, William H.H. ~ Co. 2 G
Woods, William W. ~ Co. -
Wooten, Leroy C. ~ Co. K
Worf, B.S. ~ Co. I H
Worf, W.T. ~ Co. I
Wright, C.B. ~ Co. C
Wright, F.J. ~ Co. B
Wright, Franklin J. ~ Co. B
Wright, Frederick B. ~ Co. I
Wright, G.W. ~ Co. K
Wright, G.W. ~ Co. K
Wright, George ~ Co. I
Wright, H.M. ~ Co. B
Wright, Isaac ~ Co. A
Wright, J.A. ~ Co. C
Wright, James ~ Co. A
Wright, John S. ~ Co. C
Wright, John V. ~ Co. E
Wright, Joseph N. ~ Co. K
Wright, P.N. ~ Co. C
Wright, Robert ~ Co. I
Wright, T.W. ~ Co. A
Wyman, John ~ Co. F
Young, G.W. ~ Co. H
Young, Joseph ~ Co. A
Young, Nathaniel ~ Co. I

For Further Research

The website links referenced in this appendix change periodically. Check our website for updates.

http://www.researchonline.net/linkupdates.htm

National Archives and Records Administration

http://www.archives.gov/research/order/order-vets-records.html

Confederate Records

http://www.archives.gov/research/military/civil-war/

For Confederate army soldiers, there are two major record collections in the National Archives and Records Administration that provide information on military service:

(1) compiled military service record (CMSR) and

(2) records reproduced in microfilm publication M861, *Compiled Records Showing Service of Military Units in Confederate Organizations* (74 rolls). Records relating to Confederate soldiers are typically less complete than those relating to Union soldiers because many Confederate records did not survive the war. These records are now available on CD-ROM by state. They

may be ordered from our website for $35.00 per state.

http://www.researchonline.net/catalog/service.htm

NARA does not have pension files for Confederate soldiers. Pensions were granted to Confederate veterans and their widows and minor children by the States of Alabama, Arkansas, Florida, Georgia, Kentucky, Louisiana, Mississippi, Missouri, North Carolina, Oklahoma, South Carolina, Tennessee, Texas, and Virginia; these records are in the state archives or equivalent agency.

NARA records are available from the Family History Library in Salt Lake City Utah. You can order them at your local Family History Center (FHC) (Mormon Church). The centers should have a Research Outline on Military Records which should cost about a dollar. Also there is a good book out on Military Records (NARA) by James Neagle. It should be in most FHC. In the card catalog on microfiche, you can go to the Author/Title section, look under Author = National Archives. All their film is there listed by NARA # (sample - M530. LDS microfilm is quicker and cheaper than requesting from NARA}.

To obtain Civil War military service and pension records by mail

Paper copies of Civil War military service and pension records can be ordered by mail using one NATF Form 80 for **each soldier** and **each type of file**.

You can obtain the NATF Form 80 by providing your name and mailing address to inquire@nara.gov. Be sure to specify "Form 80" and the number of forms you need.

You can also obtain the NATF Form 80 by writing to:

National Archives and Records Administration
Attn: NWDT1
700 Pennsylvania Avenue, NW
Washington, DC 20408-0001

The Cost of this type of lookup is $45.00.

CONFEDERATE SERVICE AND PENSION RECORDS

The agencies listed below are repositories for Confederate pension records. The veteran was eligible to apply for a pension to the State in which he lived, even if he served in a unit from a different State. Generally, an applicant was eligible for a pension only if he was indigent or disabled. In your letter to the repository, state the Confederate veteran's name, his widow's name, the unit(s) in which he served, and the counties in which he and his widow lived after the Civil War. Some repositories also have records of

Confederate Homes (for veterans, widows, etc.), muster rolls of State Confederate militia, and other records related to the war. For information on procedures and fees for requesting copies of records, contact the appropriate repository. Also See Online Pension Indexes for Florida, Georgia, Tennessee, Texas and Virginia

ALABAMA

Alabama Department of Archives and History –

http://www.archives.state.al.us/index.html

624 Washington Avenue
Montgomery, AL 36130-0100
Telephone: 334-242-4363

A Guide to Alabama Civil War Research is available in EBOOK and paper formats. 211 pgs.

http://www.researchonline.net/catalog/110601.htm

In 1867 Alabama began granting pensions to Confederate veterans who had lost arms or legs. In 1886 the State began granting pensions to veterans' widows. In 1891 the law was amended to grant pensions to indigent veterans or their widows.

Service records of Alabama soldiers may be viewed on line:

http://archives.state.al.us/civilwar/search.cfm

ARKANSAS

Arkansas History Commission and State Archives

http://www.ark-ives.com/

> 1 Capitol Mall
> Little Rock, AR 72201
> Telephone: 501-682-6900

In 1891 Arkansas began granting pensions to indigent Confederate veterans. In 1915 the State began granting pensions to their widows and mothers.

Two published indexes are available in many libraries:

> *Allen, Desmond Walls.* Index to Confederate Pension Applications (Conway, Ark.: Arkansas Research, 1991).

> *Ingmire, Frances Terry.* Arkansas Confederate Veterans and Widows Pensions Applications (St. Louis, MO: F.T. Ingmire, 1985).

FLORIDA

Florida State Archives –

http://dlis.dos.state.fl.us/index_researchers.cfm

R. A. Gray Building
500 South Bronough Street
Tallahassee, FL 32399-0250
Telephone: 850.245.6700

In 1885 Florida began granting pensions to Confederate veterans. In 1889 the State began granting pensions to their widows.

A published index, which provides each veteran's pension number, is available in many libraries:

> *White, Virgil.* Register of Florida CSA Pension Applications (Waynesboro, TN: National Historical Publishing Co., 1989).

GEORGIA

Georgia Department of Archives and History –

http://www.georgiaarchives.org/

Georgia State Archives
5800 Jonesboro Rd.
Morrow, GA 30260
Telephone: 678-364-3700

A Guide to Georgia Civil War Research is available in EBOOK and paper formats. 211 pgs.

http://www.researchonline.net/catalog/090801.htm

In 1870 Georgia began granting pensions to soldiers with artificial limbs. In 1879 the State began granting pensions to other disabled Confederate veterans or their widows who then resided in Georgia. By 1894 eligible disabilities had been expanded to include old age and poverty.

A published index is available in many libraries:

> White, Virgil D. Index to Georgia Civil War Confederate Pension Files (Waynesboro, TN: National Historical Publishing Co., 1996). and online:

KENTUCKY

Kentucky State Archives –

http://www.kdla.ky.gov/

> Research Room
> 300 Coffee Tree Road
> Frankfort, KY 40601
> Telephone: 502-564-8300

In 1912, Kentucky began granting pensions to Confederate veterans or their widows. The records are on microfilm. A published index is available in many libraries:

Simpson, Alicia. Index of Confederate Pension Applications, Commonwealth of Kentucky (Frankfort, KY: Division of Archives and Records Management, Department of Library and Archives, 1978).

LOUISIANA

Louisiana State Archives –

http://www.sos.la.gov/Pages/default.aspx

3851 Essen Lane
Baton Rouge, LA 70809-2137
Telephone: 225-922-1000

In 1898 Louisiana began granting pensions to indigent Confederate veterans or their widows.

MISSISSIPPI

Mississippi State Archives –

http://www.mdah.state.ms.us/

Mississippi Department of Archives and History

P.O. Box 571
Jackson, MS 39205
Telephone: 601- 576-6850

In 1888 Mississippi began granting pensions to indigent Confederate veterans or their widows. A published index is available in many libraries:

> *Wiltshire, Betty C.* Mississippi Confederate Pension Applications (Carrollton, MS: Pioneer Publishing Co., 1994).

MISSOURI

Missouri State Archives –

http://www.sos.mo.gov/archives/

State Information Center
300 West Main Street
P.O. Box 1747
Jefferson City, MO 65102
Telephone: 573-751-3280

In 1911 Missouri began granting pensions to indigent Confederate veterans only; none were granted to widows. Missouri also had a home for disabled Confederate veterans. The pension and veterans' home applications are interfiled and arranged alphabetically. Typically, the pension file is small, perhaps four to eight pages, containing a standard application form and may include letters of recommendation from family members or others.

NORTH CAROLINA

North Carolina Department of Cultural Resources

Division of Archives and History –

http://www.ah.dcr.state.nc.us/

> 109 East Jones Street
> Raleigh, NC 27601-2807
> Telephone: 919-733-7305

In 1867 North Carolina began granting pensions to Confederate veterans who were blinded or lost an arm or leg during their service. In 1885 the State began granting pensions to all other disabled indigent Confederate veterans or widows.

OKLAHOMA

Archives and Records Management Divisions –

http://www.odl.state.ok.us/oar/archives/collections.htm

> 200 Northeast 18th Street
> Oklahoma City, OK 73105
> Telephone: (405) 522-3579

In 1915 Oklahoma began granting pensions to Confederate veterans or their widows. A published index is available in many libraries:

Oklahoma Genealogical Society. Index to Applications for Pensions from the State of Oklahoma, Submitted by Confederate Soldiers, Sailors, and Their Widows (Oklahoma City, OK: Oklahoma Genealogical Society Projects Committee, 1969)

SOUTH CAROLINA

South Carolina Department of Archives and History

http://scdah.sc.gov/

8301 Parklane Road
Columbia, SC 29223
Telephone: 803-896-6100

A Guide to South Carolina Civil War Research is available in EBOOK and paper formats. 200 pgs.

http://www.researchonline.net/catalog/scresearch.htm

A state law enacted December 24, 1887, permitted financially needy Confederate veterans and widows to apply for a pension; however, few applications survive from the 1888-1918 era. Beginning in 1889, the SC Comptroller began publishing lists of such veterans receiving pensions in his Annual Report. To obtain a copy of the pension application from the 1888-1918 era, the researcher needs to know the exact year in which the veteran or widow applied for a pension. From 1919 to 1925, South Carolina granted pensions to Confederate veterans and widows regardless of financial need. These files are arranged alpha-betically. Pension application files are typically one sheet of paper with writing on both sides. Also available are Confederate Home applications and inmate records for veterans (1909-1957), and applications of wives, widows, sisters, and daughters (1925-1955).

TENNESSEE

Tennessee State Library and Archives –

http://sos.tn.gov/tsla

Public Service Division
403 Seventh Avenue North
Nashville, TN 37243-0312
Telephone: 615-741-2764

A Guide to Tennessee Civil War Research is available in EBOOK and paper formats. 180 pgs.

http://www.researchonline.net/catalog/110801.htm

In 1891 Tennessee began granting pensions to indigent Confederate veterans. In 1905 the State began granting pensions to their widows. The records are on microfilm.

A published index is available in many libraries:

Sistler, Samuel. Index to Tennessee Confederate Pension Applications (Nashville, TN: Sistler & Assoc., 1995).

Confederate Home records are also available, and there is an online index:

Index to Tennessee Confederate Soldiers' Home Applications

http://www.tennessee.gov/tsla/history/military/pension.htm

TEXAS

Texas State Library and Archives Commission –

http://www.tsl.state.tx.us/

P.O. Box 12927
Austin, TX 78711
Telephone: 512-463-5480

In 1881 Texas set aside 1,280 acres for disabled Confederate veterans. In 1889 the State began granting pensions to indigent Confederate veterans and their widows. Muster rolls of State militia in Confederate service are also available.

A published index is available in many libraries:

White, Virgil D. Index to Texas CSA Pension Files (Waynesboro, TN: National Historical Publishing Co., 1989).

An online Index:

Index to Texas Confederate Pension Applications, 1899-1975

http://www.tsl.state.tx.us/arc/pensions/introcpi.html

VIRGINIA

Library of Virginia –

http://www.lva.lib.va.us

Archives Division
800 East Broad Street
Richmond, VA 23219
Telephone: 804-692-3500

In 1888 Virginia began granting pensions to Confederate veterans or their widows. The records are on microfilm. Two indexes are available online:

Virginia Confederate Pension Rolls (Veterans and Widows) Database http://lva1.hosted.exlibrisgroup.com/F/?file_name=find-b-clas10&func=file&local_base=CLAS10

The Historical Sketch & Roster Series

These books contain information for researching the men who served in a particular unit. The focus is for genealogical rather than historical research. More than 1100 volumes are currently available. For a complete listing see our website:

For Confederate Titles by State

http://www.researchonline.net/catalog/crhmast.htm

For Union Titles by State

http://www.researchonline.net/catalog/urhmast.htm

TABLE OF CONTENTS:

List of Officers with biographical sketches
List of companies and the counties where formed
Officers of each company
Military assignments
Battles engaged in the war
Historical sketch of the regiment's service
Rosters / compiled service records of each company
Bibliography of sources

Paperback - $25.00 (Selected larger volumes are more expensive.)

CD-ROM - $15.00

EBOOK - $9.49 – PDF format of the book delivered by EMAIL – NO SHIPPING CHARGE

Shipping is $6.00 per order regardless of the number of titles ordered.

Order From:

Eastern Digital Resources
31 Bramblewood Drive SW
Cartersville, GA 30120
(678) 739-9177
Order on Line
http://www.researchonline.net/catalog/crhmast.htm
Sales@researchonline.net

Made in the USA
Monee, IL
04 July 2022